The Anthropology of Economy

The Anthropology of Economy

Community, Market, and Culture

Stephen Gudeman

BLACKWELL
Publishers

First published 2001

2 4 6 8 10 9 7 5 3 1

Blackwell Publishers Inc.
350 Main Street
Malden, Massachusetts 02148
USA

Blackwell Publishers Ltd
108 Cowley Road
Oxford OX4 1JF
UK

Library of Congress Cataloging-in-Publication Data has been applied for.

ISBN 0–631–22566–8 (hardback); 0–631–22567–6 (paperback)

British Library Cataloguing in Publication Data.

A CIP catalogue record for this book is available from the British Library.

Typeset in 10.5 on 12 pt Sabon
by Ace Filmsetting Ltd, Frome, Somerset
Printed in Great Britain by TJ International, Padstow, Cornwall

This book is printed on acid-free paper.

Contents

Acknowledgments

I began research for this book while on a single quarter leave from the University of Minnesota, and I am grateful to the University as well as the College of Liberal Arts for their support in the past years. The initial draft of the book was written during the year I was a Fellow at the Center for Advanced Study in the Behavioral Sciences; I thank the Center for that special opportunity, and the National Science Foundation for financial support (grant #SES-9022192).

The book's thesis – that we live in multiple communities which nourish endeavors – is supported by its own history, for I am indebted to many colleagues and friends. My special thanks go to Alberto Rivera, with whom I have undertaken fieldwork in Colombia and Guatemala. We have published articles and a book together, but that public authorship does not sufficiently express my debt to him. The ethnography on Guatemala and Colombia comes from our shared fieldwork, which he has allowed me to use, and I have gained enormously from our many discussions about the ethnography and larger issues. In June 1995, Arjo Klamer and Phil Mirowski spent a humid weekend in Minneapolis while we discussed economic anthropology; they will recognize themes from that conversation in this volume. In the past decade, I have also had excellent discussions with scholars from other disciplines, and I thank Jack Amariglio, Stephen Cullenberg, Antonio Callari, J. K. Gibson-Graham, Larry Lohmann, Deidre McCloskey, John Richards, David Ruccio, Vernon Ruttan, and James Scott. I also owe special thanks and appreciation to Frédérique Appfel-Marglin and Stephen Marglin for their support and suggestions. In anthropology, I have received encouragement, interest, references, critique, and suggestive ideas from Nurit Bird-David, James Carrier, Scarlett Epstein, Arturo Escobar, Adam Kuper, Keith Hart, Michael Herzfeld, Alf Hornborg, Mark Mosko, Ben Orlove, Gísli Pálsson, Rick Shweder, and Richard Wilk. My Minnesota colleagues John Ingham and Mischa Penn have been ever-supportive, and I appreciate their help and good colleagueship. At Minnesota, I also want to thank Amy Porter and Kathleen Saunders. At home, Roxane, Rebecca, Elise, and Keren have been great commentators, listeners, and readers over long periods of time.

The author and publishers are grateful to several sources for permission to reuse previously published material: some of the material in chapter 7 was first presented in my 1992 article, "Remodeling the House of Economics: Culture and Innovation," *American Ethnologist*, vol. 19, no. 1: 141–54; an earlier version of some of the information offered in chapters 1, 2, 7, and 8 was published in Stephen Gudeman and Alberto Rivera, "Sustaining the Community, Resisting the Market: Guatemalan Perspectives," in John F. Richards (ed.), *Land, Property and the Environment* (Oakland: ICS Press); a version of chapter 5 was published as "The Postmodern Gift," in Stephen Cullenberg, Jack Amariglio, and David Ruccio (eds), *Postmodernism, Economics and Knowledge* (London: Routledge, 2001).

Chapter One

Community, Market, and Culture

Economic anthropology attends to industrial life as well as ethnographic situations, because comparable processes in securing and managing valued things are found everywhere. But economy, which revolves about making, holding, using, sharing, exchanging, and accumulating valued objects and services, includes more than standard market theory suggests. Anthropology plays a special role in broadening our understanding of material life, for the less-recognized processes are displayed with special clarity in the situations ethnographers study. In this book I offer a cross-cultural model of economy drawn from anthropology, written theories, and contemporary life. My purpose is to develop a lexicon or language for discussing economic processes as well as environmental, welfare, distributional, and other contemporary issues.

I argue that economy consists of two realms, which I call community and market. Both facets make up economy, for humans are motivated by social fulfillment, curiosity, and the pleasure of mastery, as well as instrumental purpose, competition, and the accumulation of gains. By community, I refer to real, on-the-ground associations and to imagined solidarities that people experience. Market designates anonymous, short-term exchanges. We might call these two aspects of economy, the Up-close and the Far-distant. In one guise, economy is local and specific, constituted through social relationships and contextually defined values. In the other, it is impersonal, even global, and abstracted from social context; this dimension consists of separated but interacting agents. Both realms are ever-present but we bring now one, now the other into the foreground in practice and ideology. The relationship is complex: sometimes the two faces of economy are separated, at other times they are mutually dependent, opposed or interactive. But always their shifting relation is filled with tension. This book is about the dialectical relation of economy's two realms.

I shall especially try to portray the multiplicity of the community realm with its grounding in local values, and show how it and market are connected in institutions and practices. The motor of capitalism is profit-making, but I shall suggest that even the most market-driven actor – the national or global corporation – mixes the two realms and relies on the presence of communal relations and resources for its success. Economic anthropology, I think, uniquely displays the double face of economy and the importance of the up-close. The politics of this book stem from this demonstration of the importance of the communal realm, thus obliging us to rethink our ways of distributing new wealth.

I arrived at this model slowly, for, as I found in the course of my studies, economic anthropology itself is divided theoretically. My own intellectual trail led me right through the discipline's conflicting theoretical perspectives, because each time I thought I had solved a puzzle in economic anthropology, the answer prompted new questions that led to a shift in my course and to fresh inquiries about the connections between sociality and impersonal exchange. A brief recounting of these experiences and perplexities provides a miniature map of the field and its fissures.

My first research, in the 1960s, was carried out in a small village of rural Panama. I went there filled with confidence that my business school training in decision theory and game theory, combined with anthropology, would yield deep insights into the local economy. Wearing the hat of a neoclassical economist, I intended to apply concepts from the theory of markets to the activities of subsistence farmers.[1] My goal was to elicit their agricultural choices and plot them on decision trees, attaching their subjective valuations and probabilities to the outcomes. I anticipated that this exercise, intended to explain their behavior in terms of rational choice and self-interest, would open the way to a full exploration of their economy. Standard theory would be my guide even while I adapted it to the local conditions. In the language of economic anthropology, I would be a "formalist," because I was presuming that several modernist theories were universally applicable. The assumption, I thought, was a respectful one, for I inferred that rational choice was shared across cultures and that humans made reasonable sequences of selection regardless of context.

Emboldened by theory and certain of method, I set to work within a few days of moving into the village. I well remember the first interview with my Panamanian neighbor, who farmed rice and maize for household consumption. His puzzlement and gentle incredulity at my questions set me to wonder if his activity of burning the earth and poking holes in it for seeding would be illuminated by comparing it to a Monte Carlo simulation. What had happened to a robust concern with human intentions, shared practices, and verbal meanings? I kept hearing Meyer Fortes's warning about the limitations of "billiard ball" sociology. (He meant seeing social practice as physics or unintended actions and reactions.[2]) After some sleepless hours, I quit that study the next day; but then I was adrift, for I lacked a theoretical anchor. While in Panama I collected a great many data about economy, even administering a detailed economic questionnaire to a random sample of the 91 households in the village. But I could not make sense of the information, and my interests turned to community, family, and godparenthood. The rules that separate sacred godparenthood relationships from economic transactions drew my attention, for this separation protected their sanctity and permanence, yet provided a basis for trust and commitment that could further other exchanges. I now see that my struggle (having been raised in a world of commercial and Deweyan pragmatism) to understand how people could feel that a purely sacred, invisible, intangible tie committed them to one another, in the face of contrary self-interests, played a role in developing my understanding of community economy.

When I later discovered Latin American dependency theory, Marxism, and neoRicardian economics, the economic information from Panama suddenly made sense, and I wrote a study on the devastating consequences of the change from self-sufficient agriculture to market cropping.[3] It seemed to me that the three theories, though developed in Latin America and nineteenth-century Europe, offered building blocks for constructing a general economic anthropology. These theories, unlike the more abstract and individualistic ones, start with class structure or the differential command of resources, and show how this control influences the allocation of wealth in market exchange. They suggest that material life may be filled with conflict, exploitation, and inconsistencies, such as farming both for subsistence and for gain. For the Panama study, thus, I used developed theory to understand local practices and voices; but I did not consider why these theories were generally applicable nor how a theory itself may reflect or be influenced by the social conditions in which it develops.

Upon completing this study, I reconsidered my path when I asked myself how actors' voices and meanings could contribute to an understanding of economic life and theory. Influenced by the work of Geertz (1973) and Sahlins (1976), I wondered how the anthropological concept of culture could be fitted to economics. Eventually, I honed the issue to a single question: what is cultural economics? This puzzle set me off on a new trail. I worked my way through the "substantivist" view of Karl Polanyi and the institutionalism of Thorstein Veblen. Both writers are institutionally oriented, and both offer general theories of economy – one based on the universality of human instincts, the other on the ways that land and labor are shaped and used in societies. Of the two, only Veblen – pragmatist and symbolist – inquired into actors' meanings. With this theme and anthropology as my guide, I began to see economy as constructed through folk models and metaphors.[4] The developing perspective led me to question the way we usually define the economy – as consisting of goods and services transacted in markets – and to be sceptical of essentialist theories in economics. On the one side, I argued that material action may be constructed through religious, social, or other "non-economic" practices from which they cannot be separated; on the other, I proposed that there was no underlying, "true" model of economy, but multiple, meaningful formulations within particular cultures. To demonstrate the breadth of this claim, I analyzed some theoretical writings in Western economics as cultural constructions. If the theories of David Ricardo or the eighteenth-century physiocrats derived from culturally framed experience, and achieved their persuasive power partly by refashioning accepted perceptions, how different were they from the ethnographic models? Why should we accept Western theories as being cross-culturally convincing or as having a special grasp on economic essentials, the search for which may be a modern, Western obsession?

Even while finishing this endeavor, however, I had to admit that I now had a collection of separate models – illustrating the human cultural capacity – but no way to develop a comparative economic anthropology. I also knew that local practices intersect with the projects of those outside a community who may provide powerful persuasions and limits on what may be achieved. Economies, no less than theories about them, never exist in isolation (despite the reading that modern economists give to the Robinson Crusoe story and reproduce in their bounded models with exogenous variables).

I went back to the field, therefore, and undertook a research project in rural Colombia with Alberto Rivera – friend and former student.[5] Under the umbrella concept of conversational communities, we studied local language and practices, the constraints under which they operate, and the relation of changing texts in modern economics to both.[6] We found that the language and practices of the rural dwellers resembled some Western economic theories of earlier times, such as physiocracy. This discovery broadened our conversation, for we surmised that European economic theorists themselves were influenced by models in their local communities, and these same constructs were conveyed to the New World through the practical behavior of farmers, laborers, soldiers, and Jesuits, where they have been altered but remain recognizable especially in agrarian contexts. These theories were part of our learning, as was past fieldwork, so we began to see our ethnographic findings as the product of a complex conversation among the rural dwellers, ourselves, our memories, and our separate histories; and we concluded that ethnography is never an unmediated representation, objective model, or factual account but a located product. With its focus on the connection between the house economy at the margin and the corporate economy at the center, our study also presented a nascent model of community and market economy, for it showed how the house and corporate worlds are locally joined in plays of power and value difference. But as the work neared completion, moments of reflection gave me to realize that this study, focused on a region in Latin America, did not provide an architectonics for a comparative economic anthropology.

This brief account of an unplanned trail brings us to my present project. Economic anthropology, empowered by field studies and a critical view, can broaden the conversation on economy, help uncover general processes in material life, and provide fresh insights into contemporary economies. In this book, I thus engage the general and the particular, weave together some theories in anthropology and economics, and intertwine both with details of material life. I shall offer a model of economy, which the ethnography – drawing on current and past materials from Africa, India, Europe, the Americas, New Guinea, and Southeast Asia – is meant to illustrate, just as my engagement with ethnography first-hand and through texts has helped produce the model.

The Values of Economy

Economic practices and relationships are constituted within the two realms of market and community, and the four value domains that I term the base, social relationships, trade, and accumulation. The salience of these domains and realms varies across societies and historically, and the terrain is contested and changed, but economic practices are always situated in a value context.

In contrast to my anthropological model, the two realms of community and market are usually separated in contemporary discourses on economy. For example, neoclassical economics focuses on one value domain, the market, which is modeled as a separate sphere making up the whole of economy in which all goods are priced and available for exchange. This economy consists of two institutions: households and businesses (see figure 1.1). Households own labor and raw materials which they sell in markets; firms purchase these resources and transform them to products and services for sale to households. This circu-

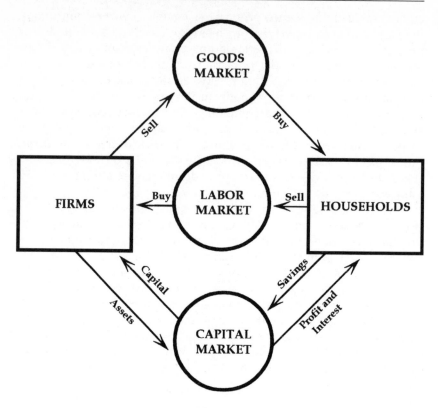

Figure 1.1   The neoclassical economy

lation of materials, goods, and services through markets is self-contained. Government holds a regulatory role but is not an immediate
player. Communal transactions, to the extent they exist or are recognized, represent irrationalities, frictions, hindrances, or "externalities"
to a system that is otherwise efficient.[7] In this discourse, efficiency is
the central value, while "development" broadly means replacing "old"
with "new" values by bringing the market realm to prominence through
new legal structures and by actions of the International Monetary Fund
and World Bank.

A second difference between my model and neoclassical economics
revolves about our differing understanding of value. Most contemporary theories of economy accommodate value relativism through the
notion of individual preference that influences demand, which, in combination with supply, determines price or a good's value. In contrast,
I propose that we live in a world of inconsistent, or incommensurate,

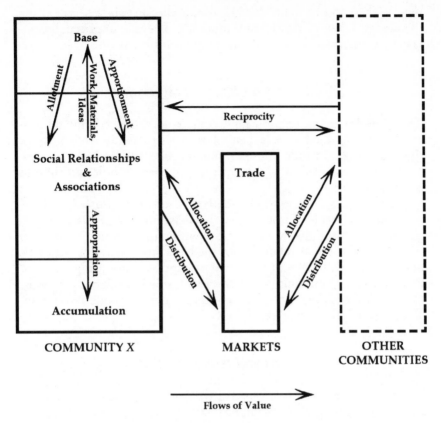

Figure 1.2   Economy as domains of value

domains of value that are locally specified. Culture is made and re-made through contingent categories, such as home and work, body and the other, weekdays and weekends, beauty and efficiency, or friend-ship and love. Different value arenas make up economy (see figure 1.2).

The base or foundation

One value domain, the base or foundation, consists of a community's *shared interests*, which include lasting resources (such as land and wa-ter), produced things, and ideational constructs such as knowledge, technology, laws, practices, skills, and customs. The base comprises cultural agreements and beliefs that provide a structure for all the domains. These locally defined values – embodied in goods, services, and ideologies – express identity in community. They are unpriced, heterogeneous, and often sorted into incommensurate spheres.

Social relationships and associations

The second domain, relationships, consists of valued communal connections maintained as ends themselves. These commitments, kept for their own sake, include house economies, lineages, and nations. Today we find this value domain expressed in corporations and clubs to some degree.

Through these relationships, the base is *created*, *allotted*, and *apportioned* to people in community. The base and social relationships, partially constituting one another, fall within the community realm of economy. The social relationships mediate the transfer of materials and services, and the material transfers express relationships. In contrast, between communities, *reciprocity* – guided by relative positions, tactics, and multiple motivations – forges and disconnects relationships through the extension of base.

Goods and services traded

The third value domain consists of the separated *goods and services* that individuals and groups impersonally trade for production or saving and consumption. Their values are expressed in varying exchange rates. Participants in this trade domain are communally constituted as corporations, individuals, partnerships, households, families, lineages, haciendas, manors, kin groups, and others. Their exchanges are often aided by use of a currency or part-currency (backed by communities), but exchange may take the form of barter (especially when the community warranty is lacking or fails).

Appropriation and accumulation of wealth

The final domain consists of collecting value. Accumulated value includes resources, relationships, goods, and money capital, all of which may become components of other domains. Amassed value is held, invested, consumed, and displayed.

Sustained and justified by economic power, social obligations, and ideologies, accumulations may arise through tribute or tithes, monopolies, and arbitrage, which secure value from the other domains. Practices in this domain of value revolve about appropriating newly formed values (from innovation), and allocating and reallocating established ones.

The accumulation domain includes many institutions and actors who operate in other domains as well: lineage elders who collect cattle, valuables, or wives; political states with leaders or rent-seekers who gather taxes and tribute; corporations; individuals; and "banks" (including government banks and the World Bank). This domain also may emerge as a distinct "mode" (in Marxist terms). For example, tributary modes, such as rent-seeking states, may depend on lineages or petty commodity producers for their continuance. The receiving sphere is not idle, however, for it may support activity in the other domains by establishing laws and service structures, "offering" physical protection, or providing access to gods who assure agricultural fertility.

In capitalism, money pervades this final domain. Value, held as private property, is measured by money and can be accumulated as financial capital which is a summation of past profit. Capital is principally acquired through trade and production. Tributary forms of appropriation, such as church tithes and state taxes, are also found in capitalism, and acquisition through brute force and state power may play a part at the margins of the system, but capitalism fully develops when the domain of accumulation persists through sequestering profit from production within trade – as rents, interest, and accounting "profit" – and using this capital to appropriate newly formed value.

Two Transaction Realms

We live in associations or communities that offer a degree of certainty and security. In the community realm of economy, the base and social relationships are salient, although the other value concerns are found: impersonal trade is directed to securing items that maintain community, and accumulation is exercised within social relationships. Communities may be small as well as ethnic groups or states held together by force and ideologies. Sometimes they are represented or personified in a single person, which can lead to authoritarianism; sometimes they are modeled as contracts between separate individuals; and between these two extremes many forms are built as people acquire, mix, and shed identities through the communities they join. The communal realm, placing each of us within a matrix of social relationships and mediating material life in which communal projects take precedence over self-interest, offers a degree of predictability. But we also transcend social boundaries to encounter new goods and others. In this second, market realm, trade and accumulation are prominent. The trade realm situates individuals and groups as separate actors who undertake short-term interactions and exchanges to achieve both material ends and gain. In this market realm, self-interest of the unit – whether an individual, a family, or a corporation – is a primary motive and value. But the market realm draws on community, for it relies on socially constituted units and relationships. These two divergent motives and behaviors, swinging between the refuge of communal predictability and the taste for uncertainty, are intermixed and sometimes conflict in economies.

The market realm revolves about short-term material relationships that are undertaken *for the sake of* achieving a project or securing a good. In the communal realm, material goods are exchanged through relationships kept *for their own sake*. Things done for their own sake are self-fulfilling or self-contained, and have no referent outside themselves. Linguistically, a reflexive verb or a performative falls in this domain. In material life, a production system that feeds back to itself or work done for the satisfaction of the craftsmanship provide examples. In rural Latin America, where household economies are found, people use a reflexive verb to speak of their joint project, "maintaining the base" (*mantenerse*). In contrast, an activity done for the sake of something else points outward, to another behavior or object that it requires for its completion, or for its justification and rationale. Linguistically, a referential statement falls in this domain, because it points to something external to itself. Buying goods for the sake of selling them and gathering a profit (*hacer dinero*) is an object-oriented activity in Latin America. Certainly, means-to-ends actions often are done in the service of a larger purpose such as maintaining a house or manifesting one's divine selection. But two thousand years ago, Aristotle observed that people often confound actions done "for the sake of" something else with activities done "for their own sake." He saw that instrumental actions, such as buying goods to sell them and make a profit, may eventually come to be done for their own sake, and he viewed this transformation as a confusion and moral mistake, an observation elaborated in Marx's (1967 [1867]) notion of fetishism, Veblen's (1914) idea of derangement, and Polanyi's (1968a) concept of fictitious commodities.

Maintaining the base and accumulating capital epitomize the different projects of community and market. Communal trade is undertaken to secure goods that sustain the base or have "use value," to employ Aristotle's expression; in Marx's terms this trade takes the form of Commodity – Commodity' or Commodity – Money – Commodity'. In contrast, market trade revolves about exchange value or increasing monetary capital (Money – Commodity – Money'). Both projects are realized in trade, which is thus ambiguous. Attractive for its possibilities yet avoided for its potential losses, trade from a community perspective has been modeled as sinful (Le Goff 1988), a sham (Aristotle 1984), and exploitative (Marx 1967 [1867]), whereas from a market perspective it appears as the cause of improved living standards (Smith 1976 [1776]), Ricardo 1951 [1817]) and the expression of free choice.

The two realms of market and community complement one another, conjoin, and are separated in acts, institutions, and sectors. No trade or market system exists without the support of communal agreements, such as shared languages, mutual ways of interacting, and implicit understandings. Communities also are inside markets, as households, corporations, unions, guilds, and oligopolies, and contain them as nation-states that provide a legal structure for contracts and material infrastructure. There are dualistic or parallel systems, as in the case of colonial regimes when a cross-national corporation makes use of a local, community economy through political power; ports-of-trade – such as Portobello in old Panama – are international marketplaces that have been given a special time and quarantined place in a local economy (Boeke 1942; Geertz 1963; Polanyi, Arensberg, and Pearson 1957). There exist inner/outer relationships when a house economy is contained within a market economy, as in rural Colombia or our own life. Sometimes a market draws a surplus from a community economy, when subsistence farming supports cash cropping or when people undertake piecework or telemarketing from their homes at very low rates of remuneration. In the West, too, there has been a long-term shift from community to market that is often described as modernization, progress, and the triumph of rationality.

The two realms may be institutionally and tactically interwoven, as in a "trade partnership," found in many parts of the world, in which two members of different groups located in different areas maintain an enduring relationship (communal), yet each aims to secure a monetary profit from the other (commercial).[8] Similarly, in the "trader's dilemma" (Evers 1994), a local merchant is caught between the aims of maximizing profit in selling, and maintaining relationships with customers with whom he shares kinship, residential, or social ties. At a larger scale, the house-business in Latin America that combines the two modes, by making a profit using unpaid family labor and uncosted resources, is neither transitional nor on the road to modernization, but lasting under certain conditions.

Most of us use both realms of economy every day. Sometimes we buy at an impersonal superstore that has no clerks and uses automatic checkouts, taking pleasure in anonymity, not having to talk with others, and securing a low price. Other days we buy at a small, nearby store so that we can support a business community or chat for a moment with a clerk or cashier, though at the cost of paying higher prices. Sometimes we go to both stores within the same hour, as if to seek a psychic balance; and some of us – ill-mannered or confused by this realm of social tactics – seek social contact in the anonymous store or avoid it in the communal one, thus producing quizzical if not curt responses in both.[9]

The model depicts as well the articulation of separate modes that have been juxtaposed through force, expansion, colonization, and like processes. Thus, a tributary mode by which wealth is appropriated may be implanted on a community realm, as in the case of Inca expansion (Godelier 1977a); tribute may be exacted within community (Meillassoux 1981 [1975]); or tribute may be demanded by an elite from communal groupings that practice petty capitalism, as in the case of China (Gates 1996). In some cases, modes of extraction themselves locally intersect (Semo 1993). Resistance and struggle between such separate modes often result.

Over the long run, the relationship of market and community is dialectical, using that term in an open-ended sense (Harvey 1996), for many activities can appear under either guise, and each is constituted in relation to the other. I focus on the features of community, but we fashion these pillars and processes in relation to market life that is also socially constituted. For example, the emergence of household-based trade on the margins of growing markets – as in the rise of informal economy – may be a dialectical response to the centralization of economic power, the growth of monopolistic practices, and state control (Hart 1992).

Commensuration: Panama in the 1960s

During my first fieldwork in Panama, I was confused by the measurement systems the people used. I wanted to quantify land tilled, labor used, other expenditures, and revenues, in order to gauge the surplus each household was producing. I thought one might return a number, such as a profit rate, to summarize their efforts. But the rural farmers were not interested in summary calculations or even financial equivalents; they used disparate, homemade measures when quantifying work processes. Each measure had a specific use, none had a direct relation to money, and I could not correlate them under a single ruler. I did not even know the history of the measures; some might have originated in the village, others must have had a colonial or Hispanic origin.

The villagers grew rice, corn, and beans for the home, and sugar cane for cash sale, all of which were measured differently. I soon learned to separate subsistence harvests from the sale crop, and then to distinguish among the domestic ones. I also found that farmers did not measure land for the domestic crops; area was deduced from the seed planted. People said, "one *lata* [a large soy bean oil can] of rice seeds one hectare," which was a number they knew from experience. This ratio was a secondary measure, however, because what really mattered was the seed to harvest ratio, which varied by land fertility and seed strain. Ultimately, everyone said that approximately one pound of rice would feed a normal size family for a day. So, by figuring backward from consumption to harvest to seed to land area that had to be cleared, a farmer could make plans for the year. For other crops, too, a seed to harvest ratio was used, but the measuring rods differed. (Farmers used small gourds to measure corn seed, although the size of these vessels differed by household; other measures were used for beans.)

After rice was seeded, it had to be weeded several times before harvesting. Sometimes two men exchanged work with the hoe, sometimes four or five joined efforts to rotate from field to field (*una peonada*), occasionally they paid workers from the village or outside. All work efforts were measured by the day or by task. Although each task was roughly a day's work, the measuring rods for the tasks varied. For example, a task in weeding rice was measured as 16 square "*varas*" (yards); a *vara* was gauged as the length between the finger tips of outstretched arms. But rice weeding could also be measured by number of rows, with the number depending on the difficulty of the work and length of rows. Harvesting tasks were different. For rice, the task measurement was number of "handfuls" gathered, though an owner counted his rice harvest by baskets and, eventually, sacks. A sack in rice, however, was not comparable to a sack in corn, for each required different amounts of harvest work, weighed different amounts, lasted for a different time in the house, and fetched different amounts if sold. To add to this diversity, when men exchanged work singly or within a group, they usually did not cross their efforts between crops or classes of work. Inequalities were balanced by individual arrangement or by cash.

Thus, I encountered measures based on fistfuls, arm lengths, tin sizes, gourds, food plates, burlap sacks, baskets of vine, baskets of reed, paces, time, length of rows, number of rows, and area. Some measures were drawn from parts of the body, others were common containers.

All were based on up-close experience; they were low-order abstractions. The measures had familiar functions. All served as units of account for judging quantity, as in a harvest, work, or seed. Some also were payments; occasionally, a rice harvester was paid in fistfuls of rice according to the number he collected. Finally, a day of labor was both an accounting unit and a payment, and it had a degree of exchangeability, as in the male work groups, although not usually across crops. But no general unit of account was used to count, compare, or exchange across all land, work forms, and crops; I could never even compare rice, corn, and beans, even as proportions the people wanted on a food plate (so that demand might measure their comparative values and set the amounts seeded). No one was concerned that the food and work measures did not mesh one with another; the measuring rods were incommensurate.

Sugar cane, raised for sale to nearby mills, was very different. I tried to calculate profit figures, but they were not important to the growers because a field would not yield a harvest until 18 months had passed, and in the interval would be used for intercropping subsistence crops; growers also possessed several fields from different years that were harvested together (a field might last 3–5 years). For the farmers, the significant calculation was land area devoted to the crop, because this footage (inspectors from the purchasing mills walked the land each year) determined the cash advance the mills provided for paying workers, part of which growers diverted to their own pockets (which they considered to be profit). Thus, a grower received cash advances during the season and a final sum based on the volume and sugar content of the combined harvests from the different fields less the money advanced. Money provided the measuring rod or means of commensuration in sugar cane, but it had no touchstone in everyday experience.

Commensuration is found in all economies, for we do not live without making categories and creating value comparisons.[10] But the measuring rods vary in generality, and this degree of abstraction is related to community and market exchange. In many cases, a local measuring rod itself may not be used in trade. Rice and maize – though counted – were not traded one for the other among agriculturalists in Panama. In addition, the labor used to produce them was measured by task and by time, but these counters were not used in trade; men exchanged labor in rice and labor in maize but not one for the other. Measured rice labor and measured maize labor constituted limited payments. In contrast, the measuring rod of cash received for the sugar cane was used to purchase any item, including labor to raise the domestic crops.

Economies are never awash in complete singularities or nonexchangeables; they always feature a degree of commensuration and exchange, as in rice for harvesting work. But commensuration and exchange are never total: some items we do not (yet) sell, such as our hearts. And within the domain of market exchange we create pathways or bounded exchanges, such as government-issued food stamps that can be traded only for a range of foods or scrip payments by haciendas that can be redeemed only at their stores. In all exchanges, we see the dialectics of community and market; and we switch circuits with such frequency and dexterity that it escapes notice: children are assigned specific chores for a set allowance in coins, although the money was first earned by a parent in the market. University professors are paid a wage plus fringe benefits in health insurance, medical plans, and retirement contributions. The totality makes up their compensation, but they cannot trade their health insurance for a retirement benefit. Each fringe benefit is and is not a commodity, measured by money; it is a ration that cannot be returned. The alchemy of money, with its power of commensuration, lies in its ability to dissolve distinctions between value schemes or measuring rods, and to create the fiction that a flattened, comparable world exists. We make and live both realms continuously.

Separations and Dialectics: Other Perspectives

In the long discourse on economy, community and market have been invoked in complex ways. Aristotle initially distinguished two economic terrains through his opposition of use and exchange. He adduced the example of a shoe, which can be worn (used) or traded (exchanged). In the first case, its particulate (or incommensurate) features are important and distinguish its value from all non-shoes; in the second case, the shoe is compared to other fungible (commensurate) goods for which it can be exchanged. For Aristotle, the two uses were morally distinct though often confused in practice. Pure trade lay outside the sphere of household economy, which was founded on acquisition for use and was limited in its ends; its purpose was to support the achievement of individual excellence fashioned in activities undertaken for their own sake by citizens of the polis.

Adam Smith did not directly refer to Aristotle when he distinguished between value in use and value in exchange to set out his famous puzzle. He observed that some things, such as water, have high use value but low exchange value, whereas other things, such as diamonds, have low use value but high exchange value (Smith 1976 [1776]: 33). Prices or exchange rates in the market did not directly correspond to use values. Smith provided one answer to this seeming paradox by advancing a complex theory of labor value to explain exchange rates.

One theoretical line, following Adam Smith, was developed by Marx. Despite his few references to Aristotle, Marx was deeply influenced by him, and much of his own work, especially his theory of surplus value, represents an elaboration of Aristotle's distinction between use and exchange value. Marx explained prices and the generation of surplus (and market profit) through the dialectical relation of the use and exchange of labor. Labor is bought at its exchange rate but capitalists gain control of its use value, which in turn produces a surplus above its original exchange value. This surplus is appropriated by the capitalist. For Marx the trade of money for goods, and especially of money for money, represents an abstraction from and mystification of the labor expenditures that underlie the production of things and the generation of surplus prior to their appearance in exchange. When gaining wealth becomes the purpose of trade, money becomes an animate object or fetish that veils the labor which supports it.[11]

By a second strand of theory developed in the nineteenth century – after Bentham, Ricardo, and Mill – the notion of use value was replaced by utility; then, by the mid-twentieth century, the concept of utility was transformed to preference or subjective preference (which underlies demand schedules). Exchange value came to mean price, which results from the interaction of demand and supply in the market, and Aristotle's distinction between use and exchange disappeared; in much of modern economics, the market domain is seen as freestanding.

Outside the neoclassical and Marxist traditions, the Aristotelian division between use and exchange has taken many turnings. For example, Weber distinguished between substantive and formal rationality (1978: 85–6). Substantive rationality designates material behavior shaped by political, religious, or ethical standards. Formal rationality refers to action based on calculation and means-to-ends reasoning. In practice, claimed Weber, these ideal types are mixed together; but he did not provide an interactive or dialectical theory of their connection, although the concept of a long-term transition from substantive to formal rationality informs many of his historical studies (1958 [1920], 1961 [1923]).[12] On Weber's historical view, the practice of instrumental rationality initially was legitimated by the rise of ascetic Protestantism (Weber 1958 [1920]), because worldly success in trade – but without consumptive expenditures – revealed that one was a member of God's elect. Once embedded in the economic sphere, instrumental rationality cast its net across a wide range of activities, and this rationalization of everyday practices powered by shifting religious beliefs, market expansion, and changing political and legal systems transformed this act of doing something for the sake of something else, such as ascertaining divine acceptance and grace, to something done for its own sake. Achieving market success, which had been practiced in pursuit of divine grace, became an act without grounding or limitation, leading to entrapment in an "iron cage." According to some views, this historical transformation in the meaning of economic practices marks the turn to modernity in the West.

The separation between the formal and substantive meanings of economy was given greatest currency by Karl Polanyi, although he accorded immediate credit for the distinction to Karl Menger (Polanyi 1977). Polanyi argued that the interaction of humans in relation to their environment constitutes the conditions and substance of society. When land and labor are placed on the market – as in developed capitalist economies – society's inner core is dissolved; yet land and labor are only *fictitious* commodities, because they are not produced by humans. Polanyi marked a divide between economies. Some are best described by a substantivist view, others by a formalist perspective. In embedded economies, land and labor are transacted through social relationships. When kinship dominates, reciprocity prevails; when political and religious institutions dominate, redistribution is found. In contrast, the modern market economy, in which all things are disembedded from their social conditions of production, is best understood through formal economics.

Polanyi's division, with its roots in Aristotle, echoes distinctions made by Vico, Morgan, Maine, and Töennies. He felt, however, that the historical shift from embedded to disembedded economies was violently destructive. When land and labor are disembedded from the social fabric and traded for money, society undergoes a devastating transformation. Polanyi (1944) provided one account of this historical shift but did not develop a model of community–market interaction or foresee the ways that communities persist and are required for markets, or how markets sometimes support and provide the conditions for new communities. His view that land and labor constitute economy's invariant elements also takes little account of local or cultural constructions of economy or the way that knowledge, technology, and customary performances influence economic processes.

Polanyi's terms, formal and substantive, resonate with important categories in philosophy. R. G. Collingwood, for example, distinguishes between moral and economic action, a division with roots in Kant and Aristotle. A moral or deontological action revolves about duty and obligation, whereas an economic action concerns means-to-ends relationships. Particularly compelling is Collingwood's specification of economic action as one in which "each party is using the other as means to his own ends by permitting the other to use him in the same way" (1989: 65); on this view, people become instrumentalities when engaged in economic practices. Collingwood implies that economic action builds on a division between self and other, or subject and object, and that the other transformed to a means becomes an impersonal object. In economic action we need never be concerned with the other's subjectivity. Impersonal trade, freed of lasting commitments, diminishes social ties and human identity.

A similar conclusion was reached by Veblen. Pragmatist, dualist, and anthropologist manqué, he made subtle use of the Aristotelian division.[13] In several of his later works, Veblen shows how the commercial world is divided between businessmen (the "captains of finance"), who want to accumulate monetary wealth, and engineers (the "captains of industry"), who develop technology and make things. He first used the distinction in a critique of J. B. Clark's theory of capital, by showing that the word capital has a double meaning. On the one hand, capital means equipment for making things; on the other, capital is a monetary accumulation used to secure a gain. Veblen showed how we sometimes apply one sense of the term to the other and confound the two. For example, as money, capital can be divided into small allotments and exchanged; as equipment, capital is non-divisible and often not mobile. Most neoclassical theories of the market, however, merge the two senses and treat capital as partible, malleable, and mobile. The theory that marginal money inputs yield marginal money products does not fit the fact that people and equipment are not divisible and often not movable! (And when one marginal person or machine is added to a process, all else does not remain constant.) Veblen linked this ideological confusion of pecuniary and industrial wealth to metaphoric thinking, and made extensive use of the division to display the cycles and contradictions of capitalism as well as the ways one form of wealth dominates the other through the instinct of predation.[14] As the captains of finance gain command of the industrial system, financial acumen itself is credited with the qualities of industrial workmanship. This appropriation of one side of economy by the other through metaphor, said Veblen, is a *derangement* that is special to capitalism. The entirety is a gloss on Aristotle's insight that activities done for their own sake and activities done for the sake of something else are separate yet confounded in practice.

In recent years, social scientists have turned to the study of human relationships, such as trust, confidence, mutuality, benevolence, goodwill, caring, and respect, that underwrite trade, the formation of credit groups, or savings associations. Putnam (1993) argues that trust, standing at the opposite pole to non-cooperation and competition, is a product of accumulated social capital.[15] His concept of social capital bears kinship to my notion of the base, but for him dyadic ties provide the foundation for material life, and so the broader communal commitments from which they derive are obscured.

Granovetter (1992a, 1992b) offers a different understanding. Drawing on Polanyi's opposition of the embedded and disembedded economy, he argues that anthropologists utilize an oversocialized conception of human action (embedded economies), whereas economists employ an undersocialized one (disembedded markets). Granovetter urges that in non-market economies there is more instrumental action than anthropologists recognize, whereas in market economies there is more embedded material action than economists concede.[16] I share this view, but Granovetter does not provide an economic theory built on the connection, interaction, and variation of the two broad realms.[17]

Anthropologists have also considered the relation between social ties and economy often by focusing on reciprocity or back and forth delayed exchanges that are buttressed by social bonds. For example, Gregory (1982) sorts economies into gift and commodity systems. Reciprocity is regnant in one, trade in the other. Commentators have since remarked that the opposition can be found within economies.[18] For example, goods may pass through phases to serve as both commodities and gifts, shifting along a continuum from market exchange to reciprocity (Appadurai 1986; Kopytoff 1986). But these latter arguments also tend to emphasize dyadic ties rather than larger realms, and they fail to offer a view of the connection between the market and communal realms. For example, Carrier (1992), in a survey of exchange on the island of Ponam in Melanesia, criticizes the absolute division between gifts and commodities. He shows how the two modes are intertwined across a range of transactions, from merchants, to local market traders, to trade partnerships, to gifts themselves. Carrier (1998) also draws a division between *inclusive* property, when an object is multiply held, and *exclusive* property, owned by a single individual. He argues that we have sorted economies and property systems so that the West seems to be home to exclusive property, whereas Melanesia is the region of inclusive claims (or "gift" economies). But on Ponam both forms are found, and Carrier urges that the two possession forms characterize the modern West as well.[19]

In a stimulating treatment of money that also resembles my views, Bloch and Parry (1989) visualize exchange in terms of short-term interests and long-term morality; one expresses rational calculation, the other manifests communal commitment. Money tends to be aligned with short-term interests but can be socially cleansed or transformed for communal uses. In addition, Keith Hart (1986), in a luminous commentary, points out that money itself is two-sided. Issued and secured by a state, on the one hand, money can be exchanged by anyone for anything, on the other. Hart applies this two-sided notion of money to fish transactions in the Trobriand Islands (Papua New Guinea), because fish can be exchanged by ceremonial transactions (the state dimension) or by individual barter (trade). The form used depends on whether or not an encompassing political order is present; individual barter takes place only within existing political commitments, whereas ceremonial transactions construct them. Trobrianders shift between the two modes as political and material conditions change. This dialectical view resembles my own.

Finally, Gibson-Graham (1996) contests the centeredness and phallocenteredness of capitalism, by which it becomes an entity or whole against which "other" economies are measured. Their strategy is double: on the one hand, Gibson-Graham argues that capitalism has no single motor but many engines, so alternative accounts and accountings of it are possible; similarly, other economic modes are not lacking or deficient in essential characteristics as defined by capitalism, just as female is not the opposite and negative of male. This approach is congenial, and my invocation of community as a repository of possibilities and incommensurate value arenas, rather than the negation of capitalism, surely provides a counterpart story to theirs. As they also argue, such a perspective has implications for the way corporate wealth is distributed, a topic to which I return in the final chapter.

From Community to Globalization

In the chapters that follow, I initially explore the communal and market realms as separate moments, attending more closely to the communal because ethnography yields insights about these forms and the time has arrived to recognize the submerged realm. The ethnographic data were collected throughout the twentieth century, and in some cases anthropologists considered the contexts of study as isolated from colonial, postcolonial, or market forces. But the work was carefully undertaken and I use it if only for certain purposes. In the early chapters, I examine the base and its associated processes, showing how it is supported, strengthened, maintained, and augmented by sensible practices. Transactions within the communal realm revolve about allotment and apportionment. In contrast, reciprocity is an interbase transaction, and it hovers between the incommensurate and commensurate. A gift extends the base to others and so bestows an aspect of community. But reciprocity also may be invoked to "explain" the presence of the base (as an initial gift) and to justify a pattern of allotment or apportionment as being in accord with the divine or ancestral conditions of that gift. Trade to maintain the base is also a necessary part of the community realm; and it is found both at the margins or borders of community and on the "inside."

On turning to markets, I focus principally on innovation and the generation of profit as the motor of capitalist growth. I argue that profit starts with innovation, but this creation of value is dependent on the presence of community.[20] The innovator not only creates a product, or a new form of production or distribution, but a relation to others. For example, Henry Ford's innovation of using conveyer belts to make a moving production line changed the relation of tools to humans, how humans use the environment, the objects produced, and how humans relate to one another in production. But his innovation also changed human relationships in respect of these changes: demographic mobility increased; tire, gas, and cement industries developed; new forms of shopping arose; consumer fascination with automobiles developed; family and corporate relations altered as wages and demand increased; and the innovation itself – the fixed assembly line – spread to other forms of manufacturing. Ford's innovation became traces that altered other relationships. When I drive a Ford, I am driving a Ford – a trace, an historical memory, a connection to the innovator. Ford is "in" the economy and society by his work, and in this sense he has a relation to me and left his mark in the world.

The innovator both works in a world of traces or memories that are a legacy of community and make up his base, and makes worlds for others. Again, I am not only speaking of on-the-ground relationships as in who buys a product; rather, the innovator adds to a base of traces and shares his world-vision with others. An innovator creates a service or product, or a new way of doing, but the creation is also a tool or mediation, because through it the innovator makes a relation to others mediated by the object. In one sense, innovation is about products, services, and profit; in another it is about creating connections, for through an object the innovator affects or influences the worlds of others. The base of the innovator becomes part of another's identity, much as the gift extends community to others. Products and services, even when bought, are gifts. Innovation, or human creating and extending, lies at the basis of all economy.

Following this consideration of market and community as separate realms and their connection through innovation, I examine conversions of value between them. In some ethnographic cases, community and market occupy separate spaces and are enacted through distinct institutions, so that objects and people are transformed on crossing between them. When capital expands, we often find the debasement of community as its values evaporate in support of the market; but the creation, maintenance, and expansion of base also may transform market life. Finally, I consider implications of this model for contemporary discussions about the role of corporate and political obligations, and for the shifting tension between localization and globalization. The corporation is both a market or legal-financial entity and a community that is nestled in larger communities. Corporations engage in formal contracts, executed in markets; but "outside" these priced transactions, and often preceding them, corporations employ "ceremonial exchanges" or transactions buttressed by goodwill, and they use reciprocity. These latter exchanges lodge the corporation in its environs and connect its capital to other bases, suggesting that the distribution of profit – which is central to the production of well-being, economic difference, and class structure – might be newly modeled in terms of multiple, incommensurate values and economy's two realms. In contrast, we may surmise that one problem with early forms of socialism in Eastern Europe was the state's inability and refusal to recognize and cope with the attractions and spirit of anonymous trade.

The model also well displays contemporary processes of localization and globalization, for the value domains run from specificity and local ties to accumulation and global connections. Globalization, in my view, is closely tied to increased financial flows or the unfettered movements of accumulated profit that can alight and be used to purchase local means of production; capital crosses labor and resource markets, taking advantage of differential prices. Globalization has grown with the lowering of transportation and transaction costs, the loosening of financial controls, and the advent of dispersed production by which industrial processes are segmented yet brought together across great spaces. Globalization is anchored, however, by local innovation and by ownership of capital that turns a profit. Globalization–localization instantiates the dialectic of community and market or the tension between keeping identity and the base, and spreading ties to others and accumulating capital.

These several and final concerns about the distribution of wealth and contemporary change return us to my larger aim of providing a new lexicon for conversing about economy, and of pointing to areas of economy in which we balance, select among, contrast, and struggle with incommensurate values. I would like to reopen and situate these discussions within an anthropological model of economy.

NOTES

1   For some of the standard arguments for and against the use of neoclassi-
    cal economics in anthropology, see LeClair and Schneider (1968) and
    Schneider (1974). Plattner (1989) offers a later collection. Wilk (1996)
    provides a recent account of developments in economic anthropology.
2   I doubt he had in mind Milton Friedman's (1953) charter statement in
    economics that actually employs this image in relation to intentions.
3   See Gudeman (1978). The literature on the several theoretical approaches
    is very large. On Latin American dependency theory or structuralism,
    see Cardoso and Faletto (1979), Furtado (1976), Frank (1967, 1969),
    and Sunkel (1993).
4   On substantivism, see Polanyi (1944, 1968, 1977), and Polanyi,
    Arensberg, and Pearson (1957); on my work see Gudeman (1986). For
    further elaboration of cultural economics in relation to substantivist and
    formalist assumptions, see Bird-David (1992a) and Orlove (1986).
5   I remain indebted to Rivera for the fieldwork collaboration and many
    conversations (Gudeman and Rivera 1990). The idea that economics is a
    communicative discourse and involves modes of persuasion had been
    strikingly argued by Klamer (1983).
6   We developed the notion of conversations from our evolving field prac-
    tices. In economics, Klamer and Colander (1990) were developing a re-
    lated use of conversation in their ethnographic study of aspiring
    professionals.
7   One reaction of neoclassical economists is to extend their theory as far as
    possible across the communal realm (Becker 1976, 1981).
8   One example is the *pratik* relationship in Haiti, as described by Mintz
    (1961).
9   We also invent, make sense of, and interpret many micro-behaviors by
    projecting the two models on practical action. Consider opening a door.
    Sometimes one does it for oneself: this is individual self-sufficiency. But
    sometimes one does it for another as an act of communality or social
    connection. Here the complications start. The communal courtesy can
    be an act of friendship, but until recently it was also a gendered act indi-
    cating male dominance, although one sometimes opens a door for a
    banker, businessman, or president, as an expression of submission. All
    are acts within community.
    Conversely, a doorman at a hotel or restaurant may open doors, which
    is a market act, especially since the prices of the establishment will be
    raised to cover the doorman's pay. This act may be seen as a projection
    of community that indicates mutuality, for the restaurant or hotel sells
    itself as an establishment of community, yet the doorman may depend
    on tips for his survival. Are the tips a market obligation in repayment for
    a service, a communal payment, or an appropriation of communal senti-
    ment?
    Women today are suing to be able to practice this male profession,

which is yet a different illustration of how the communal realm helps structure market participation. Because part of the significance of the doorman's act is its gendered nature, contestation against this power and the closed labor market must originate in shifting communal expectations. From gender to tips to the projected sense of mutuality, the significance of the doorperson's act depends on its shifting place within community and market.

10   In a different way, Kopytoff (1986) has argued the point.

11   For an anthropological treatment of fetishism in which community provides the ground against which market relations stand revealed, see Taussig (1980).

12   "Originally, two opposite attitudes toward the pursuit of gain exist in combination. Internally, there is attachment to tradition and to the pietistic relations of fellow members of tribe, clan and house-community, with the exclusion of the unrestricted quest of gain within the circle of those bound together by religious ties; externally, there is absolutely unrestricted play of the gain spirit in economic relations, every foreigner being originally an enemy in relation to whom no ethical restrictions apply; that is, the ethics of internal and external relations are categorically distinct. The course of development involves on the one hand the bringing in of calculation into the traditional brotherhood. . . . At the same time there is a tempering of the unrestricted quest of gain with the adoption of the economic principle into the internal economy" (Weber 1961 [1923]: 261–2). Smelser (1976) also suggested that attention should be given to the ways the two rationalities re-enforce, conflict, and combine over time.

13   His first publication was on Kant (1884).

14   On these several concepts of Veblen, see especially *The Instinct of Workmanship* (1914), *The Place of Science in Modern Civilisation* (1942 [1919]), *The Theory of the Leisure Class* (1953 [1899]), *The Theory of Business Enterprise* (1978 [1904]), and *The Engineers and the Price System* (1983 [1921]).

15   In addition to Putnam, see Dore (1992 [1983]), Fukuyama (1995), Gambetta (1988), Hyden (1980), and Vélez-Ibañez (1983) for cognate arguments.

16   He also extends the critique of anthropologists to theorists of moral economy (Scott 1976).

17   Daly and Cobb (1994) provide a different development of similar issues.

18   Gregory (1997) also has expanded his view; our approaches have points of similarity.

19   Hornborg (1994) develops an argument about the persisting tension between the local and global that also overlaps mine.

20   Richard Epstein (1995) offers an argument in political theory that would largely omit community impulses.

Chapter Two

Economy at the Base

Life in community provides predictability and identity through control of social, ideological, or spatial domains. But setting aside a space also frames an unknown territory to explore. Attachments create a home and its transgression, which is the dialectic of community and market.

I use the word community in a broad sense. Communities are small, intimate assemblies, as pictured by Töennies (1988 [1887]), and imagined groupings that never meet (Anderson 1991). Communities may be bound by similarity and represented by a single person who assumes political and economic powers, such as owner of an hacienda or leader of an authoritarian state; or they may be assemblies of autonomous actors whose identities precede membership. Often communities are viewed differently by their members so their boundaries are as putative as real. Most communities are continually fashioned in a changing conversation, but they rarely define a total life, because individuals usually belong to many different communities that are contextually activated and provide different identities.

Communities are often organized around activities that vary in importance and by their connection to economic functions. A self-sufficient household undertakes a range of tasks, but an eating club of friends may only share equal access to food once a month. A health maintenance organization possesses a commons of medical services but with regulated access rights for members; charitable foundations are communities that distribute wealth; Apple computer or Saturn car owners may share knowledge in their consumer communities.

Communities are hierarchically arranged, embedded, and overlapping. For example, cities comprise many communities, variously based on ethnicity, religion, schools, wealth, recreational areas, and commercial districts – each linked to a different identity. The same principle holds in smaller societies. A "matrilineal" group in northern Colombia is made up of cross-cutting matricentral units, homesteads, uterine kin, females who garden together, males who herd together, and trekking groups (Rivera Gutiérrez 1986). Community composition shifts as affiliations are changed in authorized ways or by manipulating qualifications of membership, such as genealogy, marital status, language spoken, and place of birth. In modern times, "racial" purity has been invoked to constrict membership in private clubs, nation-states, and the human race. The rules of inclusion also may be contested and altered, as in the case of struggles in the United States over which age groups and citizens qualify for community-supported welfare payments and health care.

States, as communities, may be held together by force, as in the military state, or by volition. They differ internally, ranging from egalitarian to authoritarian; and state ideologies charter different community forms. Neoliberals would limit influence of the state on individual choice, although government control of the market through interest rates and fiscal measures (the budget) may make income distribution a result of both market and communal forces. Those with more socialist inclinations may want a strong state to insure income or wealth equality, nationalists may argue for a powerful community as an expression of historic identity, and business interests may want a strong state so that legal mechanisms and police control can be mobilized as class interests crystallize.

In the contemporary world, communities stretch across national borders, sometimes with the goal of resisting market forces: animal rights groups, drawing on membership from around the world, slice the nets of fishing boats from one or another nation; money and help from different countries flow to victims of floods in the Midwest of the United States or in South Asia. Such acts depend on imagined commonality.

The community realm is built on social values that are different from those of anonymous exchange. It has several features, but they are differentially found and contextually fashioned: (1) a *base* or *commons*, and ways of maintaining the base through time; (2) *cultural constructions* conjoining base and people, and helping to define identity; (3) *situated or embedded reason* and *innovation*, which sustain and change the base; (4) *self-sufficiency*, which supports independence and identity; (5) rules for *allotting* and *apportioning* the base and products; (6) forms of *reallotment* and *reapportionment*, which mark changing positions, power, and accumulations; (7) internal *appropriation* and *extraction*; (8) expansion and contraction of borders through *reciprocity* and *force* practiced between communities; and (9) *trade* for maintenance and exploration. In this chapter I turn to the first four features of the model.

The Base

A community economy makes and shares a commons. I also term this feature the "base" or "foundation," adapting some terms from Latin America. The commons is a shared interest or value. It is the patrimony or legacy of a community and refers to anything that contributes to the material and social sustenance of a people with a shared identity: land, buildings, seed stock, knowledge of practices, a transportation network, an educational system, or rituals. As the lasting core, though changeable over time, the base represents temporality and continuity. Without a commons, there is no community; without a community, there is no commons.

Most modern economists – after Galileo, Descartes, and Locke – interpret the material commons of a people as an independent, objective entity that can be properly managed only by having expressly stated rights of access (Ostrom 1990). They re-read the commons as something separate from a human community, perhaps as a symbol of community but not the community itself. This market and modernist reading separates objects from subjects.

My use of the term "commons" is different from that of most contemporary economists and political scientists in another way. For them, a commons is real property used by market agents and contained within a market; a commons is either an open-access resource, freely available to all, or a common-pool resource, regulated by rules of use (Ostrom 1990). These theorists would show how control of certain scarce resources through social rules rather than competitive exchange supports market ends and the achievement of efficiency; thus, they argue, market actors sometimes agree for reasons of self-interest to form limited economic communities with a commons. I think this formulation represents a misunderstanding of the social sphere of value, reduces the social to self-interest, and conflates community and market through the misapplication of the language of trade. Communities of the form I examine are not devised to serve market life; irreducibly social, they operate for themselves as they relate to self-interests and the world of trade.

On my view, the commons is the material thing or knowledge a people have in common, what they share, so that what happens to a commons is not a physical incident but a social event. Taking away the commons destroys community, and destroying a complex of relationships demolishes a commons. Likewise, denying others access to the commons denies community with them, which is exactly what the assertion of private property rights does. The so-called "tragedy of the commons" (Hardin 1968), which refers to destruction of a resource through unlimited use by individuals, is a tragedy not of a physical commons but of a human community, because of the failure of its members to treat one another as communicants and its transformation to a competitive situation. Often a community economy does not despoil the environment as rapidly as a market economy does, because in doing so it despoils itself.

A commons is regulated through moral obligations that have the backing of powerful sanctions. But communities are hardly homes of equality and altruism, and they provide ample space for the assertion of power and exploitation from patriarchy to feudal servitude. As expressed in European writing from Locke through Mill, one attraction of arranging society through exchanges born of private property and individual contract, and liberated from persisting social claims and ties, lies in the freedom it offers to all members to engage in transactions that are advantageous to them as individuals.

The substance of the base varies widely, comprising more than real and productive property. For example, by communicating and sharing knowledge, scholars make a community. They hold and enjoy knowledge in common which sustains both community and individual goals. But the base may be composed of land, natural resources such as water or minerals, or a fishing or hunting domain. The commons may be a wilderness area reserved for canoeing or a stand of trees, kept from human entry, held for recreational enjoyment, or maintained for long-term use. In Latin American cities, squatter settlements may form around a water supply after which local associations begin to demand sewage and electricity services that become their commons. When Mayan communities on Guatemala's Lake Atitlán keep forest land from individual use in order to preserve their water sources and have wood for communal projects, they add to their commons and community. The base may be the inventory of a natural foods cooperative, a species of whale or snail, or a group's sacred mountain. I count talismans, amulets, totems, the Vatican's St. Peter's, yogurt culture, and sourdough starters that are passed between households, as well as tokens of chieftainship, such as a staff or stool, among the commons. The Crown Jewels belong, for example, to the reigning monarch, to the monarchy, and to the British nation; they may not be sold, because the community itself cannot be sold.[1] The commons may even be but a flickering candle that stands for lineal, familial, ritual, and property continuity – in short, a legacy (Filifer 1995). I term such central parts of the base *sacra*, a word that refers to the bottom bone of the spine but has a sacred implication as well. Mauss (1990: 43) used this Latin word for property that "a family divests itself of only with great reluctance and sometimes never."[2]

The base may have community value – as a symbol of identity, an expression of values, or a source of material sustenance such as a dam or reservoir – and it may be used for market purposes. But the commons, as a part of community, has as a superordinate value the good of all taken as a whole over the good of an individual. When evaluating individual use rights, the overriding criterion is the effect on community. There may be constant tension between communal and individual claims on a base, particularly in a country such as the United States where accepted economic doctrines are principally market-based and there is a prevailing belief that the community succeeds when individual entrepreneurs do; in the United States some argue that the primary use of the commons should be to support market enterprise.

For example, long contested are rights to log in national forests or to use federal land for grazing. Community-use spokespeople argue that "America the beautiful" is a land of "purple mountain majesties." This song of the commons, which almost became our national anthem, concludes: "and crowned thy good with brotherhood from sea to shining sea." Still, the "amber waves of grain," also honored in the song, were planted by individual farmers and so the struggle over how to dedicate the land is captured even in our sacred hymn.

But the United States does hold a large number of items in common aside from national lands and parks, certain natural resources, and a stockpile of armaments. The single most important shared item is the Constitution, which is hermetically sealed under glass and protected from thieves and saboteurs. Viewed by every schoolchild who goes to Washington – and a very large number do – the Constitution is the founding statement, the authenticating text, of the national community. It inscribes exactly what the community holds in common. Around the Constitution are arrayed a number of subsidiary or dependent structures – the White House, the Washington monument, the Lincoln memorial, the Jefferson memorial – in descending order of sacredness. These and other monuments add to the commons by amplifying some of its features and history. The Washington monument, a symbol of male power and seminal force, is built of stones from all the states; its height – enhanced by its singular location on a hill and by zoning laws prohibiting taller buildings – offers a commanding view of all other points of power. The Lincoln memorial, low and open, speaks of inclusion and empowerment of the common person. The array is continually expanded, as in the examples of the Vietnam and Korean War memorials. Marches and parades that display national communities –

from male "Promise Keepers" to civil rights or antiwar groups – typically take place in the space bounded by these monuments.

The United States' Constitution and the Crown Jewels are both sacra, but each tells something different about the community that holds them: the community may be personified in a chief and her symbols of power or represented in a written document that is understandable only by literate members of the community. In all cases, the commons is "held" in the double sense of being a group and a lasting property. A commons is maintained as the affirmation of community itself.

Sacra

The base, with its core or sacra, represents what it means to be a member of a community. The sacra – displayed as Crown Jewels, a constitution, regalia, or relics; imagined as a holy grail, ancestor, or incarnate spirit; spoken as a sacred, secret word; performed as a ritual; or kept as an item of usable wealth – may be so powerfully linked to the constitution of community that it is never traded but held for the power and identity it conveys and sustains. Sacra are found at all levels of community: national – the US Constitution; provincial – a patron saint; local – a community's physical title to common land (Lewis 1951: 114); familial – a landed domain. The family patrimony also may be more transitory, such as jewels, silver, and photographs. I would even encompass aspects of the person within the broad range of sacra such as purchased marks of identity, including cars, hairstyles, tattoos, breast implants, clothing, and names, or appropriated property through the notion that labor performed annexes that on which it is exercised.

Communal sacra, as Turner has compellingly shown, also may be kept secret to be revealed to young initiates as part of their socialization. Some sacra that make up the building blocks of the community are so important they are never revealed to young members; others are shown in a transformed, grotesque state to induce the novitiates to think on the components of their society (Turner 1967).

If sacra are identified with community, then their destruction, like the extinction of a physical commons, is a community tragedy. Harrison (1992) remarks on the generality of seizing the valuables of the defeated, and of vanquishing others by seizing their sacra.[3] The children's game "capture the flag" is organized around this principle. Malinowski, reminded of Kula valuables on seeing the Crown Jewels in Edinburgh Castle, remarked that some had been taken by England to the "indignation" of Scotland (1961 [1922]: 86). In late 1996, the Stone of Scone was brought back to Scotland, however. The stone –

reputedly used as a pillow by Jacob and then passed through Egypt, Sicily, Spain, and Ireland before reaching Scotland – had been the seat for crowning Scottish kings until 1296, when Edward I seized and put it on display in Westminster Abbey. Seven hundred years later, when finally returned to Scotland, its arrival was celebrated with piping and ceremony.[4]

Physical practices that destroy community by seizing sacra fit Herzfeld's observation on the use of blasphemy in Greece. A part of local and accepted social discourse, blasphemy as an "attack on another man's *sacra*" displays social distance as it diminishes the prowess of the one addressed (Herzfeld 1984: 659). The subjects of such blasphemy – your "God," "Virgin Mary," "uterine kin," "agnatic group," or "government ministries" – are symbols of community identity (ibid.). The verbal attacks are directed against the sacra of the other, denying their efficacy yet affirming the importance of such agreements in social life.[5]

Sacra also may pertain to several levels of community at once, and define the position of the individual in relation to a larger whole (Herzfeld 1987). A saint's image in rural Panama provides one example. In the capital of Veraguas province, which lies in the center of the country, an icon of the Virgin of Fatima, itself a refraction of the Virgin Mary, was kept and honored by vows and prayers. Villages in the province similarly held idols of the Virgin of Fatima that, as it were, constituted representations of a representation. Each of these images was known as The Traveler. On the virgin's feast day, the village idols were brought to the provincial church to participate in a joint blessing and procession that seemingly revivified them. During the rest of the year, each idol circulated among the houses of its village according to the apportionment rule that the traveler could not remain in a home for more than one night nor return until it had visited all other homes in the community. While at a house, the saint offered the inhabitants a measure of protection against evil and environmental dangers, and household members could solicit her help. A supplicant was obliged to slip a monetary offering into the locked box that was attached to the saint's pedestal, and in theory the donations were collected at the yearly celebration, although people said that others usually stole what they had offered: the box never seemed to contain much cash.

The traveler was a sacra at several community levels: provincial, village, household. Each village idol was a copy and token of the provincial sacra (that was itself an image). In their roles of both replica and token, the individual icons represented the sharing of a larger provincial base; yet, this larger base was continually fragmented, if not contested, by the existence of separate village bases; and the apportionment of the village base was contested by the blasphemous act of stealing prior donations that helped ensure personal and household connections to the saint. As in the cases of looting and blasphemy, this segmentary and social display of separation and contestation had performative force because attachment to the Virgin was shared.

Some communities may not have sacra; the meaning of sacra – from a central myth to religious icon to a constitution – may be disputatiously interpreted; or a community may have several sacra that are differently esteemed by members. But at the core, the community dimension of economy is indelibly social, for it cannot exist without the agreement that is its commons. I return to a partly Durkheimian perspective in which both economy and society have a sacred foundation, but not in the modern sense of the term. The sacredness of society here refers not to a putative equivalence between it and a divinity but to its investiture with authenticity and legitimacy by acts of faith in others that, largely implicit, are the means – the only means – by which social agreements are sustained. If in today's language we call these acts sacred, this should be understood only as an analogy or translation: society, economy, and belief are conjoined in the commons as a singular commitment, and they are often represented by objects that are kept for their own sake, apart from any justification on the grounds of market efficiency. The central activity in community is maintaining the group and its values; its axial moment is commitment.

The complete commons of a community usually is a heterogeneous collection of objects. But sacra, as remembrances of the suture of society and economy, cast their significance on ordinary items of wealth including those traded within the sphere of commercial value. At the center lie the most valuable objects that stand for community itself. Protected and surrounded by prohibitions, such as the ordinance that the United States flag should not touch the ground, be burned, or flown upside down, these objects are not for sale nor even for circulation within the community; they are the restricted and "inalienable possessions" (Weiner 1992) that constitute the true patrimony.[6] Malinowski himself early reported that although armshells and necklaces continually circulate in the Kula exchange, a few may be permanently withdrawn as local "heirlooms" (Malinowski 1961 [1922]: 100). Surrounding such sacra may be other important valuables that are sometimes circulated, if only among a select few within a community. A named professorial chair circulates among the chosen within a university; the right to occupy this sacral object surely symbolizes the joining of high scholarly credentials with a university's endowment – both of which lie at the center of the community's perpetuation. Similarly, each household group among the Iban of Sarawak possesses a sacred and central strain of rice, known as its *padi pun* (Freeman 1958, 1970 [1955]). Great effort is made to reproduce this rice, year after year, and to yield a surplus; the *padi pun* is never lent to others or traded. Planted in the very center of a rice field, it yields its strength to all the rices that are planted around it. Directly encircling the *padi pun* in a rice field are certain subsidiary strains of rice that are "semi-sacred," rather like its offspring. When an Iban household group splits up, as it must when children are born and families grow, the succeeding unit takes one of these subsidiary strains to its new locale, where that rice, invested with the sacra of the previous group, becomes its *padi pun* and core rice. In addition to both these sets of rices, ordinary ones are seeded at the periphery of a plot. As elements of the commons, their plenitude is said to depend on the efficacy of the heirloom. But these rice strains are eaten, saved, lent, exchanged, and given to others. A surfeit of ordinary rice is traded for gongs, that are stored in the house. Savings and heirlooms, gongs embody the power of a household's *padi pun*, and this power is said to strengthen and grow over time as represented in an accumulation of gongs.[7]

The base in a system of social value is the counterpart of capital in a system of commercial value. But differing in qualities and different in their uses, many parts of the base have no common measure, unlike capital, all parts of which are measured by money and deemed commensurate in exchange. A key feature of competitive, market capitalism is making profits and accumulating them as capital, whereas the central process in community is making and sustaining a commons. But like capital, a base is a savings against contingency. Indeed, savings often have a Janus-faced appearance. For example, preserving the European house, the family's summer cabin, or the Latin American hacienda means maintaining both a commons and capital. Landed gentry are legatees of a community that has rules of admission such as male primogeniture, and they are owners of commercial property that yields a rent but cannot be sold if the house is to survive. Capital and legacy, personal inheritance and heritage, the European estate and the hacienda may be exchanged for cash only at the expense of losing the patrimony, of severing the continuity of a community.[8]

The discourses on capital and the base also are not so separate as might be supposed. Compare, for example, two primary theorists of the commons and private property: Aristotle and Locke. Aristotle argues that the commons, including both the constitution of the polis itself and material property, is shared by all citizens; and this is so, because man is a social animal and cannot live alone. Locke, whose arguments in the *Two Treatises* (1960 [1690]) are designed to counter Aristotle, installs personal labor as a sacrum and makes the individual into a bounded or atomic unit. Humans create value by remaking and so taking over portions of the natural world through their labor; and this appropriation (from an open-access commons) becomes private property and personal wealth which can be sold or alienated at individual volition. Locke effectively makes the individual the container of a commons: the single person, by mixing his labor with objects, appropriates them for himself just as a larger community mixes things and people, and so joins them. In some respects, Locke condenses a community notion within the person. The individual becomes a community of one: different worlds yet intermixed.

Common Constructions

Around the world, many constructions of the commons and its connection to people are found. But in countless instances, the base of a group is modeled as part of community itself, not as a separate, mechanically driven object, as in the Newtonian construct of capital.[9] Such cultural models do not distinguish between the human and non-human constituents of community, or between people and material; the social, spiritual, and material sustenance of the community are one.

Cultural models of the base, underwriting the commitment of a group of people, are often built around forms drawn from immediate experience. With regularity, people use (1) family figures – mother, father, parents, ancestors, a lineage; (2) the human body and its parts; or (3) the house to construct the commons.[10] For example, among the Nayaka, hunters and gatherers of South India who are divided into small groups, the environment, including the forest, rivers, and hills, is a parent.[11] Ever-providing, it gives without constraint to its children who are the living. This Nayaka image is linked to their allotment practices; they view themselves as siblings and members of a joint household, and so share items – asking for them and keeping no accounts of what is taken and given; the same does not hold for their relations with traders, plantation employers, and shopkeepers who are not part of their intimate community. Their model has implications for ecological practices also, because just as the Nayaka trust and depend on the environment – as they would their parents – they must respect its bounty and take no more than their share.

In parts of Africa, the environment is represented as a lineage of ancestors who, having traversed and lived in the area, and having developed the techniques of agriculture, fructify the land in which they are buried. Ancestors also may be reincarnated in game animals, so that crops and game animals are made available in return for rituals performed or payments made to the ancestors. Similarly, a chief may be seen as the incarnation of a line of chiefs, and the chief's regalia – the community's commons – may be invested, may be saturated, with this sacredness. The well-being of the chief may be deemed necessary for both the material and social health of the community. In other parts of the world, a food – such as yams – may incarnate a lineage or continuing domestic group and can be grown only by its members, who in turn will have no sustenance if their seeds are lost; seeds also may have souls that must be respected; or the abundance of natural resources – reflecting the benevolence of a mother-like figure or the malevolence of a devil – may be made available through their wishes tempered by human supplication and conduct. In still other areas, human-like spirits animate game that is hunted, and success is assured by propitiating the spirits first and expressing gratitude after; the health of animals may depend on the goodwill of saints; abundance of water may require the performance of rituals to the deities (Sikkink 1994, 1997).[12]

Similar ideas are found in early Western economic models. The physiocrats of France, who were predecessors of modern economics, asserted that "the land is the mother of all goods." They thought the instrumental work of the "husbandmen" or farmers helped bring forth a material bounty, but claimed that this act of midwifery was non-productive or "sterile." They saw the land itself as giving, with God as the ultimate donor. (They also reasoned that owners of the soil or nobles held rights to the agricultural surplus secured from the giving agent.)

In some cases, as among the physiocrats, a community constructs its relationship to a base through the notion of giving. In parts of Latin America, farmers say the land "gives" (when it is productive) and "does not give" (when the soil is depleted); they add that harvesting is a "taking." Similarly, the forest of the Nayaka "gives" like parents. Sometimes, a return for such giving must be made by offering rituals, thanks, or parts of the harvest, but often not, and the repayment is a token of the product secured. Harvest rituals are important events also for many Europeans and European-Americans, who live in a predominantly market economy where nature's bounty is conceived to be humanly earned. Thanksgiving is the nationally shared, community holiday of European-Americans in the United States. At a common meal, eaten to excess at a specially festooned table, mutual ties are remade, dependence on a heritage is displayed, and thanks are given for the continuance of community life in the New World. Each household practices the same ritual, consuming the same food at the same time, in the larger community that is the nation-state. A community enactment of thanks for abundance persists even in the life of those caught up in the practices of market life.

In all these cases, crops are raised or animals are hunted by instrumental practices. But the end or community is often projected on the means so that the instrumental, "for the sake of" activity is done "for its own sake" as a social performance. For example, the goal may be to maintain the house, lineage, village, or religious sodality, and this communal entity is projected on the means of production so that the divinity, ancestors, saint, spirit, or other being is modeled as lending productivity to the instrumental act, as in the case of lineage ancestors who fructify land. The instrumental act, encompassed within a social purpose, displays community participation and commitment as it materially reproduces the group. It is a reflexive or partially self-referential act.

The Weberian account of the Protestant ethic and meaning of economic action is similar. According to Weber, in the early stages of Protestantism instrumental practices were undertaken to achieve economic gain, but this success displayed one's membership in God's elect. Not gain itself but commitment to being saved justified the relentless pursuit of money that revealed one's destination; the "for the sake of" activity was partially undertaken "for its own sake," which was to display commitment.

Caring for the base

Making and keeping the base is a central concern in community, for the base makes a community as it is made. An endowment that welds together people and things, the base is passed across generations and provides the beginning for its legatees. As a Panamanian villager said, when I asked how he made a living, "You have to have a beginning." In rural Latin America, the base is a group's hoard or savings for the unpredictable. A heterogeneous collection, it includes natural resources and products, completed work, remainders or leftovers, as well as castaway items scattered around the homestead that seem to have no immediate use – it is a repository of the old, the new, and the unused..

In Spanish-speaking areas of Panama, Colombia, and Guatemala, the base consists of material things, human character, work, and the divinity. The concept of "force" or "strength" (*la fuerza*) unites the several parts of the base, provides the mooring for a household, and offers a rationale for caring for the base.[13] Strength has divine and mundane referents. It is life energy; the word might also be translated as *vis vitae* or vital essence, to use an older terminology. A property of all living things, force is found in plants, animals, and humans as well as some natural products, such as charcoal, whose strength has not yet been gathered (*recoger*) by humans. The elements of nature – soil, sea, and rain – are the sources of strength for all living things. Plants secure their force from the elements, and animals replenish themselves from plant life. But these conveyors are not the foundations of the chain, because strength is ultimately a product and manifestation of God's power (*el poder*). The force of living things, constituting the stuff of life, owes itself to God's might.

Born with strength or vital energy, humans expend force in living; languor resulting from work or physical illness signals a diminution of *vis vitae*, and death results from its extinction. People must continually secure vital energy from their surroundings. The often-heard expression "meeting the needs of the house" refers to this necessity of gathering and preserving force in the base. Market wants, however, are sometimes dressed up as household needs, through linguistic appropriation and persuasion when the two spheres are interwoven. I once saw a sign outside a store in Central America that advertised grains, cooking oil, and salt as items of "first necessity" and cigarettes and alcohol as items of "second necessity"!

Humans gather strength from nature by working, and work gives a household rights to what its members gather. This connection between work and property has a theological justification. According to the people, the world manifests God's power; and he possesses all for having made it, from rocks to vegetation to humans. Having been made in God's image, humans likewise possess the products of their work, including the strength of nature that they secure. But human work must be sustained by strength, and just as God possesses the world because he supplied its strength, when humans supply the force for working, they possess both the activity and its products. Thus, by keeping a base and drawing on it, a household group owns the work of those it sustains and the products of their efforts that in turn maintain the base.

But good practices in the fields and at the hearth are not sufficient to sustain a group, because a household also must be "well-run." A major aspect of caring for the base is being thrifty or making savings. A household exercises parsimony in its consumption of foods and use of goods; people try to prolong the life of items in use and to expend as little as possible. The art of being thrifty may be practiced on anything, from whittling a new grip for a machete from a tree limb to mending handles on a basket by using vines.

The practice of parsimony (coupled to past innovations) provides "leftovers," "leavings," or "remainders" that become savings. In agriculture, when crops such as maize, rice, potatoes, or beans are well managed, the harvest covers what is needed for seeding, foodstuffs, and fodder, and yields a remainder. The base of a household is composed of a collection of disparate remainders – sacks of maize, beans, and animals – that add value and are monuments to past innovation.

People use the word economizing (*economizar*) for the act of being thrifty and practicing parsimony (*hacer economías*) (Gudeman 1978; Gudeman and Rivera 1990). I understand being thrifty and economizing to refer to a means–ends relationship but one in which the focus is on minimizing expenditures or the means. Economizing is an instrumental act (a "for the sake of" activity), but refers to what is not expended and so can be saved. For example, once a harvest is parsimoniously achieved, its expenditure as a means to satisfy hunger is also economized. In the countryside, economizing is practiced for the sake of keeping the base; it points to an end valued for its own sake. In the market, economizing refers to the means–ends relationship itself so that more means may be committed if greater ends can be secured; the ratio of ends to means is judged not by the savings created but by efficiency–producing the most product per unit means or using the least means per unit product. Market economizing, which is making a profit, has no separate referent; it points to itself for legitimation. The household and market meanings of economizing have different senses.

The Latin American construct of the foundation provides one example of how human economy and environment, people and things, are welded together. No distinction is drawn between human-made and resource capital. The ideas of strength and force, with their divine justifications, provide the mooring and identity for the household.

Situated Reason

In Panama, I learned early that the word "foundation" or base refers to the physical underside of a house and, by metaphoric projection, to the material parts of a group's resources. By further extension, it designates the people of a house, for the person with a good foundation has the character and reason needed to manage a domestic economy. In seeking a marital partner, one searches for a person with a good foundation, and building a foundation means having children who develop into reliable individuals and perpetuate the family legacy. The foundation, Latin American villagers observe, is inside and outside a person, so dissolving the body's borders and constituting individuals in relation to their base. A person's foundation both consists and is a product of "situated reason" that develops in relation to others.

Across the centuries, situated reason has proven difficult to specify and define. It constitutes part of what Aristotle meant by *phronēsis* (practical wisdom) and *technē* (art), and what Locke intended by "complex ideas," Diderot by "art," Veblen by "workmanship," Schumpeter by "innovation," and Lévi-Strauss by "bricolage." Schön (1983) terms it reflexive reason or art; Scott (1998) very effectively describes such acts as *mētis*; and Marglin (1990, 1996) explores these practices under the label "techne" as opposed to "episteme," which is formal, logical and abstract. But many of these constructions, while emphasizing situated reason's flexibility, do not fully capture its community placement. More recently, cognitive psychologists and anthropologists, influenced by Vygotsky and Bateson, and by pragmatism, have been exploring this communal practice under terms such as situated learning, shared reason, or social cognition.[14] Others have attended to the idea of "everyday history-making" (Spinosa, Flores, and Dreyfus 1997). Hutchins (1995) explores learning in context to suggest that cognition is a function and part of a total social and material environment. Neither fully innate nor entirely learned but a composite of the two, situated reason is symbolically mediated and develops within the context of supporting adults and culture.[15]

Local reason is socially and historically dependent. For example, in Panama, the ways of working are part of the communal heritage. Children "play" at cutting and loading sugar cane, building houses, seeding a field, carrying water and cooking, and many other adult activities that they witness. More generally, a child learns by doing, by watching and copying others, and by receiving a guiding hand. Apprenticeship in working is central.[16] In Colombia, harvesting potatoes is learned by watching an adept, and by bending over, moving along a row, pulling potatoes from the earth, sorting the tubers by eye, putting them into the appropriate basket, and pulling the baskets along until a row is completed – receiving an occasional comment in the process.

These skills, put together as individual styles or ways of working, do not have a "logical" or deductive form that can be generalized and mechanistically applied to different situations. Potato harvesting is different from picking maize, beans, tobacco, and other crops, each of which is a distinct activity. No rule unites each job as a whole. Harvesting potatoes is not even learned as a whole, but over time, and some people may come to be more accomplished at one stage, such as digging, whereas others may be adroit at sorting. Everyone comes to have a different way of using, moving, balancing, and adjusting her body in the work.

This reason-in-action changes in the performance or doing. As the people say, they have to "conform" or "adjust" in their work. A woman cooking a pot of potatoes is in continual motion as she adjusts the size of the fire, blows on it, selects a different type of wood for cooking, keeps an eye on the boiling water, adds potatoes or slices in half ones already cooking, fans the smoke out of the kitchen, and checks the flavor of the broth as she sprinkles in condiments or adds salt or water to suit the tastes of her household. I have watched farmers adjust their practices through the year as they try to judge the changing weather; household necessities; amount of rice they need; which plots to seed; when to seed; which seed to use (for seed strains have different times of maturity, resistance characteristics, and consumption features); as well as when, how often, and how well to weed. No meal preparation exactly resembles another; no farming year is precisely like the prior. Each requires adjustments, and as these are tried, they become part of a person's repertoire of skills or foundation.

In Latin America, practical reason is often described as doing something *al tanteo* – grappling, touching, and feeling one's way forward. This way of working "by feel" or "hit-and-miss" (*tantear*) has no rule. A method of coping by adapting and adjusting, and by experimenting on a small scale using materials and relationships at hand, each new trial adds to the store of knowledge, which accumulates in a meandering fashion. *Tantear* conveys the sense of change and suggests this reason lies in the entirety composed of people, their environment, and legacy: one person's enactments become examples for others. Situated reason is reflexive, for it is learned in the doing and each completion provides an example to be changed, and, as practices change, so shifts the environment. Using situated reason, people adjust but draw on accepted models, they experiment yet have predictability.

The concept of situated reason dissolves the borders between mind and body, person and surroundings, individual and community. I once visited the workshop of an older artisan in Latin America who made roof tiles in quantity for sale. The shop was filled with used and unused furnaces of varying sizes and types, countless molds, and innumerable finished and broken roof tiles. As I listened and observed, it became apparent that this collection was not rubbish but a legacy for working. The materials were tangible reminders and tools for solving problems, a kind of library. "Mind," in this sense, was not contained within the artisan's brain but in the ensemble without which his physical capacities could not be exercised.

This unbounded, situated rationality supports innovation and maintenance of the base. A base is built of innovations that occur through openness to contingency which local reason affords. Seeds, foods, medicines, clothing styles, designs, songs, and agricultural techniques are the historical products of innumerable trials. In Latin America a rural house, like an urban workshop, may be filled with discarded tools, old items, and half-made pieces. Not evidence of a people's "carelessness," as a city-dweller in Colombia once said to me, the discards embody past efforts and constitute a physical memory that may be activated, altered, and put to use. Discards represent past associations and provide materials for potential connections.

In Latin America, I have watched people innovate outside market contexts. In rural areas, farmers who are raising crops for their households try different ways of seeding – by combining seeds, planting them closer together or farther apart, or changing the orientation of the rows. Men make fishnets for their own use and find new ways of arranging the knots and styling the network, often in response to the fibers they are using. Every rural house is built with slightly different materials, depending on availability, and the dwellings are uniquely shaped often in accord with the family itself; as houses are extended and rebuilt, such differences become monuments of innovation and part of the household base.

Even so simple an act as making a chimney cap suggests that innovation is a function of context not calculation. In rural Guatemala a family found that rain was entering its new, metal chimney pipe, and spoiling the cooking fire and creating smoke. Casting about for a thrifty solution, they found a discarded metal bowl in the yard. Turning it upside down, poking holes in the rim, and looping wires through these and around the chimney, they fashioned a chimney cap. This object would not have been devised had not metal bowls appeared in the market, had the household base not contained a discarded bowl, and perhaps had not a child put a food bowl on her head after eating.

These adjustments to the base that occur within the privacy of a community often pass unremarked by both observer and theoretician. Yet, even if local innovations bring no monetary profit to their makers, they are certainly akin to development in the market, such as making a new medicine or food, or reorganizing a factory line. A community innovation increases well-being, a market innovation raises the monetary standard of living. Both are products of situated reason and add value.

This basic reason is very different from "rational choice" and rational man. The concept of "*homo economicus*" has several guises. According to some, the core concept in market discourse is rationality – perfect or imperfect, bounded or not. "Economic man" or the rational person, isolated and self-interested, chooses among alternatives by calculating their benefits and costs, maximizing the yield, and ignoring their public effects on others. The rational person pursues private gain and uses no-cost public goods whenever possible. Central to this idea of rationality are self-interest and calculation, implying that humans act to maximize means-to-ends connections and have the ability to price – that is, to use a common measure for all goods and preferences: we harbor the desire and possess the faculty to calculate and quantify things, persons, and relationships. When actual behavior does not correspond to the assumptions, theorists modify the variables defining self-interest or presume that real behavior is affected by non-rational externalities, such as imperfect information. The idea of rational choice, a more focused notion, often refers to consistency in choice or revealed preferences; and even such ideas as commitment to others and to moral implications can be added to this idea of "reasoned assessment as a basis of action" (Sen 1978).

Situated reason is not an alternative to reasoned assessment or instrumental calculation, whether guided by self-interest or commitment to others. But situated reason, dependent on community, is always an important part of economy. Rational decision-making presumes an ordered world in the sense that items or units exist and are commensurate. Situated reason makes a world, and opens new worlds, dissolving oppositions between self and others, self and objects. It is part of economy at the base.

Reason and property

An intriguing case suggesting a relation between situated reason and real property comes from a recent study by Anderson (1998) in the former Soviet Union. He shows how the Evenki people who live in Arctic Siberia legitimate appropriation from the environment or create property. For Evenki, appropriation is a kind of "taking," justified by "knowing the land." On my reading, such knowing can be glossed as "know-how." For Evenki, know-how is locally learned, instrumental activity. Each knowing is separate, such as how to catch reindeer, where to cut trees, or how to survive inclement weather; and knowing has an element of making-do, of being able to adapt and adjust as an event unfolds. For Evenki, having an ability or capacity means that one can cut trees, hunt animals, or use the land in relation to the skill or craft possessed. In this sense, the Evenki model is one form of a labor theory of value that justifies appropriation from the external world. But the Evenki notion is more communally rooted than the Western one that descends from Locke, for knowing-how creates status and commands respect from others; and knowing-how implies a sort of reflexivity with the surrounding world. For example, a hunter must never be boastful or sharpen his butchering knife before stalking game, because animals can hear. The prohibition requires that the hunter see himself as might animals. Similarly, the injunction not to be greedy in using resources is as much a reflection on a person's relation to others as it is on his relation to the environment. Know-how is an activity done both for the sake of something else and for its own sake. Knowing the land legitimates using it to sustain one's self and family, and knowing the land expresses identity and self-realization in the heritage of skills. This double instrumental and fulfilling act creates real property through the exercise of human properties.

Self-sufficiency

Anthropologists have made a central contribution to the understanding of economic behavior through their study of economies organized for self-sufficiency.[17] In most instances only a sector of an economy is self-reproducing. In the case of non-reproducible goods, such as heirlooms or land, self-sufficiency means keeping the base for oneself or the group, whereas with reproducible goods, such as food crops, self-sufficiency may be achieved by creating a loop from production to consumption to production. Self-sufficiency helps create and maintain the commons, and marks independence and the borders of a group.

The discovery of self-sufficient economies raises a fundamental question. Why, and when, do people exchange – and why do they keep to themselves? Braudel (1982), in his inclusive study of the rise of markets, simply assumes that people exchange. Adam Smith proclaimed that humans have an inherent tendency to truck and barter. Durkheim (1933), by dividing societies into those based either on mechanical or on organic solidarity, set out precisely this difference between self-reproducing systems (mechanical solidarity) and systems of trade (organic solidarity). He supposed there was a long-term movement from one to the other, caused by demographic expansion, population concentration, and the social excitation these yield through heightened encounters between people. Today, economists usually explain that exchange is prevalent because it lowers risk, secures needed resources, expresses self-interest, or expands choice. Above all, economists argue that task specialization followed by exchange is the most efficient way to meet material wants. For their part, anthropologists sometimes theorize that exchange establishes peace pacts between groups,[18] secures prestige for those with special access to external goods, or expresses moral closeness between otherwise separate individuals.

My view is different. Humans build communities that yield a measure of certainty but produce boundaries that represent possibilities to
explore and transcend. Exchange is part of human grappling with the
environment. Making or remaking what one has and assimilating the
world of others is the dialectic of material life.

In practice, the amount of labor, resources, and production devoted
to exchange or non-exchange shifts. For example, in times of down-
turn in a market economy, a household may forgo buying frozen beans
that can be readied in a microwave and purchase fresh beans that
require more preparation. As conditions worsen, the beans may be
grown in a garden at the house, so that only seed and tools need to be
purchased; finally, even the seed and tools may be home produced. In
the shift from frozen to fresh to home beans, participation in market
exchange declines as time devoted to the communal production of
goods increases.

The base and its sacra provide the building block for self-sufficiency.
In lowland Panama, the people say that no meal is complete without
home-grown rice, and only rice gives strength to humans; in the uplands of Colombia, the same was said of potatoes, but different crops
were honored in other parts of the country.

The Kekchi Maya of southern Belize provide a compelling example
of the connections among base, self-sufficiency, and identity.[19] Existing at the margins of markets for more than 400 years, Kekchi economy
has long been a shifting combination of self-sufficiency and the trade
of labor or products for cash. Although the line between the two sides
has changed as the importance of each has grown and diminished, the
Kekchi display how self-sufficiency in a crop provides security and
continuance for a community.

For Kekchi, corn is the true, necessary, and staple food, and is consumed at every meal, either as dumplings or tortillas.[20] In Kekchi, the
verb *to eat* is the active form of tortilla, and any meal without corn is
termed a snack. Revered and respected, corn is dried and stored at
home; its quantity measures a household's wealth and security. Even
when a man has an important source of cash income through trade or
market cropping, he raises corn for the house. Kept for consumption,
offered at house altars, and exchanged between households only on
ritual occasions, no other crop is treated with such care or provides so
many metaphors for daily life as corn.

Most households try to raise more corn than they need for eating,
because some can be sold and the excess is fed to chickens and hogs
which can be taken to market when emergency cash is needed. But
hogs also are eaten, especially on ceremonial occasions such as the
building of a new house. When a new home is built, blood from a hog

is splashed on the corner posts and a hog's head is buried beneath the hearth, while pork served to guests is a sign of warm hospitality. But hogs are savings banks for corn, and so it is this food, with its conversion to hog meat, that ultimately provides the true base of the house and sign of hospitality. Raised for the sake of maintaining the house, corn is symbolically projected into its foundation.

The handling of rice, which the Kekchi raise as a cash crop, offers a striking contrast to corn. Corn fields are possessed by older, married males, whereas the largest rice fields belong to unmarried men. Rice is individually owned, raised, and controlled, even when the separate producers share in the work of raising corn for the same house. A young man may work in and be fed by his father's corn field but sustain his own rice plot in his free time. No obligations fall on an owner to share his rice within a house just as the rice owner cannot obligate family members to work for him. Accounts are kept of the rice labor one man performs for another, and debts are cancelled by a return of work or money.[21] In contrast, corn help is never repaid in cash, although when there are work conflicts between corn and rice, the former takes priority. Lastly, no rituals surround the growing of rice. Rarely consumed and hard to keep, rice is not fed to pigs.

The planting of rice as a cash crop is recent and falls outside the system of communal control and religious importance. Rice is rather like an item secured in external trade. Attractive for what it brings, which is cash, and a danger for what it undermines, rice occupies a position similar to that of Aristotle's external trader whose practices can undermine community or the polis. Rice also fits the pattern of diffusion that Veblen (1914) pictured; when a crop spreads from one culture to another, he argued, it is often freed of its established rituals and takes on new functions. But rice and maize are closely connected for Kekchi as two sides of one economy, because household self-sufficiency in corn subsidizes the very low return they receive for selling rice.

Today, whether the Kekchi "sacralization" of corn is a result of ideology, market resistance, or risk avoidance, corn is the basic – in eating, agriculture, ritual, and myth. Whether Kekchi self-sufficiency in corn is a reaction to the dangers of market dependence or the product of tradition is irrelevant, because the two implicate one another. Yet, the Kekchi illustrate how self-sufficiency of a single crop lies at the core of community economy. Corn self-sufficiency, providing independence as well as assurance against uncertainty, has become a badge of household position and village membership. The fine line the Kekchi draw between the home and market crops highlights the importance of their community economy.

Rice in Borneo

Studies from the island of Borneo (Sarawak) also demonstrate how the reproduction of a crop provides for the reproduction of community; here as well social position and power are attained by augmenting harvests kept for the group.

We have seen how the Iban keep a central strain of rice that gives power to other strains and indicates continuity and strength of the family. These same themes appear among the Kelabit who live on the Baram river in Sarawak.[22] The Kelabit also occupy longhouses that are divided into hearth-groups. Each hearth-group is a distinct community that strives to be self-sufficient, especially in rice. Formed around a nuclear family, the hearth-group passes through a developmental cycle. Two adult couples, both able to grow rice and live by it, should not and do not live together.

For the Kelabit, rice is the central food and item of symbolic importance. Most foods come from animals and plants that are said to live on their own, but not rice, which requires human cultivation. Rice is owned and eaten only in the hearth-group. Cooked at a group's fireplace, which is the "inside," "deep," or "true" part of the dwelling, rice is consumed collectively, because eating together indicates commensality and mutual dependence. When working in distant fields, people prefer to return to the dwelling for the midday meal, but if a meal is taken in the fields, hearth-groups sit together, facing inward with their backs to those in other groups. A Kelabit resists eating the rice of others and eating his own rice at someone else's hearth. (In contrast, other foods can be cooked and eaten anywhere.)

Grown for the sake of maintaining the group, rice provides it with "goodness." The larger the hearth-group, or the more people dependent on the rice supply, the greater the goodness attained. Goodness I take to be something like flourishing, well-being, or living well in Aristotle's expression for living appropriately in community. It is a value in community economy but not measurable. On certain ritual occasions, such as naming feasts, when it becomes appropriate to eat the rice of others, the "really good people" are able to provide rice to many others or even to all of Kelabit, so projecting the everyday experience of their hearth-group on the larger society.

Failure to produce enough rice for hearth-group subsistence does not lead to starvation but to dependence on others or being forced to eat other foods which results in a loss of goodness. Rice labor performed for others also is reciprocated or goodness will be lost. In contrast, game, vegetables, and cultivated foods are shared between hearth-groups without loss of prestige, and this sharing does not create debts or the need for reciprocation.[23]

A Fragmented World

Stretching from Latin America to Borneo to Africa and elsewhere, the evidence is remarkable.[24] Raising rice, potatoes, maize, or yams – the food varying by area – becomes a performance and mark of identity. These ethnographic cases cast doubt on claims that humans inherently seek to exchange in anonymous market transactions. People tend their gardens to make community. Keeping to the self expresses one side of economy, but it persists in all economic formations and defies market theory that presumes humans by instinct or natural desire produce only for exchange.

Our own practices – dispersed and fragmented – illustrate the pull of keeping sacra and maintaining community identity, and they challenge standard theory as well. The United States keeps large stocks of unused oil, even while buying abroad. Japan resists importing rice from the USA, because consumption of the more expensive local variety has become an expression of commensality, the family, self, strength in life, and land sovereignty (Ohnuki-Tierney 1993, 1995). Trade negotiators from the USA have had difficulty understanding this Japanese discourse on identity and community economy – especially since Japan has become a symbol of market efficiency in other domains – but when self-sufficiency in rice makes independence, why exchange?

Some brief ethnography from a village in Hungary before the post-socialist turn illustrates the persistence and importance of a base, and its changes as well as its involvement with market life. Until the last quarter of the nineteenth century, wealth was seen to reside in the soil; dependent on agricultural returns, a person gained status through land possession. Technology was relatively stagnant, cultivation was extensive, labor was a necessary input but not viewed as value-creating. This system was largely a feudal or manorial heritage. Land was the sacra. Then, in the late nineteenth century, given several agricultural and economic crises, villagers began to diversify and experiment with crops, and shifted to more intensive agriculture. Locally, the marker of independent status shifted from land control to possession of one's labor, and right through the interwar period people sought to control their own labor, although land ownership could aid in its possession. Contracting to work on a manor, for example, was avoided as far as possible. Such servitude was likened to contracting a uxorilocal marriage, and manor workers were compared to animals and disdained like gypsies. The people explained that through work a person produced both the material world and honor, although individual statuses were not directly comparable.

After 1947, with the advent of socialism, central planning became paramount, but by the mid-1960s there was a move to decentralize in hopes of achieving greater efficiencies. A small-scale market economy grew outside the massive communal form, and this development led to a split between the generations. The older generation held that possessing one's activity was central to maintaining esteem. The younger generation saw work in terms of time and remuneration; it was a calculated or rationally directed activity. The older generation sold goods on the market but did so by trying to raise a surplus of regular and home crops and animals. They were practicing the art of economizing. In contrast, the younger generation raised new crops, depending on market prices and the possibility of profit. Economizing for them meant calculating the relation of means and ends; control of one's own labor was important only because work was a commodity and means. Leaving aside the recent post-socialist transition, we see changes from late feudal forms to early capitalism to socialist planning (that spawned a market reaction) which reveal the persisting yet changing role of sacra, the base, and its constructions from land, to labor, to instrumental rationality. Some changes set one generation against another as the economy's balance shifted from community to market.

Today, most of us live in both realms. We buy goods but retire some from circulation as legacies – jewelry, linens, clothes, dishes, bibles; and we pass along objects made by ancestors. Self-sufficiency in food also can be an ideal for us, even if infrequently practiced. Some years ago, I visited a very successful corn farmer in Iowa. Still a young man, he had expanded his family farm by effort and intelligence – specializing in corn, keeping up on technologies, trading at opportune times, and using government assistance programs. On a cold November day, he drove me across the land, stopping here and there to pick up a stone or piece of wood, as he explained how he had purchased inexpensive stone-filled, soggy land that others thought unreclaimable. Over the years, he had acre by acre removed the stones and devised drainage systems. We visited his storage barns, tested his giant combines and other equipment, and saw his airplane and computer by means of which he followed the commodities market. Finally, we sat down to a huge Sunday dinner at which he proudly announced that every item on the table – pork, potatoes, corn, milk, vegetables, ice-cream – had been produced on the farm. In eating with him, we shared the base and identity of a self-sufficient, multimillionaire.

NOTES

1 An excellent discussion of such inalienable objects is provided by Annette B. Weiner (1992); what she describes as "inalienable possessions" corresponds closely to what I term the commons, the patrimony, or the core of the commons.

2 See also Davenport (1986) and Geary (1986).

3 In his work on medieval sacred relics, Geary (1986) also notes how these objects often substituted for political power and could be stolen – the ultimate theft occurring in the sacking of a city. In one of his remarkable essays, Radcliffe-Brown (1958 [1952]) saw that totems were really part of a larger class of social symbols having to do with community identity. He observed that in the case of "sex totemism," one gender might express displeasure or take retribution on the other by killing an animal of its totemic species.

4 Minneapolis Star Tribune, Nov. 16, 1996 (p. A4).

5 The point that ritual and performatives might express identity and distributions of power was initially argued by Leach (1954).

6 James Carrier reports the story of a man who set fire to a flag. "I'm protesting," said he. "If the flag is really precious, why do we sell it at K mart . . . when it was sold, that's when it lost its meaning" (Carrier 1995: 115).

7 Du Boulay presents a fascinating picture of Greek mountain life in which the sacra is the land, house, fire, hearth, and ultimately the woman who tends the hearth and makes the food on which the house relies. Money was gained and worn as an indication of the "strength" of the house (1974: 37).

8 Common objects may assume this same Janus-face quality. McCracken (1988) tells of Lois Roget who keeps her family's possessions. The goods all have community significance as items associated with ancestors or locality through place of purchase, making, materials, or prior owners. Each object is labeled by its communal characteristics. Ms. Roget draws in the next generation by using goods – plates, an oil lamp – on special occasions or in rituals that remind participants of and make community. Her great concern is that her descendants will not keep and revere their heirlooms and the sacra of community. Will they transform them in the direction of the market pole? I am indebted to James Carrier for bringing this story to my attention.

9 Mirowski (1989) explores the use of Newtonian models in modern economics, demonstrating that these are built on contextually persuasive metaphors.

10 For a discussion of some of the epistemological issues, see Ingold (1996a, 1996b).

11 The Nayaka material is drawn from studies by Bird-David (1990, 1992a, 1992b, 1993).

12 I explored some of these constructions in Gudeman (1986).

13 Studies by others suggest that variations on this theme are found from Mexico to Peru and Chile, and in Portuguese-speaking Brazil as well (Bourque and Warren 1981; Foster 1967; Orlove 1995, 1997; Scheper-Hughes 1984, 1992). With Rivera, I suggested that force is a European folk idea (Gudeman and Rivera 1990). Durkheim (1995 [1912]) used the notion of force to express the pervasiveness of the sacred in social life and its manifestation in totems; for Durkheim, force was the strength of society so that in worshipping a totem society was venerating itself. In this light, the reflexivity in Durkheim's argument was not that of assuming society to be the supersubject of thought but of inserting a European notion, force, into the formulations of other people.

14 See, for example, Bateson (1972), Goody (1995), Lave and Wenger (1991), Rogoff and Lave (1984), Resnick, Levine, and Teasley (1991), and Vygotsky (1978). The work of Cole (1991, 1996) is especially relevant. I am particularly grateful to Tim Ingold (1996c) and Gísli Pálsson (1993, 1994) for their discussions of "enskilment" which is closely related to situated rationality.

15 Developmental psychologists term this form of learning, by which social groups channel and support the cognitive development of their young, the zone of proximal development (Vygotsky 1978), scaffolding (Bruner 1985), and guided participation (Rogoff 1990).

16 Rogoff (1990) describes how Mayan children observe their mothers making tortillas or weaving and then begin to do so themselves, receiving a kind of guided participation or ever-decreasing scaffolding in the learning process. See also Rogoff, Mistry, Göncü, and Mosier (1993).

17 Karl Polanyi (1968: 7) claimed anthropology's outstanding discovery was that economy may be submerged or embedded in social relationships, which is to say that community economies exist.

18 Albert Hirschman (1977) might argue that this anthropological generalization was anticipated several hundred years ago in Europe by the idea that *doux commerce* civilizes unruly passions.

19 For the Kekchi, I have relied on Richard Wilk's (1991) study.

20 Most Kekchi land is held through a reservation system instituted in the earlier part of this century. Use rights are granted to the first person who clears the forest and propitiates the Mayan deities, who, as true owners of the land, grant use of it to humans. Land is the communal heirloom.

21 The Kekchi – drawing on a familiar metaphor – claim that the village should act like a family; and villagers have common work obligations (*faginas*) for the village itself. An adult male may spend from four to eight days a year repairing bridges and buildings, or clearing pasture for the community; he is caring for the village commons.

22 See Janowski (1995).

23 The same values are encountered in other parts of the area. For example, among the Gerai who live in West Borneo, household self-sufficiency in rice is the basis for achieving "standing" (Helliwell 1995). Rice here, too, is a metaphor of the human, and "standing" means achieving economic independence or autarky of the household. Rice surpluses, that

provide the measure for standing, give protection against future contingencies and are traded for display items such as ceramic jars and jewelry. A group successful in achieving self-sufficiency is "good," whereas one that cannot produce either children or sufficient rice is "debased" (*busong*: a degraded, unsuccessful, unbalanced state (Helliwell 1995: 369, 370)). Only slaves cultivate for others rather than for self-sufficiency.

24 For valuable descriptions from Greece, see Du Boulay (1974: 28–38) and Theodossopoulos (1999). For other accounts, see Bohannan and Bohannan (1968), Fortune (1963 [1932]), and Smedal (1989).

Chapter Three

Sharing the Base

In a market people exchange goods, buying and selling at the best price available until satisfied they cannot better their personal holdings. Exchanges in community are different, for they revolve about ways of dividing a shared base, are guided by multiple values, and have to do with fashioning identities as well as material life. Ethnographic illustrations of sharing the base possess the virtue of openly displaying these general processes, for the same activities often are more hidden in industrial economies.

I distinguish between allotting and apportioning the base, both of which are ordered by multiple values. Allotment designates the way a stock or permanent fund, such as land, is parted for use; apportionment refers to dividing a flow, such as a harvest.[1] But the dividing line between the two may be thin, as in the case of water, which is both a stock and a flow; and they may be elaborated through secondary repetition, or reallotment and reapportionment. Within the same economy, the division patterns also may vary by goods and services, or by community size, from household, to village, to political territory. In addition, the allocation process is often tied to instituted power or manipulated by power-holders to buttress their social status or fill their coffers; and in many areas, where market transactions have recently expanded, gender control of wealth has become asymmetric, because it depends on who gains access to market returns (which, generally, is men). Thus, the allocation pattern in community economy is usually a composite or combination of different value scripts: basic foods may be divided according to need within households; land access may be allocated by first possession or by lottery, but only to citizens, adults, or males in local lineages; festal beer may be shared equally in villages; and captured swans, tusks of slain elephants, and joints of butchered animals may be paid respectively to a queen, chief, and mother's brother.

Allotment

Land, often the most important component of the base, is variously allotted. In some Guatemalan villages land is held both as private property by households and in commons by religious brotherhoods or *cofradías*, so that individuals may have access to arable land in both systems.[2] Within a brotherhood, usufruct usually passes from father to child, but retention of the use rights depends on serving the *cofradía* whose saint blesses the land. On the saint's day, the *cofradía* sponsors a procession and commensal celebration; and the ritual leader of this service, known as the *cofrade mayor*, bears considerable costs. The position rotates annually among males in the *cofradía*, and, if a man refuses to serve, he loses rights to till the commons. If a brotherhood member moves away and cannot participate in its activities, his rights also lapse, in which case the *cofradía* allots his plot to a new member. Participation requires time and expenditures – there is a transaction cost in the market lexicon – but serving the saint is considered to be a "pleasure" and necessary to ensure land fertility and well-being with others. The values of communal maintenance, participation, and equality are expressed in this allotment system.

Many African lineages also held land in commons, but these patterns were different, and land borders were fluid as lineage claims were linked to expansion, mobility, and accumulation. Consider the patrilineal Tiv of northern Nigeria as they were organized in the 1940s.[3] Tiv resided in compound groups led by a senior male who coordinated farming activities and controlled the spiritual resources on which local prosperity and fertility depended.[4] Compound groups were clustered in larger territories formed about lineage segments that controlled access to land. Every man had the right to farm the land and participate in the affairs of his local patrilineage. If he wished to seed more land than needed to support his family, he sought permission of his compound head, who uniquely might accumulate more land, labor, and wealth than others.[5] Only while a man farmed a plot did he have exclusive control of the land. Left fallow, the plot became available for other members of the lineage segment, and a temporary resident also might be given farming rights. But land was never rented to others, and selling land would have been like selling one's lineage position. For the Tiv, land – sealed to a community and its lineal ancestor – was locally allocated by male elders on the basis of right and need.

The Jukumani, an ethnic group in the highlands of Bolivia, display different values in their allotment of land. They mark the boundaries of their land with great precision, and their complex division pattern employs allotment, reallotment, tribute payments, reapportionment, appropriation, and expansion of territory, all of which may be abused by rent-seeking leaders.

Jukumani economy is a product of pre- and post-Conquest times.[6] They arrange themselves by *ayllus*, which are named landholding groups, organized around patrilines. The land is allotted at the village level and tilled by families who inherit use rights. No one can sell land, and on the rare occasions when someone has tried, the perpetrator has been berated, exiled, or killed (and supposedly eaten). The land, protected and nourished by the earth mother (*pachamama*), is part of community; to sell the earth abrogates social relationships – hence exile or extinction of the offender as the retribution.

Each village controls seven fields, and every landholder has rights to parcels in each field. A field contains a tribute plot for village officers, and there are more tribute plots for leaders of the four central *ayllus*. Once, all Jukumani had to work four days per annum in these plots, raising potatoes and maize for the leaders. This tribute was reapportioned by leaders in raw 'form during the year and in cooked form during festivals; some was sold to pay for common religious and legal services, but much was appropriated by leaders for personal purposes.

Jukumami are divided between "original ones" (*originarios*), whose ancestors lived in the area in the early 1800s, and "people of the margin", or *kantu runas*, who arrived later.[7] Only original ones have usufruct, and they are taxpayers. (If a landholder fails to pay community taxes or sponsor festivals, he or she may be demoted to being a person of the margin, with a near agnate taking over the land.) In the past, after seeking the permission of a landholder, a person of the margin could use a plot's edges for grazing animals and for sowing in exchange for four days of labor. Today, he may be required to pay cash as well, although marginal people also have taken over some of the leaders' tribute commons. People of the margin must always establish a legitimating tie to gain land access: in the past, a marginal one might care for aged landholders or contract a uxorilocal marriage with a full community member. Today, under demographic pressure, the authorizing tie is more narrowly defined: it must be a patrilineal connection. Thus, the expression *"kantu runa"* means at the margin in time of arrival, of a plot of land, with respect to a kinship group, in economic power, and in village obligations.

Traditionally, people of the margin could move on to land of non-Jukumani and augment the borders of their group. Such expansion is no longer possible, so, with population growth, a new community identity has come to be recognized – "child of the margin" (*kantu wawa*), or one who has an even less complete status than a person of the margin. A child of the margin gains access to land by providing agricultural labor and helping a landholder meet his ritual obligations; the labor debt and forms of address used make his relationship even more asymmetrical than that of a person of the margin. Together, the two types of marginal people help define Jukumani identity, because through their changing rights to the base, the Jukumani negotiate the meaning of community.

From Stock to Flow

The cases from Latin America and Africa illustrate ways in which access to an immobile base is allotted. Sometimes the base is both a permanent stock and a flow, which requires both allotting and apportioning. In the highlands of northern Spain the village of Ramosierra holds a yearly division in which rights to a flow obtained from a stock are simultaneously apportioned and allotted to community members: chance and equity are the guiding values.[8]

A large stand of pine trees were unexpectedly donated to Ramosierra in the 1400s by King Juan II of Castile in return for military support. Obtained by grant, not purchase, the trees require little upkeep, but are annually culled so the wood may be sold. Rights to the timber are apportioned in the Pine Luck, which is a central community activity, for the return can support a thrifty family for a year.

Rights to participate in the Pine Luck are limited and passed by inheritance. Participants must be married, over the age of 25, and resident in the village for more than six months each year. The inclusion rules have broadened, narrowed, and been manipulated through the years, but participation in the Pine Luck always connotes full communal membership; it cannot be purchased. The apportionment itself works by chance. A group of senior males divides the forest into lots equal to the number of qualified rights-holders. Lot numbers are drawn as names of participants are called out. A lot need not consist of contiguous trees but may comprise stands from several areas; and legatees may coalesce split rights to share a physical lot. In theory, lots should be equal in monetary value, although in fact the variance may be considerable. Equity and luck are the apportionment values; and, in fact, wealthier villagers secure their riches from outside the community and its commons.

Apportionment

Apportionment patterns are closely linked to their guiding values and tactics. Goods and services may flow from all to all in a community, from all to one, or from one to all. Equal food sharing in agricultural households illustrates the first pattern. Tribute and payments to leaders, as in the case of Jukumani, represent flows from all to one and the exercise of power. Finally, a single person, such as a hunter or collector, may share his bounty with others. The Nambicuara of Brazil provide an example.

Nambicuara, who hunt, gather, and practice agriculture, live in nuclear family households near kin and within a village circle. The primary production unit is the nuclear family, but it is not the unit of consumption. In the early 1970s, the ethnographer Paul Aspelin studied the division of foods among ten families in one village.[9] The Nambicuara's two most important or basic foods are meat and manioc soup, and these foods are always shared. Other foods are pooled and consumed within families, and shared with others only on demand. Aspelin's data, based on more than 100 observed cases, show that meat and manioc soup are apportioned according to relative size of the recipient unit or per capita. Kinship distance and personal friendship have no effect on who receives what. The Nambicuara explain that some do better in hunting, others in gardening, and all should be able to benefit from the successful producers. Their equity values assure that everyone has equal access to basic foods, which helps to reproduce the community. Aspelin also discovered that the people's rule-of-thumb measurements corresponded closely to his calibrated scale, although smaller families received slightly more than their expected share and larger families received less.

Through this apportionment pattern the group marks its changing boundaries. Villagers can be excluded from the division as a sanction for stealing, committing incest, or failing to contribute; but new households in the village are given a portion before contributing, and significant changes in social position also are marked by food sharing. Game and manioc soup do not represent the totality of Nambicuara foods, but this apportionment pattern of the basic foods provides a model and support for the rest of communal life.

A similar apportionment pattern, involving the distinction between stocks and flows, tangibles and intangibles, and community and market has been reported for the Hadza of Tanzania. Woodburn (1998) recounts how Hadza share meat from big game. In brief, the meat is divided into two parts – god's meat and people's meat. God's meat flows to the meeting place of initiated men. The second portion, in turn, is four times apportioned: the meat is first taken on demand at the spot of butchering, next it is brought to the camp and divided again, then it is cooked and divided yet again, and finally the leftovers are themselves distributed. To receive meat, people must claim or demand a share.

In the Hadza case community and market are separate, for Hadza also practice anonymous or socially disembedded exchange but with non-Hadza. Among themselves Hadza do not barter, debts are avoided, and objects are transacted through social relationships. The core of the communal realm is not reciprocity but apportionment from a common or shared "base." For the Hadza, this base is made up of a consumable or flow (meat) not a stock or permanent fund, and it is apportioned in four stages by demand. The right to demand meat is socially established and morally supported; however, the apportionment is not determined by set rules that prescribe a particular division, such as social position or gender. The Hadza also have some durable goods or permanent funds that they allot on demand and transfer by gambling, but the focal moment of the community realm is manifested through flows of butchered meat. Finally, outside or at the borders of Hadza community, barter and trade take place, but this trade may be partially converted to a form of sharing as it is assimilated to community.

Analytically, then, there are several kinds of property rights or incommensurate values among the Hadza; these holdings are distributed variously by stocks and flows, by transfer rules, and by the object's and participants' places in community. The Hadza distribution pattern exemplifies the larger generality: on the inside of any community, division of a common good holds; reciprocity is an act between communities; trade is found at the furthest reaches. Communal exchange rests on shared morality but it implies and is always linked to impersonal trade that it supports.

Reallocating the Base

As social positions change, flows may be reapportioned, and reallocating the base shifts social standing. For example, among the Zahau Chins of highland Burma, social positions are signaled and changed when oxen are sacrificed and shared at feasts given in honor of the spirits.[10] Offered only by male household heads and organized in sequence by importance, animal sacrifices provide givers with prestige and the right to receive increased bridewealth, as well as membership in the village council. By completing the entire cycle of feasts, a man attains the highest position in the spirit world.

At a sacrifice, the ox is cut into nine named joints, with a varying number of parts. Each distributional unit consists of pieces from a joint or several joints together. The quality of the joint, the size of share, and their combination determine the value of a portion. Feast-givers distribute the entire animal by apportioning pieces to specific categories of kin, to "official" best friends, to helpers, and to themselves (one joint). The village headman and blacksmith also receive lots, as does every male household head, though the value of this share (measured by size and joint quality) varies with the feasts that the receiver himself has sponsored. Finally, the widow of a past feast-giver receives her husband's share for one feast after his death; other widows and the destitute get small pieces from all the joints. Overall, every household receives from the sacrifice as a sign of communal membership and a measure of the giver's own commitment to communal welfare.[11] The value schemas are several: repayment for village and feast work; maintenance of social relationships; recognition of feasts already given; equity; and charity. Recipients secure confirmation of their established but different social positions as the feast-giver gains standing. But this division pattern is also an instrumental act, for serving as a bulwark against the uncertainties created by warfare, raiding, and headhunting in the Chin area – and functioning like a local currency – meat allotted to others is a way of safeguarding, storing, and retrieving accumulations of wealth.

Sharing and Social Value

Some years ago H. Ian Hogbin (1938–9) provided a compelling example of a reapportionment that has little to do with material value and everything to do with social position. Marking one extreme in division processes, it casts an interesting light on our own practices as well. Reporting on the Wogeo, who live on a small island off the north coast of New Guinea, he described a type of feast, involving village, clan, household, and gender relationships, that has no rationale other than the mutuality it creates.

In one instance, a man offered a minor feast to mark the occasion when his youngest son was first allowed to wear a rattan belt. Deciding on the date of the feast, he invited several neighboring villages and then laid a prohibition on collecting chestnuts until the feast. Some five days before the feast, the men of the feast-giver's village spent two days gathering chestnuts; women put them in baskets. Three days were spent removing the husks and picking up coconuts.

On the feast day, the people of the host's village brought their collected products and put them on mats in front of the feast-giver's house. Next, the chestnuts were poured into three large baskets and 50 coconuts were placed beside each one. Soon people from the other villages arrived. They had collected chestnuts and coconuts and pooled them in their villages and divided the pooled product into smaller amounts for carrying. Upon arrival, they placed their chestnuts in a large basket with the coconuts alongside. One village supplied no coconuts, so some were added from the host village's supply.

When all was collected, the apportionment began. The host called each village forward in turn, and the basket from one was redistributed to another. Women of the receiving village emptied the large basket of chestnuts and filled their carrying baskets while men picked up the coconuts. All then returned to their villages where the chestnuts were pooled in front of the headman's house. He, then, redistributed the goods so that each household received an equal share. Finally, women cooked the chestnuts, and people ate them in such large quantities that many suffered from indigestion.

Thus the reapportionment: women and men in households collected chestnuts in small baskets (1) and took them to their village leaders (2), who agglomerated them in large baskets and then divided them into small baskets for carrying to the host village (3). At the host village, the small baskets of chestnuts from each village were agglomerated in large baskets, and then redistributed by village (4) and divided into smaller amounts for carrying home (5). In the home villages, the small baskets were again agglomerated and then the chestnuts were redistributed equally to households (6), where they were consumed (7). One village received slightly more than it brought, the host village slightly less. The entirety was surrounded by gaiety.

How are we to appreciate this process in which communal reapportionment is stripped bare? The event may serve to energize work efforts; perhaps it helps to equalize ecological differences between villages and demographic differences between houses. But explanations drawing on efficiency and comparative advantage in trade have little persuasive force, because most participants leave with what they brought! Why cart goods from home only to return with them?

Falling outside the explanatory limits of market models, the Wogeo exchange involves sharing by "pooling" and "interchange." The reapportionment makes and marks the values of communities: age, gender, households, clans, villages, and collections of villages. But the feast also changes the positional value of the feast-giver through the size of community he can mobilize – to eat its own produce.

Reapportionment and Exchange Rates: Aristotle's Solution

Through apportionment and allotment, prized goods and services are transferred in accord with communal values. The Wogeo present one case in which flows balance but positions shift through apportionment. What about the reverse? Might goods be transferred by community allocation without altering social positions? Certainly, market trade achieves this result, but these exchanges turn communal connections into impersonal relationships. Is it possible for community members to exchange goods to adjust and maintain their holdings yet retain their relative social standing?

On my reading, Aristotle explored the possibility of this form of transfer in his writing on economy and exchange rates in the *Politics* and the *Nichomachean Ethics*.[12] But no part of Aristotle's economic texts has drawn so much attention as his treatment of exchange rates in the *Ethics*. Everyone claims it is confusing; few are admiring. Eric Roll says Aristotle's argument is "obscure" and that Aristotle thought exchange-value existed "apart from price and prior to any particular act of exchange" (Roll 1973: 34). Marx claimed that Aristotle failed to propose a labor theory of value, but Schumpeter (1954) thought he was groping for one. Finley concluded that Aristotle "was not seeking a theory of market prices" (1970: 14) but failed to make clear what Aristotle was doing. Karl Polanyi offered the several claims that Aristotle was not concerned with price theory (1968b: 106), that he wanted to provide a formula for the just price (ibid.: 79, 97), that the just price was an exchange equivalency (ibid.: 97), that equivalency was tied to the relative standing of the exchange partners, and that "set prices" restored self-sufficiency (ibid.: 108). But Polanyi also suggested that personal status was the same as productive skills and that exchange rates had to be set in proportion to them (ibid.: 107): this argument not only implies that Aristotle was groping toward a labor theory of value but contradicts Polanyi's initial claim that Aristotle was not concerned with a theory of price.[13]

I offer a different interpretation. First, Aristotle did not provide a theory of market price. The words "price" and "just price" do not appear in the *Ethics*. Aristotle was examining rates of exchange within community, that is between households within a village or polis (larger political community) but not in the marketplace. Of course, he knew that competitive markets existed. Aristotle is seldom cited for his early and perceptive understanding of monopolies and their effect on pricing. In the *Politics* he relates the story of Thales of Miletus, who, forecasting a large harvest of olives, leased all the olive-presses in his region;

when harvest time arrived, Thales reaped a fortune. Aristotle also tells the story of a man in Sicily, who, by cornering the market in iron, doubled his money. Aristotle distinguished between these sorts of impersonal financial transaction, in which profit is made at the expense of others, and trade within community undertaken to achieve sufficiency. His concern in the *Ethics* was to explain at what rate items should be exchanged within a community.

In my view, Aristotle used the image of apportionment from the commons to build a model of exchange within the polis. Exchange rates, he argued, should replicate this apportionment pattern, so allowing the polis to maintain its pattern of just deserts, remain self-sufficient, and provide a context for the achievement of excellence and well-being. Aristotle's picture of community economy and exchange was the reverse of the contemporary market model. According to market theory, the intersection of supply and demand determines prices, that in turn set returns to the factors of production and hence the allocation of wealth and relative standing of individuals. By contrast, in Aristotle's economy, social position determines the allotment of the commons, which sets the pattern for exchange rates. For Aristotle, just or proper rates of exchange maintain the realm of social value. Let us follow his argument in detail.

In the fifth book of the *Ethics*, Aristotle examines justice, which is a virtue and the key excellence. His treatment of exchange rates and allotment within the context of justice is significant, because allotment and exchange require the use of ethically bound, socially aware judgment or reason that takes account of communal relationships.

In the *Ethics*, Aristotle described two forms of justice: "rectificatory" and "distributive." Rectificatory justice has to do with correcting injustices in transactions between individuals, as in cases of fraud. Relying on arithmetic calculations (adding and subtracting), this sort of justice restores the initial conditions between two parties so that one does not gain at the expense of the other. In contrast, distributive justice refers to allocating honor, money, or "the other things that fall to be divided among those who have a share in the constitution (for in these it is possible for one man to have a share either unequal or equal to that of another)" (1131^b33–4).

Distributive justice entails the use of geometrical proportions and at least four "terms" – two individuals and two shares. This form of justice is reached when equal proportions are established between shares and individuals: the ratio of the shares must be the same as the ratio or relative standing of the persons (1131^b27–31). The method may sound mechanical, but Aristotle acutely observes that such ratios are "the origin of quarrels and complaints – when either equals have and are

awarded unequal shares, or unequals equal shares" (1131ª23). He adds
that people agree the distribution should be made on the basis of merit,
but rarely concur about its meaning. Democrats argue that merit comes
with free birth, aristocrats think excellence determines just deserts,
and oligarchs identify merit with wealth or noble birth. Recognizing
that the rules of allotment are contingent and negotiable, Aristotle
does not provide a warrant for one or another measure: his interest
lies in the pattern or form of the division.

Implicit in Aristotle's model is the assumption that positions and
goods can be coordinated through social agreements and a sense of
justice drawing on wisdom (*phronēis*) (Nussbaum 1986: 210). Instrumental calculations cannot bring together incommensurate values, although Aristotle does not explain how the comparisons are made.

It was Aristotle's next step, however, that proved confusing to economists. He suggests that individual exchanges within a community be
modeled "after" the allotment pattern of the commons. In effect, Aristotle argues that two exchangers should first pool their separate products and then divide them in proportion to their own just deserts in the
community. Each two-part exchange, as between a shoemaker and
farmer, is a token or emblem of community allotment. Not prices in a
market, these trade values reproduce the communal order. For example, the shoemaker would receive that share of the pooled shoes and
grain that he would receive from the commons, and the farmer would
receive his share as well. If the shoemaker received $\frac{1}{100}$ of the commons, to which he made an agreed contribution, and the farmer $\frac{2}{100}$,
they would trade in the ratio of two to one. For intracommunity trade,
proportional returns must be established: "The number of shoes exchanged for a house [or for a given amount of food] must therefore
correspond to the ratio of builder to shoemaker. For if this be not so,
there will be no exchange and no intercourse" (1133ª22–4). Emphasizing the difference with market trade in which value is determined in
exchange, Aristotle adds,

> There will, then, be reciprocity when the terms have been equated so
> that as farmer is to shoemaker, the amount of the shoemaker's work is
> to that of the farmer's work. But we must not bring them into a figure
> of proportion when they have already exchanged . . . but when they
> still have their own goods. (1133a32–1133b3)

Aristotle clearly understood that market price is established in impersonal trade. He is discussing trade within community in which social
relationships, a scheme of value, and knowledge of the other precede
and set the conditions for the exchange.

Meikle (1995) offers a very different interpretation of Aristotle's treatment of exchange rates. He thinks Aristotle is addressing something like commodity exchange as we experience it in competitive markets.[14] His reading, emphasizing the commensuration of goods alone, leads him to claim that Aristotle was unable to resolve how exchange value is determined, for neither need – holding a community together – nor money could provide the measure.[15] Thus, he claims, Aristotle "has no theory of value at all. His contribution is not to have offered such a theory, but to have given a precise formulation of the problem which a theory of value has to solve" (Meikle 1995: 190; see also ibid.: 27). Aside from our different contextual placements of Aristotle's narrative (market versus community), I suspect that Meikle's concern with the question of commensuration in the market or finding the single standard by which all exchanges are to be measured is both a modernist interest and contrary to Aristotle's perspective, which, as Nussbaum emphasizes, has much to do with making adaptable judgments. The confusion over exchange rates arises not because Aristotle failed to establish a common measure for exchange but because subsequent observers confound the realms of community and market, which is precisely Aristotle's later observation.[16] As Yack (1993: 59) urges, arguments over "correct standards" of justice are the stuff of politics for Aristotle and, I might add, typical in the communities known to anthropologists. Who contributed to the commons and in what amount, the pattern of its distribution, and who qualified for a share and in what proportion was a topic of political judgment and one on which different states varied, observed Aristotle. The varying answers – from arranging distribution by age, gender, or autocracy – provided the standards against which individual exchanges in community could be measured. By according priority to maintenance of the given order, however, Aristotle did provide a conservative view, making it difficult to challenge social and political differences such as patriarchy or slavery, especially when the virtue of predictable, trustworthy relationships was being said to be upheld.

Managing Generosity at Home

Although modern economy seems devoid of allotment practices, and prevailing ideology obscures their presence, we do practice them in many arenas. For example, in the domestic sphere, age cycle events are marked by apportionments. Goods are transferred within communities and across generations at bridal showers, weddings, baby showers, birthdays, confirmations, graduations, and other celebrations;

and the content of the transfers – domestic goods, personal items, lasting heirlooms – signal degree of closeness of the parties. In addition, larger distributions, such as bequests or preinheritance transfers, reallot the base itself. The use of this way of transferring wealth is contested not by market forces but by larger communities, such as the state, that would tax the wealth itself.

Food everywhere is an expression of community relations. A family's refrigerator – stocked by the "bread" winner – is a commons to be shared by all, as any parent with teenagers knows. A pie, cut equally at the table, signifies family sharing, although earlier in the meal choice pieces of roast may have been reserved for the elder male. Many of these tactical arrangements are projected across relationships with friends and others. For example, potluck dinners vary in their organizational principles: everyone brings a pasta, a different course, or an ethnic dish so that the food commons, open to all, represents a joining of foods, thus uniting a church group, or school parents and teachers.

The complex customs of restaurant eating require cultural learning and social tactics. At an all-you-can-eat buffet individuals pay a standard price but serve themselves on the basis of want; a restaurant may also serve "family style", with everyone at a table sharing food from common bowls, transferring the desired amounts to their private plates. At some restaurants tables may be shared with other diners, and even when tables are private, salt and other condiments on the table make a commons with fellow diners. But the commercial layout is only the beginning. A group of friends at dinner may decide to share all the ordered foods, taking on the basis of want; pairs may share by splitting their orders equally; or each person may order a separate meal as private property yet exchange reciprocal, incommensurate bites with others at the table. And for each of these patterns of consumption, the bill may be divided unequally by food ordered or equally regardless of foodplate. In addition to the food, one person may donate the wine or its cost may be shared despite inequities in consumption, and a single dessert may circle around the table with precisely equal bites taken by all. These distributional practices are piled one on another at a single event, encoding need, want, mutuality, equality, and unequal monetary control in a flurry of juxtapositions. Learned over time, and mastered by some, these practices can subtly signal and deny community with others, if only for short moments of time.

Economists argue that the transaction costs of managing a communal distribution are high, but these costs are nothing other than the maintenance of social relationships or mutuality itself, for the base is part of community. Imagine the reverse: calculating at home the cost of each food, the amount served, and its time of preparation in order to divide the meal; and recall what precisely calculating each person's restaurant bill does to the sense of friendship established by eating together – both destroy community. Of course, not all communities create mutuality or equality. Corporations – located between market and community, featuring accumulation, and held together by economic power – have apportionments of the widest disparity. White males have always done better than others; and chief operating officers – vaunting their economic contributions – receive off-scale returns that reflect their power more than their market contributions or communal commitments.

At the national scale, we use many forms of apportionment, and heated discussions take place over the level and breadth of our national commitment to welfare, medical, social security, and educational programs. These arguments concern the size of the commons to be created, its proportionate division among community members, and who is to be included in the recipient group as well as the way activities and people should be shifted between market and community. Single mothers, divorced mothers, and illegal immigrants are allowed into and expelled from sharing communities in accord with political conditions and the rhetorics of persuasion. The rights of these "marginal ones" reveal more about the identity that the larger community establishes for itself than they do of these occasional members.

Arguments about community apportionment today are posed often as a trade-off between efficiency and equity. I suggest the opposition is misleading, because equity has many meanings, and community distribution can yield both equity and inequity. But community equity also cannot be "traded" for market efficiency, because they pertain to different realms of value. The "trade-off" concerns the relative place of community and market values in an economy.

These same issues concerning the relation of market to community, and the place of power and status, are manifested by mixed institutions such as charities, museums, and especially the private foundation. Charities solicit funds from market beneficiaries, reapportioning them for different purposes. The solicitation itself may be a communal performance: friends or neighbors present themselves at the door of one's house; charities sponsor balls and dinners for which potential givers pay large sums to attend so they may pledge in the presence of esteemed fellow givers. Monetary power, mutuality, and reapportionment are conjoined as individuals transfer money from the market to the community realm. Museums (as well as hospitals, hospices, and old age homes) acquire named rooms and art collections in personal acts that memorialize the giver and his taste in collecting. Organizing balls, serving on boards, soliciting money, and collecting art require time turned from lucrative to community work, further representing ways that monetary reward is turned to community merit as market life expands and requires the construction of new communities.

At the apex of this transformation of market capital to community base lies the private foundation. Usually funded by a wealthy businessperson, who parts his wealth between descendants and foundation, this unique community is subject to national laws yet is independent and self-perpetuating. The words "foundation"and "endowment" signal that it is a gifted community. The responsible foundation delineates a mission, defines its recipient communities, and apportions shares from its base to academics, inner city youth, artists, third world nations, environmentalists, or family planning agencies. The foundation community is saturated with prestige from the grantor (who mediates between market and community), to the trustees (or elders), to the boards of experts who, using their contextual knowledge, select the recipients, who themselves bear the honorific title fellow, member, lead investigator, scholar, or grantee. Is this communal process, which holds and apportions wealth and social standing, which absorbs immense amounts of time from market leaders, and which is saturated with transaction costs, truly different from managing the exchange of chestnuts in front of a gathered crowd or allocating and receiving cuts of meat and prestige at a village sacrifice?

NOTES

1   See Georgescu-Roegen (1971) for a discussion of stocks and flows.
2   For an historical consideration of rural economies and land in Guatemala, see McCreery (1994).
3   The Tiv were studied by Paul and Laura Bohannan in the late 1940s and early 1950s. At the time, they numbered about 800,000 persons. I have drawn principally on their book (1968), and two earlier articles by Paul Bohannan (1955, 1959).
4   "The community is the basic reference point," say the Bohannans (1968: 108); community and space "give the fundamental values within which production takes place" (ibid: 109).
5   Tiv have communal work obligations. A school or marketplace is cleaned by the males of a lineage; a compound group clears the paths near it. In the fields, men, especially brothers, often work together, following their "hearts." A neatly laid out yam farm, symmetrical, with straight rows, "gladdens the heart," which is part of living well.
6   The Jukumani information is drawn from the study by Ricardo Godoy (1990). See also Godoy (1991). For comparison see Platt (1982).
7   "Original ones" is stated in Spanish; "people of the margin" is expressed in Quechua.

8   The material is drawn from Michael Kenny's work, *A Spanish Tapestry* (1961). The year for which he reports financial flows was 1958.
9   See Aspelin (1979). For comparisons, see Henry (1951) and Siskind (1973).
10 This material is drawn from Stevenson (1937, 1943). Leach (1954) states that feasts and carcass allotment are similar among the Kachin of Burma. A thigh-eating chief, among the Kachin, receives the hind leg of every four-footed animal killed in his domain along with other forms of tribute, and he has the right to hold a *manau*, which is like a Chin Feast of Merit. See also Buck (1930), for a description of the ceremonial division of animals and fish in Samoa, and Marks (1976), Richards (1939), and Wagner (1956: 48) for descriptions of meat redistribution among Bantu-speaking people. For elsewhere, see Carrier and Carrier (1989), Duby (1968 [1962]), and Neusner (1990).
11 A system of loans and social adoptions provides further room for maneuver.
12 I have used the translations of the *Politics* and the *Ethics* in the Princeton University Press edition (1984). In this version of his complete works, the *Ethics* was translated by Ross and revised by Urmson; the *Politics* was translated by Jowett. To develop a better sense of the translations and translators, I have read Aristotle in other translations, including those by Rackham (1926), Barker (1946), and Thomson (1953), and have drawn on the translations of expert commentators, such as Finley (1970), MacIntyre (1988), and Nussbaum (1986), who also provide divergent readings. All references to Aristotle use the system developed by Bekker in 1831: the numerals, such as $1094^{a}1$, are printed in the margins of the Aristotelian texts; in this case, the reference is to the first line of the *Ethics*.
13 Lowry (1969: 64–5) also assimilates Aristotle to a modern understanding. For a different interpretation, see McNeill (1990).
14 For a similar view, see McNeill (1990), although he argues that need and reciprocity are the determining elements of exchange in the polis.
15 "It is impossible to come to understand the later and derivative form of the exchange of unequals until one has understood what equality in exchange means; and it is impossible to understand that until one has solved the underlying problem of commensurability, which is the presupposition of systematic exchange-relations existing at all" (Meikle 1995: 84). Aristotle's analysis fails because he does not explain how products are commensurable and so cannot show how a ratio between them might be determined. Before exchange, there must first be a shared property (ibid: 22). Here especially, Meikle's metaphysical focus, categorical distinctions, and abstraction from practical context differentiate his view from the more socially based one I offer.
16 Marx accused Aristotle of not understanding the problem of commensuration and not seeing that labor was the common denominator, because he lived within a system of slavery that obscured labor's contribution (Marx 1967 [1867]: 59–60; 1970 [1859]: 68).

Chapter Four

The Great Estate: Power, Extraction, and Expansion

The exercise of power affects allocation, because the extraction of wealth sustains leaders, and chiefly power can lead to increased extraction. A compelling example of appropriation and allocation within a single institution is provided by the great estate or manor.[1] The great estate existed before, during, and after feudalism.[2] As successor to the Roman villa, the great estate represented a shifting mix of community and market realms, and was the dominant economic institution in Europe for a millennium or more. Striving to be autarkic or self-sufficient, the great estate offered a defense against external political and economic uncertainty. But great estates were also part-communities, because they existed within larger political and religious formations. Eventually, they were eclipsed by the rise of towns, guilds, and profit-making entities.[3] Still, with their reliance on slaves and dependent peasants as workforce, great estates were internally powerful if not violent institutions, especially during times of increased labor use.

During the period that I consider, trade and markets were expanding and encompassing larger domains of material life. This extension, along with demographic growth, environmental changes, the spread and contraction of diseases, and shifts in the technologies of production and everyday life, enormously affected the great estate and had much to do with its alterations (not to mention the way nuances and shifts in political and religious conceptions, and altering sensibilities of the natural world and the possibilities for its control, modified the institution). As it spread across the vast landscape of Europe, the great estate varied by ecological zone, political climate, language region, and according to whether it served religious or secular purposes. But these influences on the great estate and its variations, which have been finely recounted by historians, I bracket to one side to look at several broad patterns of reproduction, transformation, and organizational limitation that the great estate manifested during its fifteen hundred-year history. I focus on the great estate's community aspect to exemplify how communities may grow in relation to demographic pressure, technological innovation, and the exercise of power.

Models and Historical Change

The base of the great estate was land over which it held rights or control. Frequently acquired as a gift from a political authority, but sometimes seized and often inherited, land was used primarily for agriculture, although pastoralism also was practiced. Agriculture, usually focused on the production of basic foods, was largely self-reproductive or cyclical. The great estate maintained an inner core of self-sufficient basics.

Wealth, or the accumulated parts of the base, took several forms. Tools changed and improved over this long period of European history, but in earlier times they were neither abundant nor long lasting: the great estate did not hold a high proportion of its wealth in permanent funds aside from the land. Foods were kept as stores and used to feed the house and its retainers and workers. Some produce was traded, and in some places and times the great estate accumulated display wealth, such as jewelry and the house itself.

The great estate grew by improving its technology and acquiring more land or base. Duby (1974: 177, 181) argues that as lords in the eleventh and twelfth centuries increased their demands for consumables to expend and display, new tastes helped impel agricultural intensification. Manors also grew by amassing more land, so supporting more people, including workers and consumers. This form of growth, however, encountered limits set by managerial and information control; rather than dividing its tasks and increasing the division of labor, the expanding manor replicated itself on a smaller scale.

Physically, the great estate had many forms. For example, a ninth-century royal estate at Annapes, near Flanders, consisted of a palace, built of stone, with three chambers; in addition, there was a house with eleven small rooms, a cellar, and two porches. The courtyard contained seventeen houses of wood, stable, kitchen, bakehouse, two barns, and three storehouses, while a palisade surrounded the entirety. As for equipment, the estate possessed two axes, two augers, a hatchet and adze, two scythes, two sickles, and two iron-tipped shovels as well as numerous wooden tools. But there was only one set of bedding (Duby 1968: 364). Peasant and dependent units were considerably

Self-sufficiency

Figure 4.1   Great estate with slaves

smaller and built around nuclear families; for example, in the same period one household, which used 68 acres of land, contained two married brothers and spouses (with three and five children), a married sister with spouse and six offspring, and an unmarried sister (ibid.: 33).

Drawing on the work of several historians, but simplifying to display the community structure, I distinguish five periods or models in the history of the great estate showing how a community economy replicates, internal hierarchies are formed, and flows of wealth are controlled. At all moments in this history, the goal of self-sufficiency remained central.

Model 1: In early times, up to the eighth century, the great estate may have been a single economic unit that used slaves (see figure 4.1). According to Postan (1972: 85), the great estate was most likely a continuation of the Roman villa; it existed at the outset of the Dark Ages and spread throughout Europe, although actual evidence for its presence does not show up until the eighth and ninth centuries. This autarkic community consumed what it produced, using as labor force the slaves who lived on and were maintained by the estate. Holding slaves was a legacy of the Roman villa (Duby 1974: 31–3; Postan 1972: 90), and perennial warfare, with forays into neighboring groups, ensured an ample and continuing supply of captives. Known as *mancipia*, these persons belonged outright to their masters, as did the offspring of female slaves. Duby concludes that slaves were found throughout Western Europe, their position being "the same as that of the farm animals" (1968: 37); like tools and horses, slaves could be sold. Thus, they were acquired by violence, procreation, and market trade.

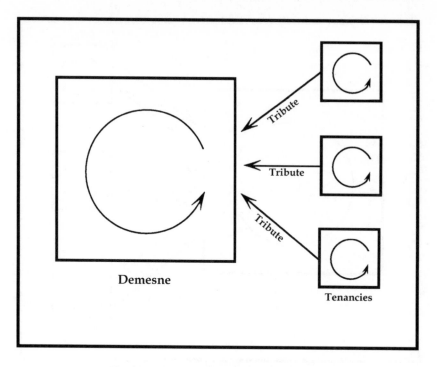

Figure 4.2   Great estate with manses

Model 2: By the eighth century, evidence suggests that the estate was often divided into a core and outlying parts (see figure 4.2). Duby terms these the *mansus indominicatus* and the peasant *manses* (1968: 35). They are also known as the reserve or demesne and the tenancies or manses. Demesne (or domain) refers both to all land held outright by the estate and to the portion of land attached to the main house; usually, the term designates the center of the estate, consisting of the best land and the domicile of the owner with his family and retinue. It was the sacra.

The land, a permanent fund, was held by the lord who granted use rights for tribute. Slaves worked the demesne and were maintained there, but some were settled on outlying manses that were also in the estate-holder's possession. Over time, these slaves achieved some freedoms from the center, and eventually some of their descendants became tenants or peasants who, though not working their own land, were technically freepersons (Duby 1974: 39–40; Postan 1972: 160). Occupants of the manses provisioned themselves from their work, and they owed payments in kind, labor, and coin to the landowner.

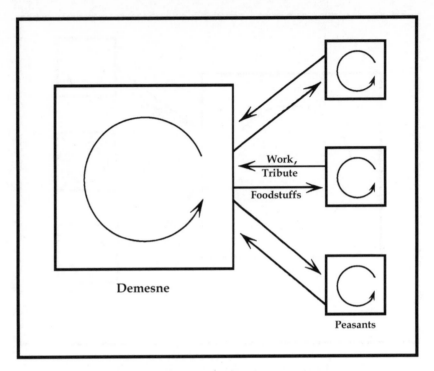

Figure 4.3   Great estate with peasants

Simple yet complex, this community economy displays replication of units by division into smaller, dependent ones. The practice reduced expenses of maintaining the core and diversified the base through spatial expansion. The smaller landholders were not always able to provision themselves from the land made available and might be partly fed from the demesne's stores even while they labored for and sent tribute to the encompassing unit. There was flexibility in the flows between center and periphery as occasion demanded, so the totality might strive to be autarkic. But especially interesting is the way the pattern of the main house was projected on the manse – each would strive to be self-sufficient – yet the larger and the smaller were different because the demesne controlled the base of the outlying manse.

Model 3: In the ninth and tenth centuries, the pattern grew more complex (see figure 4.3). The demesne land contained the reproductive core of the great estate, but its extent expanded or diminished in relation to the available labor force, and some peasant houses were set on the demesne itself. Householders supported themselves by work-

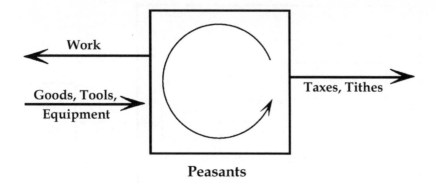

Peasants

Figure 4.4 Independent peasantry

ing on land allocated to them outside the demesne, but they were obliged to work the demesne land for the owner. When working on the demesne, they were supported from its foodstock, receiving their supply in raw form. The work obligations were heterogeneous and set by time of year, agricultural tasks, number of days owed in the year, and needs for group work (*corveés*). In addition, males usually owed tribute in firewood, chickens, or eggs; women often had to provide cloth to the manor. The demesne had no single measure, such as a set fee in coin, that was used to calculate the diverse obligations; there was no system of commensuration by which one obligation could be compared to another. The tribute amounts were variable and negotiated, so estate management required the exercise of practical reason.

Demesne flows were allocated by the owner, but the products gathered in the tenancies might be directly consumed. In some cases, the great estate contained several manors for the landlord plus tenancies. When lords were unable to maintain their household from the central demesne, they and some members of their household moved in rotation from one manor to another. And while striving to achieve self-sufficiency, the great estate also exchanged some of its output for goods that it lacked, such as cereals, wine, and salt, and for luxuries.

Model 4: A truly independent peasantry, living in villages apart from the great estate, and occupying both unused and unclaimed land, began to develop by the ninth and tenth centuries (see figure 4.4). Entirely new from the standpoint of land control, yet not in economic form, these units constituted small-scale replicas of the great estate with its project of self-sufficiency. But few of these small entities achieved self-sufficiency, partly because they had to pay taxes and tithes.

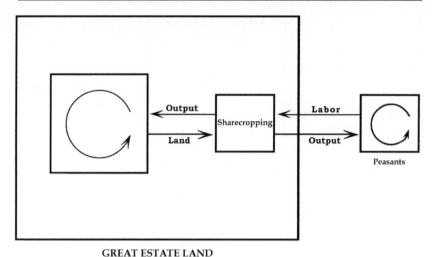

GREAT ESTATE LAND

Figure 4.5   Sharecropping

They also lacked control of ovens, mills, and other tools that were held as monopolies by great estates.

Model 5: Through the eleventh to thirteenth centuries another form developed when great estates began to expand cultivated areas (see figure 4.5). Independent peasants, lacking access to a base, formed sharecropping arrangements with manors. One side provided land, the other labor; the output was divided, often by halves. Sharecropping constructed a temporary base between "independent" units. But the relationship was asymmetric and allowed the owner of the land to receive a flow of goods at no expenditure. The estate's portion might be traded for money or market goods.

Throughout the period, covered by the five models, bases consisted primarily of the demesne, which was the most productive land, and the manses; and the base was strategically used to build different forms of community economy. Smaller units used alloted land to reproduce themselves and to pay rental and service obligations. This (sometimes partial) self-sufficiency of the smaller units allowed not only for provisioning of the larger but extraction of a surplus. In the earlier forms, most flows stayed within the community economy. In the later ones, flows received by the demesne were directed to the market with the objective of diversifing the base and displaying its wealth. Through trade also materials and tools to increase the land's productivity could be secured. The entire institution was held together through varying combinations of military power, religious allegiance, and land control.

Self-sufficiency, Rations, and Reason

The great estate, throughout much of its evolution, was not directed to securing a monetary profit. Evidence from early tracts on estate management and accounting indicates that even the notion of an over-all physical remainder or surplus grew slowly; the emphasis was on economizing and rationing what was at hand. A careful reading of guides on estate management compiled in the 1200s and later, such as Walter of Henley, the *Seneschaucy*, the *Rules* by Robert Grosseteste, and the *Fleta*, clearly reveals the housekeeping project. Profit calculations for the central part of the estate or demesne apparently began at Westminster Abbey only in 1292. Known as the *commodum* or *verus valor*, profit was figured as the difference between yields and expenses when calculated in real goods and then converted to monetary value. Many flows in a complex estate, such as direct consumption by the lord on a peripheral farm or shipments from outlying farm to center, which were struck on tallies, escaped this calculation.[4] The ideal was to be self-sufficient. Duby, for example, provides a striking quotation from the *Capitulary de Villis*, which was written in the early ninth century: "it should not be necessary to seek for, or to buy anything from outside" (Duby 1968: 44).

The project of the great estate was not only to maintain itself but to expand, by increasing the number of its dependents and its base for defense and display. According to Duby (1968: 36), the intention was to establish housekeeping on a large scale, to be lavish, and never to be short of consumable goods. The powerful man could eat as much as he wished and provide others with food, always striving to increase the numbers dependent on him and the size of his immediate house-hold. Not material accumulation but expanding the community was the goal.

Two forms of the great estate existed, however: the lay and the religious. In both, the end was consumption by the dominant. The first tended to be lavish in display. The second sometimes was too, but it supported people who spent time in religious devotions. In monasteries, rationing of flows was more important than in lay estates as the intention was to sustain a group of people who did not need to devote themselves full time to production.

Duby (1968: 379–81) provides excerpts from the Statutes written in the early ninth century by Abbot Adalard for the monastery of Corbie that reveal several important features of the monastery's internal economy. First, the physical flow of goods through the rooms of the monastery provided a schema for budgeting or apportionment.

Categories of distribution corresponded to domestic spaces. For example, according to the Statutes, some of the agricultural and other returns flowed to the chandlery (which alloted receipts in cereals), some to the cellar (which stored foods), some to the chamber (which managed money and clothing), and some to the gate (which handled external relations). Like sluice gates and reservoirs, each room, overseen by a manager (the chandler, the cellarer, the chamberlain, and the porter and hosteller), received part of the flow to carry out specific functions. The community's partitioning of goods was modeled after tasks carried out in house spaces. At-hand experience – the image of the domicile – was used to model the apportionment. (In rural Latin America today, the harvest flow may be divided into seed for the granary, food for the kitchen store, fodder for the animal barn, and products to pass "through the doors" in trade – see Gudeman and Rivera 1990).

Centuries after the Statutes were written, the house model of apportionment was still used in England, but by this time the relation between physical locale and budget unit had been severed so that the budgetary term no longer designated where a flow was used. For example, Mertes, writing about the English household in the 1400s, observes that "pantry" was an important accounting division under which expenditures for grain, pastry, and bread were entered; but, she adds, the pantry was only a room near the dining area where foods were kept briefly before being served. Furthermore, although grain was accounted under the pantry category, it was made into bread in the bakehouse, and some grain flowed to the kitchen for processing: the function of the pantry as a spatial area had nothing to do with the pantry as a budgetary category. Mertes then notes that departments such as scullery, saucery, slaughterhouse, and pastry-making also appear in the budget books, yet the terms did not refer to existent rooms but "accounting fictions" (1988: 36). Finally, even the referential link between budget category and activity was broken, for she adds with some surprise that "Under 'hall and chamber' one consistently finds only entries for coal, wood and other fuels" (ibid.: 38).

Once one realizes that household budgets are forms of community apportionment, and that people frequently use at-hand experience to organize the division of the flows, the mystery disappears. Product portioning in the manorial, monastic, and household economies was formulated, in the 800s and earlier, after the physical plan and real tasks of the domicile. Five hundred years later, architecture diverged from the budget categories which now referred to monetary allocations, but the set of labels derived from the physical images remained as a convenient scheme for modeling divisions in household finances.

A second (and fascinating) feature of Adalard's Statutes, excerpted by Duby, concerns the calculation of the portions or rations. For example, the daily ration of bread, the basic food, was about three pounds per monk. The 12 poor people who were admitted to the monastery every night each received a loaf of bread, as did the two hostellers who oversaw their lodging. In contrast, a total of 12 loaves was divided among all the traveling clerks and sick who arrived every evening; the hosteller had to apportion this fixed sum according to the number being fed. Thus, for the primary inhabitants and some others, there seems to have been a notion of basic subsistence, a set amount to be apportioned per capita; for others, the amount depended on the number of other recipients. But this varying sum also was partly determined as a proportion of the revenues, and it might have a baseline. For example, according to the Statutes:

> To accompany the bread of the poor . . . we add a fifth part of the tithe that the porter receives from the cellarer in eels or in that fresh cheese, which according to rule, the ten shepherds deliver, or from that given in tithe by the demesnes. And also a fifth part of the tithe in cattle. . . . Furthermore, we decide that a fifth part of all the money, which comes to the office of the gate shall be given to the hosteller by the porter. As for the money, we desire that it shall be distributed in such a way that every day not less than four deniers shall be given away. And if the fifth part shall not be sufficient for this distribution, the abbot, if he wishes, shall make up the other part; and if there shall be more, it shall not be held back. (Duby 1968: 380)

In this apportionment, incommensurate values concerning social position, need, equity, and equality were involved, and the division was compounded of both proportions (or ratios) and fixed sums. Very different from market distribution that occurs through pricing, this rationing scheme was guided by social values and the need to economize. We might speculate that rationing began in monasteries as opposed to estates of the nobility which had as their project the display of largesse and abundance.

The root of the word "rations" is ratio, which – aside from its mathematical connotation – means reason. In monasteries, land was allotted, food was apportioned, and the group was maintained by economic reason or ratio. By the use of this situated reason, disparate means were brought together in a monastery's projects. But this rationality, framed by the need to economize, was different from the more abstract and instrumental form used to select among means or ends in order to achieve the highest ratio of the latter to the former, for the means in the monastery were incommensurate.

Contemporary Estates

Today, the great estate survives in fragments. It was certainly found in Europe through the end of the last century if not later (Petrusewicz 1996). The Latin American hacienda also was modeled after the European form.[5] In Latin America, however, the "grand house" displayed a more strongly dual character with an inner core devoted to the production of goods for self-sufficiency and a second side directed to the production of a market crop, such as sugar cane or basic foods needed at mines and cities. Each of the five estate models I outlined, however, has had its analogue in Latin America:

Model 1 was utilized directly after the conquest when native Americans were enslaved.

Model 2 displays the era of the *encomienda* – up to about 1650 – when Europeans were "entrusted" with the "care" of native Americans who, living on reserves, were compelled to work on the landed estates allotted by the Crown.

Model 3 exhibits the period when tenants, known variously as *conciertos* or *yanaconas*, lived on the land of the great house and owed tribute and labor. This system endured well into the twentieth century.

Model 4 marks the epoch of the independent smallholder, which in some parts of Latin America, such as Colombia, began in the 1700s.

Model 5, the system of sharecropping, applies today. It is used to produce market crops, such as tobacco, or market and subsistence foods, such as potatoes.

Today, Oxbridge colleges that accumulate fine china and silver, and use rents to provision their High Table dinners reflect the European great estate. Today, also, we buy houses in which to "settle down" – and display our wealth outside market transactions. And how different from past times is the modern farmer who, while attending closely to grain markets and drawing government subsidies, holds ideals of self-sufficiency? Indeed, how different is the Silicon Valley firm, such as Hewlett-Packard, which claims to act like a family, had a founding father who wandered through its spaces like a *primus inter parus*, and provides a subsidized, egalitarian cafeteria for its employees (Saxenian 1994: 50–1)? It draws on the model of an economic community but only partly recapitulates it in market conditions.

NOTES

1   For a complex example of the way payments might be taken and redis-
    tributed in a religious community, see Neusner's analysis of the Mishnah
    (1990).
2   Postan (1975: 83) observes that the manor was a medieval institution
    but its medieval characteristics were "grafted on to an economic root-
    stock which was not specifically medieval, since it was also to be found
    in other periods of human history and in other parts of the world. This
    root-stock was that of the great estate."
3   I have drawn on Bloch (1961), Denholm-Young (1937), Duby (1968,
    1974), Gies and Gies (1990), Mertes (1988), Oschinsky (1971), Postan
    (1975), Rösener (1992), Southern (1967), and Weber (1961).
4   See Denholm-Young (1937) and Oschinsky (1971: 220).
5   See, for example, Cushner (1980), Johnson (1971), Keith (1976), Klein
    (1993), Matos Mar (1976), Tord and Lazo (1981), and de la Torre Arauz
    (1989).

Chapter Five

Reciprocity and the Gift: Extending the Base

My thesis, that maintaining and allotting the base constitutes the central act in communal economy, runs counter to standard anthropological arguments.[1] According to the accepted wisdom, reciprocity is the primary building block of community, because this practice makes and perpetuates dyadic relationships that are the irreducible core of society. Neoclassical economists, elaborating a different view, see dyadic ties as evolving from individual interests that are created prior to the development of social forms. In opposition to both theories, I think that providing gifts and enacting reciprocity are tactical acts that extend the base to persons outside a community. As tokens of apportionment and forays in expanding a community's borders, they are secondary processes. Not a rule but a process, reciprocity is one way of groping with uncertainty at the limits of a community: offering a gift probes, defends, secures, and expands the borders of community. Reciprocity reflects the tension between commensurate and incommensurate exchange; balanced between the two, it asserts and denies both.

The word "reciprocity" is used differently by economists and anthropologists. For economists, reciprocity refers to two-directional exchanges, monetized or not. Anthropologists use reciprocity for a more restricted set of practices – specifically, non-cash, non-market exchanges – and set it in opposition to commercial trade. Often anthropologists equate reciprocity with the gift on the argument that a gift obligates the recipient to offer a return, setting in motion a temporal, lasting cycle of obligations, which is reciprocity. But sometimes anthropologists avoid the term "gift" because in market economy the gift has the connotation "without obligation." For economists, there are no free lunches; for anthropologists there are no free gifts.

I use reciprocity for non-market, lasting, two-way exchanges, and gift for an initial present. An unrequited offering remains a gift. (Of course, uncertainty about whether the recompense will occur, not to mention delays in making it, blurs the line between reciprocity and gift.) Reciprocity involves the exchange of base – or things, people, and their parts – between persons of different communities. Falling in the sphere of communal transactions, it is never about objects alone but relationships forged through them. The examples of reciprocity are many: teenage friends in the USA share clothes; the Trobriand Islanders pass valuable necklaces and armbands along paths that link their kula communities; Tiv send yams to kinsmen in times of lean; some Latin American rural farmers offer tithes to the church when the harvest has been bountiful.

The many cases of reciprocity recorded by anthropologists challenge the idea that economy must be completely organized through markets. But into what theoretical framework should we fit reciprocity? Most of the theorizing on reciprocity was set in motion by Marcel Mauss, whose slim volume *The Gift* (1990 [1925]) is given a new reading by each generation of anthropologists. They usually urge that reciprocity is the pillar of social life and suspect this finding is overlooked by economists. I think anthropologists are caught in a dialectic with Western economists. Both offer essentialist or modernist views: one is relational, the other atomistic. One side emphasizes altruism, the other egoism.

The gift is not opposed to the commodity, nor does their opposition provide a typology of all economies, such as "the gift economy" and "the commodity economy" (Gregory 1982: 19). Economies are built on the interlocked realms of communal and commercial value, not gift versus commodity. Allotment makes and signifies mutuality and shared identity before the act of giving extends their bounds.

Genealogies of the Gift

The Gift by Mauss is a central narrative in economic anthropology. Many in the field believe this present from the French master disrupts exchange theory based on the idea of individual self-interest. But *The Gift*, elliptical and packed with learning, is difficult to read and interweaves several themes. A gift always has an ambiguous status. If a gift is freely given, it has no social impact, because no obligations are set in motion. The truly free gift conveys no history or social memory (Derrida 1992). But if the recipient of a gift is obligated to make a return (which is Mauss's argument), then we need to explain why and to say something about the nature of the required return. The requital also may be delayed. For example, we may be invited to someone's house for dinner, which sets up the obligation to reciprocate. But when? And what constitutes a return? Surely there must be a shared standard by which to judge the exchange of dinners? But if a value standard exists, what makes a gift transaction different from a market exchange? And why do people such as the Trobriand Islanders carefully distinguish reciprocity in the kula from the regular trade of objects (*gimwali*)?

To show how reciprocity fits my argument. I need to set these themes into a broader conversation on exchange. Overall, two discourses about reciprocal exchange have developed. The economists' conversation, which culminates in modern market views of exchange, starts with Adam Smith, runs through Ricardo, and is still being embellished. In the *Wealth of Nations* (1976 [1776]), Adam Smith offers three reasons why people exchange. In the first chapter, he sketches a model of the division of labor using the example of the pin factory to suggest that specialization by task leads to increased productive efficiency and wealth. Interdependence or exchange *within* a unit increase productivity. In the second chapter, Smith says that humans have a propensity "to truck, barter, and exchange" (ibid.: 17). This psychological rationale for exchange refers to transactions *between* individuals who naturally seek market interactions. Finally, Smith observes that we do not get our dinner from the benevolence of the baker or brewer. Avarice impels market trade (ibid.: 18), but from self-interest everyone benefits and the wealth of nations increases. This final rationale for exchange – involving self-interest, profit-seeking, and maximizing gains – underpins much of neoclassical theory today. The exchange is balanced in value, according to the measuring rod of money.

Anthropological explanations of reciprocity developed in this century. There have been many contributions, especially in the last decade or so, but I shall attend to a principal strand that begins with Malinowski and Mauss, includes Lévi-Strauss, and counts as legatees Polanyi and Sahlins.[2] Many of the recent contributions build on their voices. Like the conversation of economists, the anthropologists' is essentialist but with a difference in the selected foundations.

In *The Gift* Mauss implicitly uses an evolutionary perspective. Drawing on the available ethnography, especially from the Trobriand Islands and the Northwest Coast, as well as classical texts, he often reads variation in space as a product or representation of temporal change: the cross-cultural comparison has a historical scent. As Parry has acutely pointed out, *The Gift* contains many speculations on evolution and betrays a deep interest in origins (Parry 1986: 457). In fact, Mauss's method was Aristotelian – according to which the genealogy of the observed pattern, made available by analysis of its components, points to the original or basic social form.

For Mauss, the initial exchange, preceding all other forms, was that of total prestations in which individuals and entire groups, such as clans, "exchange everything with one another," including food, goods, rituals, dances, women, and children (1990: 70). But this "ancient system," this "elementary type," or "base," which provides the morality for all instances of the gift, can hardly be found today (ibid.: 7, 70; see also pp. 36, 42, 46).[3] Afterward, as society developed, the gift appeared. The gift is a transaction between individuals as representatives of groups. It does not involve whole groups – though it occurs between them – and is more limited than a total prestation: not everything comes and goes. The gift consists of objects, services, or performances. With the gift established, credit, barter, and then market exchange appeared. Mauss hangs the argument on a logico-temporal ordering from total prestations to market transactions. The gift makes and re-enforces the mutuality that once was expressed by total prestations, whereas market exchange – being disconnected from all social ties – disrupts commonality. Mauss's solution to what he perceived to be anomie in modern society partly caused by the predominance of market trade was to reinstate the morality inherent in gift exchange.

If we read Mauss's genetic scheme backwards, however, an absence becomes apparent. Turning the arrow in reverse from market exchange to gift to total prestations, we are led to ask: what preceded the stage of total prestations? This moment must constitute the big bang or original period of society. Mauss says little about this antecedent time, but he does offer a hint by referring, at the essay's close, to "the basis of society . . . our common life, the conscious direction of which is the supreme art, *Politics*, in the Socratic sense of the word" (1990: 83). Prior to the stage of group prestations, clans, lineages, households, or villages must be in place. The unvoiced component of *The Gift* is community economy with its allotment rules. The morality of reciprocity develops from this social form.

Mauss did not originate the idea of reciprocity. He used Malinowski's (1922) Trobriand ethnography to develop his general argument, and Malinowski himself had pointed to the importance of reciprocity. In a central chapter of *Argonauts of the Western Pacific*, Malinowski observes that *"the whole of tribal life is permeated by a constant give and take"* (1961 [1922]: 167) and proclaims:

> The view that the native can live in a state of individual search for food, or catering for his own household only, in isolation from an interchange of goods, implies a calculating, cold egotism. . . . [Such views] ignore the fundamental human impulse to display, to share, to bestow. They ignore the deep tendency to create social ties through the exchange of

> gifts. Apart from any consideration as to whether the gifts are necessary
> or even useful, giving for the sake of giving is one of the most important
> features of Trobriand sociology, and, from its very general and funda-
> mental nature, I submit that it is a universal feature of all primitive
> societies. (ibid.: 175)

The difference with Mauss is slight but important. Mauss argues that
reciprocity occurs in all social formations; Malinowski sees it as a
characteristic of one class of societies that he labels "primitive." This
equation of the primitive with reciprocity, as opposed to the modern
with the market, still finds its way into discussion.

Lévi-Strauss, in *The Elementary Structures of Kinship*, develops the
reciprocity argument of Mauss but in a Cartesian direction. For Lévi-
Strauss, reciprocity reflects basic forms of the human mind (1969
[1949]: 75) which are three: first, the necessity of the rule, then "the
notion of reciprocity regarded as the most immediate form of integrat-
ing the opposition between the self and others; and finally the synthetic nature of the gift . . . [which makes] individuals into partners
(ibid.: 84). For Lévi-Strauss, reciprocity is the kernel of the social contract: no reciprocity, no society. It is the foundation of all human institutions, which imperfectly express it (ibid.: 76). In this argument, which
asserts the universality of reciprocity across all societies, Lévi-Strauss
not only expanded Malinowski's view but rid himself of Mauss's concern with origins. He also decisively raised the stakes in the battle
between anthropologists and economists over the origins of economic
forms: after Lévi-Strauss the choice was set between two essentialisms
– irreducible dyadic bonds (for the anthropologists) and atomic individuals (for the economists).

Karl Polanyi has to be added to this story, because he has been so
influential in anthropology and because we cannot fully understand
Sahlins' argument, which I also consider, without grasping Polanyi's
contribution on which it is based. Perhaps Polanyi did not write with
the erudition of Mauss, the grace of Malinowski, or the force of Lévi-
Strauss, but he is persuasive for his ideas if not his data.

Polanyi is an empiricist. He surveyed the literature on "ancient"
and "primitive" economies to extract underlying features in the data
and construct typologies (1944, 1968). Polanyi offers a tripartite typology of all economic forms with an ill-fitting appendix. The divisions
are these. First, there is reciprocity, which is built on the principle of
symmetry and found in societies where kinship is dominant. These are
"primitive" societies. Second, there is redistribution. Built on the principle of centricity (or inward and outward movements), redistribution
is encountered in systems where political or religious institutions are

dominant, such as "ancient" societies. Finally, market exchange, built on haggling, is characteristic of modern market society. Polanyi admits that the three patterns may be found together but does not develop a theory of their co-presence, although one always dominates and colors the others. The first two forms – reciprocity in the context of kinship systems and redistribution in the context of politico-religious systems – are instances of the "embedded" economy: material functions are carried out through kinship, religious, or political relationships. Only the market, in contemporary society, constitutes a "disembedded" economy.

Hidden in Polanyi's comparative typology is an historical and evolutionary perspective that starts with reciprocity in primitive societies, moves to redistribution in archaic ones, and finishes with market exchange in modern economies. This scheme of development (from the embedded to the disembedded economy) fits the general anthropological argument that reciprocity comes before the market and redistribution.

An especially problematic feature of Polanyi's theory was the economic form that could not be placed in any of his categories. A careful reader of Aristotle and of ethnographic texts, Polanyi knew that some economic units are inspired by the model of autarky. He called it "householding," although the principle of achieving self-sufficiency can be applied at any level. Where can this economic form be fitted? Because Polanyi's typology is formed around modes of exchange, the self-sufficient economy has no place in it, as Polanyi uncomfortably recognized. Community economy was relegated to a position off the typological map.

Finally, there is the contribution of Marshall Sahlins (1972). In many respects, his argument is Polanyi's but stripped of time and laid out in space. Sahlins presents a scale that would correlate reciprocity and trade with close and distant social relations. At one end, there is "generalized reciprocity," which refers to "putatively altruistic" transactions such as the maternal suckling of children (1972: 193–4). Kinship obligations fall into this class as well. (This equation of female + sharing + community = non-economy reproduces the standard view that "economy" is the realm of males.) Moving away from such closeness, there is balanced reciprocity – the give and take of the gift – which is less personal and "more economic" (ibid.: 195). At the greatest social distance lies negative reciprocity, the attempt to get something for nothing, as expressed in barter and theft.

For Sahlins, reciprocity is the explanatory force behind the entire scheme, as demonstrated by his stretching of the verbal category to encompass all transactions from altruism at mutuality's core to stealing at its periphery. Thus Sahlins takes Polanyi one step further, by deriving allotment, apportionment, and redistribution from reciprocity. For Polanyi, reciprocity in the familial sphere is historically and logically prior to reallocation within a polity, and both come before competitive exchange in the market. Sahlins, in his reformulation of Polanyi's argument, locates allotment as a secondary phenomenon, indeed as an instance of generalized reciprocity: for Sahlins, even the domestic sharing of foods, household pooling, and maternal care are forms of reciprocity. Chiefly dues and tribute are instances of reciprocity too, because when power relations come to dominate material processes, prior bonds of reciprocity are brought together by a central authority and transformed to a scheme of redistribution which is only *"an organization of reciprocities, a system of reciprocities* – a fact of central bearing upon the genesis of large-scale redistribution under chiefly aegis. But this most general understanding merely suggests concentration in the first place on reciprocity" (ibid.: 188). Reciprocity for Sahlins is the building block of exchange, economy, and society.[4]

Extending and Retracting the Base

In different ways Polanyi, Sahlins, and Mauss hint that reciprocity may not constitute the foundation of economy and society. There remains an opening in the anthropological discourse. I suggest that reciprocity is an expression of community, and a way of extending it, but that community itself – contingent, negotiated, vulnerable – and the commons it holds – material or immaterial, spiritual or natural – together with the allotment rules it maintains are the absent elements in the anthropological discourse. Sharing is an act of making and maintaining community, and without it there can be no reciprocity. Allotment does not come "after" reciprocity; rather, moments of reciprocity or the gift are tokens of existent community and a mode of allotment.

Reciprocity (or more exactly, an initial gift) distributes the base and projects it to others. The gift extends the commons to someone outside the community, offering temporary participation or even permanent inclusion. Reciprocity is never contained within a community. The gift and reciprocity are used to probe across its borders, for a variety of motives, such as establishing mutuality and peace, expressing dominance, manipulating to advantage, displaying power or wealth, and bringing in new members. The gift is an experiment in making community, as in the case of the Wogeo where chestnuts are apportioned and invoke return flows from people who regard themselves as members of community. Gifts suggest the possibility of changing a community's boundaries by including new people within the allotment or by creating a larger and new association, as is done by the Nambicuara with meat and manioc soup, and by the Jukumami and their "marginal ones" with land. A probe into uncertainty, the gift can make community, fail, or be replaced by trade.

Consider again the dinner party. We invite a circle of friends to dinner, and later they invite us back. This round of invitations surely exemplifies reciprocity – or does it? A dinner offered is commensality, because it represents the sharing of foods that sustain a household. Raised to a higher standard of cuisine than a normal supper, and often the product of hand labor, the convivial dinner puts a household's base on display and distributes it. "Eat what you want and still there will be leftovers," states the household. The party apportions the base outside the group's borders.

But attendance at a dinner party usually produces an obligation to reciprocate, raising the question: what should be returned, and when? In some circles, guests bring their host a bottle of wine; usually it remains unopened through the evening. The wine is like an intermediary gift that signals acceptance of the dinner and promises further reciprocation, but it is not the full return itself. So we have two cycles; distinct parts of the base – wine and food – are circulated against one another; one is consumed, the other is held. Indeed, I harbor images of a few unopened bottles of wine endlessly circulating among households. As for the food, sometimes a dinner is not reciprocated, and the wine alone must constitute the reciprocation: embarrassment lingers while status is gained and lost by the different parties. Usually, the dinner is returned (along with a countervailing bottle of wine carefully selected to be different from the one received); but because the return dinner cannot be measured exactly against the original, the double cycle is perpetuated in this play of gaining status and making community with others.

Gifts, thus, extend community to others, including them as users of the base, which is another way of expressing what Mauss meant by "the spirit" of the gift. To worry about Mauss's use of the word "spirit" for the Maori term *hau*, and whether his interpretation, translation, and generalization of a local word is valid, misses the significance of the argument (Sahlins 1972). The spirit of the gift is the offering of community through its base. Mauss was perceptive to commingle objects and people as things to be exchanged, because together they make community (1990 [1925]: 14); they are the constituents of the base.

My argument partly overlaps Annette Weiner's (1992), who recently offered a contribution to the reciprocity debate.[5] She distinguishes two kinds of goods: alienable and inalienable possessions. The latter constitute sacra of the community or the core of the commons. For Weiner, to part with these goods is to lose something of one's identity, and she emphasizes that inalienable possessions are "for keeping."

But Weiner separates persons from objects so that inalienable possessions are not people, "parts" of people, or persons in relation to objects, but material things alone. Thus, she does not fully develop her claim that "loans" of inalienable possessions are ways of "making kin of non-kin" (1992: 26), which surely is a central point. Goods mediate borders by extending and contracting relationships that make community. In this negotiation, the power of community can be expanded by including others in it or by compelling them to recognize its place. This strategic act is forceful because the gift is a token of the base and community.

One can never know if an offered gift will be accepted and returned. If the gift is reciprocated, the return says much the same as the offering, and more. The return accepts the commensality, yet signals difference and independence. The result, or reciprocity, is two overlapping bases. For this reason, in many situations reciprocity is an exchange of inequivalents; because each gift is a token of a base that belongs to a distinct community and the two bases are incommensurate, the exchange is made up of unlike things.

This reciprocal extension of communality suggests the possibility of forming a larger, encompassing community. Each fragment of a base offered is both a part of a whole (the existent community) – for gifts kept in circulation are a distributed base – and a part within a possible whole (the imagined community). The wine, unopened and continuously circulated, comes to stand for the hospitality of all dinner parties in a potential community. Similarly, when high school and college students borrow one another's clothes, and use and keep them for long intervals, in complicated exchanges, they are distributing their bases and making a new community in the doing – all from the bits and pieces of their domestic ones. Reciprocity incorporates this tension between separation and unity, self-sufficiency and interdependence. There is always a delicate balance between distance and closeness, detachment and warm sentiments in the double act.

The unhinging of this tension converts reciprocity to separate communities, to commercial trade, or to war. For example, in a study of the North Mekeo of New Guinea, Mosko relates how the giving of raw meat between patriclan members of a deceased person and his mother's patriclan severs or decomposes the reciprocal cognatic relationship that had been symbolized and embodied in the deceased who was their common product. This return act ends their reciprocity and retracts community boundaries, though allowing for new extensions and connections in the future (Mosko 1985, 1989). In the case of war, Harrison (1992), describing group rituals or ceremonies as a kind of communal property, notes that victors often seize the tutelary gods or ceremonial privileges of the vanquished, such as names, dances, masks, and designs, that have been used in reciprocal exchanges. In this seizure, the core of the opponent's commons is destroyed, and so is community and the possibility of extending it to others.

On the other hand, to sell communal valuables that are used in reciprocal exchanges converts the realm of social value and well-being to that of commercial value and just living. Thus, at a dinner party, the price tag on the gift of wine must be rubbed off, and the prices of the food, linen, glassware, and silver at the dinner table cannot be revealed, except at the cost of disgrace. Contemporary stories and films that feature the selling of the non-salable sacra – the upright public servant who allows himself to be bribed for a just cause, the spouse who sells sexual access to save her husband or marriage – shock the viewer not for the high price that some services command but for the commensuration that is established between different realms of value. These are morality tales, and they cut several ways, for it is equally shocking when wealthy people convert publicly shared sacra to private property by shooting rare animals to secure household trophies, by purchasing a famous painting for private viewing, by robbing an archaeological stele from Guatemala, or by buying the rights to log rare trees. In reverse, to hold and revere an old, ordinary car converts everyday market goods to sacra – a process satirized by Warhol in his painting of a soup can.

An initial gift, then, is a trial-and-error practice, because the giver operates in the realm of uncertainty about its acceptability and appropriateness, and whether it will be returned. Gifts are converted to reciprocity for different reasons. Reciprocity can cement a relationship and establish community. The gift may express affection and mutuality but also a power difference, for the giver is able to cede part of her base without requiring a requital. The dinner party establishes commensality, and it may be a token in the struggle for status where the giver's ability to gather resources, from money to cultural skills, are put on display, whereas accepting this hospitality without reciprocation signals inferiority (see also Herzfeld 1987). So, for tactical reasons such as gaining power, keeping mutuality, and maintaining independence, reciprocity occurs. Similarly, refusal to reciprocate can indicate lack of desire to create mutuality, or it may signal inability to do so. Not a rule or norm of social life, not a feature of mind, a function of self-interest, or an essential foundation of society, reciprocity is part of a system of practices in which participants express, conserve, lose, and gain position in the sphere of social value.[6]

Sister-Exchange

An ethnographic example showing how reciprocity functions in relation to communal apportionment has been provided by the late Alfred Gell. Having produced a fine study of the Umeda of New Guinea some years ago (1975), Gell (1992) reformulated his understanding of their marriage practices in a way that fits my thesis.

The Umeda live in West Sepik Province of Papua New Guinea. In pre-contact times, the Umeda were self-sufficient. Dependent on hunting and gathering, they made stone tools and sago-pounders, and produced salt, paint, and lime as needed. Umeda worked in family groups among whom items were "shared." Gell called this social pattern an Indigenous Service Economy; quite simply, it was a community economy, within which there were apportioning relationships between husband and wife, and parents and children.

Pre-contact Melanesia was criss-crossed by trade routes. Trade took place between groups, especially ones that did not intermarry; and goods moved, via trade partnerships, up to 50 miles. In highland areas, most goods traded were not subsistence articles: trade was not impelled by the need to overcome ecological deficiencies, and groups did not depend on it for their persistence. External trade was a source of excitement, exotic imports were esteemed, and exchange relationships were valued (Gell 1992: 149, 148). In many cases, local specialization in the production of goods did not precede trade but was fostered and elaborated in response to the possibility of expanding impersonal exchange. Trade was undertaken for its own sake as a means of affirming and overcoming the limits of community.

The Umeda also practiced bride-service. Each new son-in-law had to live with and work for his wife's family for an extended period, hunting and pounding sago for them; and he was sustained by them. A son-in-law was incorporated, for a time, within the economy of his wife's family. Even after, an independent and mature hunter sent portions of the kill to his wife's parents; these pieces of meat were "shares" to which they had rights (ibid.: 155).

The Umeda practiced sister-exchange as well, and a relatively high proportion of marriages were arranged between sets of siblings. When a man was able to effect a sister-exchange, he owed no bride-service or food shares to his wife's parents.

The existence of these two marriage practices raises the question:

was sister-exchange "primordial" and an example of the reciprocity that lies at the base of making society, or did it develop after the institution of bride-service? Reciprocity theory in anthropology, from Lévi-Strauss onward, suggests that sister-exchange constitutes the weld of Umeda society; the reciprocal exchange of women was the foundational transaction between separate families. Umeda bride-service is a substitute for a woman. In his reconsideration of the ethnography, however, Gell pointed out that sister-exchange was never an ideal or rule among the Umeda (it may have begun very recently). Sister-exchange developed as a substitute for serving a bride's family, because men deem the latter to be onerous, even oppressive. Being compelled to live with and serve one's in-laws is shaming (in fact, the word for brother-in-law is "shame" – (see Gell 1992: 154). For a young man, having to work for his bride's father's group conflicts with his desire to be an independent hunter and family head. Reciprocating sisters, thus, is a way of escaping the obligation to work for another community, a strategy for establishing one's own, and a method for moderating, if not eliminating, the loss of social esteem.

Let me fit the ethnography more closely to my argument. The "original" transactions in Umeda were apportionment within groups and trade between them. A marriage expands a community's borders, and among Umeda the receipt of a spouse obligates males to participate in another household by contributing labor and food to its commons while subsisting from its flows. The men become members of a community in which they cannot build a separate base and social standing. For young men, the reciprocal exchange of sisters solves the contradiction between the subservience they experience when becoming a member of another community and the esteem they seek as heads of their own. Exchanging sisters emancipates them from their spouse's community and offers a quicker way to build a base.

The Umeda ethnography fits my argument that the gift and reciprocity are strategic moves across the borders of community. The gift of a woman, by obligating the groom to return labor, benefits the bride's father's economy at the expense of the groom's. Returning a sister is a way of avoiding loss of prestige and escaping an obligation while helping to establish the groom's community more expeditiously. Gell himself argued that sister-exchange was modeled after the impersonal, external commodity exchanges that Umeda had long undertaken. He sensed correctly, I think, that community and trade interact, and that by reciprocating sisters young men could liberate themselves from long-term obligations. But reciprocity and the gift are not pale reflections of commercial trade; they are part of a people's strategic negotiations with the base.

The Badge of Society

In an effort to counter the culturally compelling arguments of econo-mists, anthropologists have seized perhaps too eagerly on the concept of reciprocity. They might have looked more profitably to the prec-edent notion of community, for the gift is a foray across group bounda-ries. It connects social worlds or islets of incommensurability within a plural universe.

There is no single way to calculate the return to be made at holiday time when our neighbors bring their personally canned jam for our en-joyment. What did it "cost" them to make it? How much pleasure does it give us? Do we want to offer a return and continue the relationship? The contingencies in a gift are many, the uncertainties for both parties cannot be calculated and reduced to numerical risk on a commensurate scale. But the gift is filled with information, and what we do know is that with a gift of jam neighbors are saying something about connec-tions between their household and ours; they are expanding their com-mons to include us. They are distributing their base outside its normal circle so that the bringing itself is unexpected – why else do we wrap presents except to say that the present, the prestation, is a surprise? Of course, reciprocity can also be an ideology that masks material imbal-ances in an exchange (George 1996: 78). And there can be Trojan Horse and poisoned gifts (Parry 1989; Raheja 1988), for to invoke Schumpeter, giving gifts can be a mode of "creative destruction."

The gift, through the mutuality it extends or the antagonism it en-genders, expresses one or another aspect of community. Prestations, done by touch and feel, are trials of extending community and its com-mons. I think this way of viewing the gift actually brings us closer to Mauss's account, in which the notion of community and the com-mons plays a central part. Nothing mystical, no sacred force in the gift causes it to be given, received, and returned; the gift is a gesture of commensality not commensuration, yet filled at times with countervailing impulses of competition. Strictly a secondary and com-posite phenomenon, reciprocity is not the core of society but its ex-pression. Anthropological theories have it backwards: reciprocity is neither a primitive isolate nor the atom of society but its badge.

NOTES

1   Woodburn (1998) offers a recent restatement of his related argument; see also Price (1975).

2 For some of the more recent discussions, see Gregory (1982), Parry (1986, 1989), and Strathern (1988).

3 "The system that we propose to call the system of 'total services'. . . constitutes the most ancient system of economy and law that we can find. . . . It forms the base from which the morality of the exchange-through-gift has flowed" (Mauss 1990 [1925]: 70).

4 See also Humphrey (1998).

5 Weiner's views were developed in earlier essays; see, for example, Weiner (1978, 1980). For a discussion of Weiner, see Godelier (1995a, 1995b). In an extended discussion, I would emphasize that the Trobriand *dala* is a community with a base that is partly circulated to others. Weiner translates it as lineage that refers to matrilineal identity, "plots of land, hamlet sites, and other paraphernalia (e.g., body and house decorations, magic texts, dances, distinctions of rank) that were carried or claimed by the original founders" (1980: 76).

6 From a different perspective and in a different way, Bourdieu (1977) has argued this point.

Chapter Six

Trade and Profit

In the market, goods circulate and profit is secured. In theory, these transactions are unrestrained by past relationships. But in practice is trade detached from social bonds, and how is trade connected to the accumulation of wealth?

In setting out a description of market features, we inevitably encounter special difficulties. Does one describe what markets are really like or present a model of them? And if the latter, which one, for there are competing market models – Austrian, Marshallian, rational choice, new institutionalist, evolutionary – that influence what one "sees"? Given the important place of economics in Western societies, the dividing line between market fact and market model also is thin, because models of economic behavior – taught to generations of students – affect market performance just as its everyday operations and changes influence theory (Klamer and Colander 1990; Seguino, Stevens, and Lutz 1996); the two are mutually implicated. But among the theoretical perspectives, some commonalities provide a contrast with the communal realm. I want to explore not only how anthropology adds to standard theory by contextualization but how profit arises through the creation of value, and this innovation process – bringing gain in the market – is deeply embedded in the communal realm. Economic growth depends on community and culture.

The Trade Domain

Markets – relying on the exchange of rights to property – never exist "outside" a cultural and social context. Property rights themselves have local justifications. In Northern Cyprus, after 1974, when Turkish Cypriots from the south took over land from Greek Cypriots who fled south, they developed various narratives justifying land possession (Scott 1998). Right by conquest, by original ownership, by improvements added, by purchase, and by compensation: all were invoked in the competing claims, and the ability to mobilize state power through personal relationships was a key factor in securing land. The trade of rights is also embedded in community. Even the possible instance of "silent trade" proves to be no exception. The story of silent trade apparently suggests the universality of exchange and the unnecessary presence of community. According to the story, one person leaves objects in a clearing for a stranger who places a counter offering and leaves; the first individual returns and takes the offering or leaves it for more; the other person then returns, and the negotiation continues until an acceptable rate of exchange is reached. According to the story, trading is a natural impulse of humans that takes place without shared language or law. But the transaction is culturally framed: each transactor focuses on the quantity and quality of the goods, measures them against value scales, and assumes the other is doing the same. The silent trade story presumes a shared market culture.

Anthropologists have explored many ways that markets are culturally situated.[1] The physical layout of marketplaces may reflect social groupings, such as caste, gender, and ethnicity (Gell 1982). Markets may rotate regularly, from town to town, with each locale offering a specialized product for sale. In the northern Andes of Colombia a system of markets reflects ecological specialization: from a lowland site on Monday to the high plains late in the week, this marketplace system offers a range of goods from fresh fish and tropical fruits to maize, potatoes, and mountain goats. Local markets also may develop special terms for their ways of conducting exchanges (Malinowski and de la Fuente 1982), and there are specialized markets for land, labor, capital, corn futures, and even gypsy horses (Stewart 1992).

Participants in markets vary considerably. Trading may be limited to those who control a specific language, possess plentiful resources, or have a "seat," as on the New York Stock Exchange. A single marketplace can include highly capitalized traders with large and expensive arrays, and those who lack investment funds, sell inexpensive goods, and seek high turnover. In local markets of Latin America, contiguous sellers seemingly offer the same commodities, such as grains or clothing, but each builds up a distinctive array and ways of selling: the market seller develops a style, legacy, or base (just as a mutual fund manager develops an investment style). Latin American vendors also have diverse backgrounds and projects. Some own a stall, some are kin of the owner, and some are paid employees. A few people may possess several stalls with different wares and rotate opening one and then another out of interest or as market conditions change. Some sell as they practice a craft, such as making leather goods, fashioning rubber sandals from old tires, or sewing clothes. Some work in the market once a week, partly to underwrite the experience of seeing others, and some want to make money everyday. Others sell to keep a remainder; they offer fruits and vegetables – buying and selling the stock in a day – to take home the profit in foods for the evening meal.

Formally viewed, market trade is dyadic, yet each transaction is undertaken in relation to other market exchanges to which it must adjust. When this adjustment among like trades occurs systematically, a market system is formed (Rothenberg 1992). Theoretically, a complete market has a large or infinite number of buyers and sellers, competing one with another, each of whom has perfect information about the conditions of the market. In this competition, each participant tries to gain the commerce that another would secure, for, at a particular time, the market is a zero-sum game. Because the goods in circulation are limited or scarce, participants try to optimize use of their resources: buyers endeavor to maximize preferences or utility; sellers want to secure a high price.

Markets, according to many models, are systems for allocating goods. Efficiency is the key word, for on most accounts a truly competitive market in equilibrium is Pareto optimal, meaning that no participant could be made better off through exchange without making someone else worse off; for example, if by trading between themselves, two parties would each be better off, the trade is made – and so exchange always continues until an equilibrium is reached. Efficiency refers to the relation between means and ends. The endowments each actor brings to the bar of exchange are the means that are traded to achieve the desired ends. The perfect market sorts participants' preferences in relation to their endowments. When this model of market exchange is projected on production, it implies that production is efficient when the factors or inputs of production are best arranged to yield the desired ends. Whether in the realm of production or exchange, efficiency designates instrumentally rational acts.

The "fundamental" Pareto finding (Stiglitz 1994: 7) about efficient markets has been so influential among economists and in the popular wisdom that today economic rationality means efficiency. Who can argue against "being efficient" without being labeled "irrational"? And to say that one does not want to be efficient or rational is a nonsensical, if not impossible, utterance in popular discourse. Efficiency has become the supreme value in market economy.

In an efficient market, goods circulate through trade free of social relationships. Government and community have no role in the provisioning of goods, except to help correct market failures, such as managing pollution problems through the imposition of Pigouvian taxes (a solution that is contested by some modern theories – see Coase 1988). In efficient markets, trade engenders no permanent ties, even if – in some eighteenth-century accounts – it did nourish "gentle" manners and the civilizing virtues of prudence and probity (Hirschman 1992: 43; 1977). As nineteenth-century liberals proclaimed, the liberating act of trade can expand and help reform communities and oppressive rules.

This general portrait of the market, however, has been subjected to various critiques.[2] By one account, information in the market is almost never perfect, and this imperfection has far-reaching effects on the competitive paradigm and conclusions about the market that are drawn from it, such as Pareto optimality (Stiglitz 1994). According to a different analysis, information is limited and rationality is bounded by the conditions in which it operates; given their circumstances, market actors may "satisfice" rather than maximize (Simon 1957, 1959). For example, we often buy a reasonably priced good without knowing if it represents optimal value, or we buy the same lunch again and again rather than search for a more perfect combination of cost and food preference: we settle for less than the optimal choice calculated in market terms. Different observers urge that maximization should not be assumed, because human efforts in production are discontinuous, and slack in work is ubiquitous (Leibenstein 1966, 1976). Still others argue that market transactions have costs (Coase 1988), and this friction leads to the formation of market hierarchies and groups, which interrupts the picture of a seamless market in which exchanges are always freely formed (Williamson 1975). Further provisos on standard assumptions have been offered, including the presence of imperfect competition or monopolies (Chamberlin 1933; Robinson 1933).

My hesitation at accepting the typical market model *tout court* arises for a different reason: its inability to account for accumulation. Efficiency – the valued feature of market interactions – is instrumental rationality seen as a collective feature of traders who balance endowments and satisfactions. But it does not explain profit.

The Puzzle of Profit

More than half a century ago Joan Robinson observed that she had looked for a neoclassical theory of profit but could not find one.[3] Since Adam Smith first outlined the contours of the market economy 200 years ago, profit-making has been seen as the driving motive within capitalism, shaping the behavior of individuals and firms. Economists after Smith have had much to say about the source and level of wages, rents, and interest, but still there is no accepted theory explaining how profit springs into being. As Robinson later wrote with Eatwell (1973: 183), "The central problem of economic philosophy [is] the nature of profits."

For anthropologists, the question of profit's origin fits into a larger problem: what is the source of surplus in any economic system (Dalton 1960; Harris 1959)? Anthropological theories concerning state-building through use of material power and the rise of class-based societies presume the generation and unfolding use of surplus. In asking about the origin of profit, I thus implicate a class of terms – including gain, surplus, excess, superfluity, remainder, and leftover – that refers to something above expenses secured in production or exchange and that can be consumed, saved, or invested.

I use the word "profit" only for a market system. Making profits is a main purpose of market activity and closely connected to accumulation, for profit held and added to past amounts becomes capital. The question "how is capital made?" is thus the same as "what is the source of profit?"

In pure trade between two actors, *no monetary profit is gained*, although each receives increased satisfaction of wants. Trade may be unbalanced when assessed by a chosen metric, but profit is not created, and the gain of one actor must be another's loss.[4] In competitive equilibrium, it does not pay for an outside firm to enter a market, because profit "at the margin" or for a new entrant is zero. Similarly, when the trade sphere encompasses production, outputs are traded for inputs that are transformed to outputs; market units purchase labor and resources with the aim of converting them, and selling the goods and services: trade becomes an "industrial" process. But these participants are not necessarily creating *new* value or gaining a competitive profit for their efforts (although expansion or growth may occur through control of a productivity niche). In conditions of competitive equilibrium, profit making is a zero-sum game. I think this realization was the core of Joan Robinson's complaint about the lack of a *neo-classical* theory of profit.[5]

How is profit brought into being? What can anthropology reveal about this process – ethnographically and theoretically? On my view, value creation lies at the core of profit-making, and is both a techno-logical and evaluation process. This zone is filled with warranties and legitimizations because the distribution of wealth and the place of power are implicated by profit's creation.

We have seen that people have models about the way the base is made or how value is added or augmented in the foundation.[6] In many ethnographic instances, the accounts are formulated in rituals or myth, or embodied in beliefs about kinship and social relationships. Humans posit a productive source in nature, ancestors, spirits, magical utterances, souls, or powerful beings that provide the core of the commons. Some early Western accounts of production and profit resemble these ethnographic ones as attempts to explain the origin of value. For example, premodern discourses, from mercantilism (sixteenth century) through physiocracy (eighteenth century), Ricardo, and Marx all focused on how accumulation takes place. In most of these models profit is created "outside" human will; it was a potential that humans might control but did not owe itself to their making. Several of these models, in fact, invoked the notion of gift to explain profit, because it came from outside the structure of normal value.

Mercantilist thought revolved around a beggar-thy-neighbor model of profit.[7] Mercantilists assumed productivity remains constant over time so that trade within and between nations is a zero-sum game. Thus, the profit of one merchant comes from another. Heckscher cites a series of mercantilist writers who argued either that one person's or one nation's gain must be another's loss:

> Montaigne (1580): "The profit of one man is the damage of another . . . no man profiteth but by the loss of others."
> Montchrétien (1615): "It is said that no one ever loses without another gaining. This is true and is borne out in the realm of commerce more than anywhere else."
> Bacon (1625): "It is likewise to be remembered that, forasmuch as the increase of any Estate must be upon the Foreigner, (for whatsoever is somewhere gotten is somewhere lost)."
> Colbert (1670): "It is not possible to increase (the stock of one country) by 20, 30, or 50 million without at the same time taking the same quantity from neighbouring states." (Heckscher 1935: 26–7)

With its focus on market traders who appropriate the wealth of others, the mercantilist model represents an elaboration of Aristotle's view that only nature or the externality provides. For mercantilists, profit comes from the holdings of others, and it is anchored by fresh inputs from nature in the form of gold and silver.

The central theses of mercantilism correspond closely to those of the house and small business in Latin America. Both the mercantilist state and the rural house practice thrift and limit consumption to purchase less than what is sold and build a reserve. Both construct riches as arising outside the realm of exchange. For the mercantilists, the mining of gold and silver produces new wealth. For the rural house in Latin America, nature's "force" provides wealth that increases the base. Both point to a source of wealth that lies outside community. As Latin

American agriculturalists say, one "takes" the strength that nature "gives."[8] Profit is a gift to the system and a result of predation within it.

In the latter part of the eighteenth century, the French physiocrats developed one of the first theories of surplus, but in some respects it was a continuation of mercantilist notions. According to the physiocrats, the reproductive parts of nature, such as crops, animals, and forests, yield a "net product" which is the amount above the expenditures used to secure it. Ultimately, its presence is due to the divine power who set nature in motion. "The land," said Quesnay, "is the unique source of wealth. . . . [A]griculture causes wealth to increase" (1963 [1766]: 232); and Mirabeau claimed that "the land is the mother of all goods" (1973 [1760]: 120). But Turgot neatly stated the model when he suggested that land returns are "a gift of nature" and the earth offers "a pure gift to him who cultivates it" (1898 [1770]: 14, 89). Turgot's use of the word "gift" fitted the general physiocratic argument. Profit was a gift from God, although humans had to "husband" it thriftily.

Several generations later, in the early 1800s, David Ricardo elaborated his theory of rent and profit that effectively constituted the beginning of marginalist theory in economics. Ricardo demonstrated how rent could be seen as the differential or marginal return on different pieces of land: more fertile plots yielded a higher rent, less fertile pieces a lower one. At the margin, or on the poorest plot – the last piece – no rent was secured. Ricardo claimed that rent was the return on the original or inherent qualities and powers of the land (1951 [1815], IV: 18, 34). He did not assert that rent was a gift to humans, yet its source lay outside the realms of trade and human control. This construction of rent had an unforeseen impact on his model of profit.

By Ricardo's early argument, rent and profit are inversely linked: when rents rise, profits fall; as rents decrease, profits expand.[9] But – and this implication Ricardo never confronted – given his claim that rent is due to the inherent qualities of nature, profit also must be a return on nature's powers, because it increases or decreases inversely with rent as the ambit of farming shrinks or expands. What was rent at one time could become profit at another when the land margin contracted. By Ricardo's logic that rent turns into profit, nature's fertility is the size determinant, if not the source, of profit (Gudeman 1986).

Ricardo soon revised his theory, and within two years he shifted the agent of profit from nature to humans. In *The Principles* (1951 [1817], I) he developed a labor theory of value in which human effort creates value. Ricardo did not completely account for the origin of profit by this model, but he did set the stage for Marx who brought the theory to one culmination.

Marx was a Ricardian. He adopted Ricardo's nascent labor theory of value but added a dimension of signal importance to account for the generation of surplus. The centerpoint of his theory revolves about the distinction between labor-power and labor, and the creation of surplus value or profit.[10] Marx argued that surplus value (or money profit) is generated in production. To show how profit arises, he distinguished between labor-power and labor. Labor-power is what a worker brings to the production process; it consists of the capacities he can expend in work. Labor is the exercise of this capacity or what a person expends in labor during the working day. A worker sells his labor-power or work potential to a capitalist, receiving its value in money. But the capitalist actually purchases or secures command over the worker's labor. The capitalist pays for the exchange value of labor-power but gains control of its use or the worker's physical efforts.

For Marx, the crucial point is that a worker can produce by his actual labor more value than is needed to maintain his labor-power (and was paid for it). Value expands in production that is under the capitalist's control. In the transition from exchange value (the original market purchase) to use value (productive work) and then to exchange value (the market product), surplus is produced. The difference between the value of what it takes to produce labor-power itself and the value that labor-power produces makes up the surplus. Human labor is the source of profit.

But how did Marx anchor or justify his theory? He was relatively silent about this special human capacity, except for a few observations in *Capital*: "The property therefore which labour-power in action, living labour, possesses of preserving value, at the same time that it adds it, is a *gift of Nature* which costs the labourer nothing, but which is very advantageous to the capitalist" (1967 [1867]: 206; italics added). Marx "naturalized" the source of new value or surplus as inherent in the human. Like the mercantilists, physiocrats, and early Ricardo, Marx sought a foundation for profit outside the market domain.[11] Crucially, this species capacity of producing surplus is a "gift" – nature's donation.

From mercantilism through physiocracy, Ricardo, and Marx, early modernist writers were concerned with accumulation and profit. To explain profit and its accumulation as capital, they posited a source outside the economy: the divinity, precious metals, land, a special capacity of the species. In these discourses, profit was exogenously given, although once within circulation it could be transferred through modes of predation, such as financial or political power. These theorists visualized the market domain as autonomous but devoid of new value, so fresh value had to be rendered as an external gift to the existing system of value.

Modern neoclassical theory is different. In this model, firms are the principal actors. Transforming inputs to outputs, their production functions are determined by technological knowledge that is known. A firm rationally selects among the envelope of possibilities, trying to maximize returns given product demand and factor supplies at existing prices. In conditions of uncertainty, choices are set by statistical inference: past outcomes are projected to the future and weighted with probabilities and monetary outcomes, so determining selection. The system is in value stasis.

In recent years, some theorists have provided a more dynamic model of the growth of capital and value. For example, adapting an argument from Arrow, Solow shows how learning by doing or continuous improvement can be captured in a formal model. The result is impressive, except Solow is forced to divide incremental "endogenous" improvements that occur in the doing of production from unpredictable "exogenous" innovations that alter the course of production itself and introduce new value. The sharpness of the dichotomy is dubious but displays the limits of this modernist discourse: "Candor requires me to say that I suspect there is an additional irreducible elment in innovation that, if not 'truly' exogenous, whatever that means, is at least not to be fully explained by the calculus of expected profit" (Solow 1997: 28). In my view, explanation of value change and profit falls outside this discourse.

A Theory of Profit

The process of value creation is fundamentally the same in the community and market realms – in one it yields remainders, leftovers, extras, or surplus, and in the other it yields profit, which is the monetized version of incommensurate remainders. Both remainders and profit are created by innovations or "new combinations" of products and services that expand a value system. They consist in forging new products, methods of production, or forms of organization, or in finding cheaper sources of supply and new markets. Innovations, by making new connections between means and ends, create knowledge-in-practice or "technology." In one realm, they strengthen the base; in the other they expand capital.

My argument extends the theory of Joseph Schumpeter, although he hinted at the presence of the community realm:

The successful carrying out of new combinations also results in a value surplus in the non-exchange economy, not only in the capitalistic; and in fact a value surplus in the sense of a quantity of value to which there is no corresponding claim of imputation by means of production, not merely a surplus of satisfaction as against the earlier position. (Schumpeter 1934 [1926]: 142–3)[12]

Schumpeter lauded the entrepreneur as the architect of innovations and profit. On his view, economic *growth* occurs by expanding the use of existing technologies and land and labor (as in early Colonial America). But *development* takes place only through the efforts of entrepreneurs who make "new combinations" (ibid.: 65); and the success and failure of entrepreneurs determine the progress of the economy. As Schumpeter once emphasized, the entrepreneur "triumphed for others . . . and created a model for them which they can copy" (ibid.: 133).[13]

In the market, profit is the monetary leftover that an innovation secures. A successful innovation, by creating new value, draws a revenue that is larger than the cost of the factors used in its production. After the productive factors have been recompensed, there is – in Schumpeter's terms – a "remainder" or "leftover," and this incremental value, though never predictable, composes the profit. Because profit is the return for innovation, and it results from entrepreneurial practices, gains – on Schumpeter's account – are rightly taken by the entrepreneur who put the innovation into practice.

Schumpeter's model of profit actually corresponds closely to the Latin American ideal of building a base (perhaps he was influenced by visions of a house economy). In Schumpeter's words, profit is the "remainder" gathered after costs have been covered; in the Latin American community lexicon, material "remainders" are secured after expenditures have been "replaced." In both cases, the innovation extra is relative to the prior cycle; once realized its value joins capital or base.

In his early writing, Schumpeter argued that entrepreneurial activity was composed of making "new combinations." He briefly observed that it "consists precisely in breaking up old, and creating new, traditions" (1934 [1926]: 92), but the emphasis was on the creative side.[14] Several decades later (1976 [1942]), Schumpeter still fancied this view but now referred to it as a process of "creative destruction." Some may link this more negative formulation to Schumpeter's pessimistic prognosis for capitalism; others may see similarities to the dialectical idea of breaking the fetters and revolutionizing the forces of production. But Schumpeter's oxymoron, "creative destruction," can also be

appreciated in light of the fact that the entrepreneur draws on ana-
lytic, synthetic, and critical capacities. Perhaps Schumpeter did not
sufficiently emphasize that the entrepreneur operates in a social context and that, as it shifts, similarities and dissimilarities may be sharpened, which may stimulate other innovations. A successful innovation
also shifts the context for which it is made, opening the way for further change. Still, in his model, there is no necessary connection between the before and the after in the creation of a product. Schumpeter's
signal contribution was to connect the act of innovation to uncertainty. Because the acceptability of an innovation, as well as the
possibility and size of profit, are unpredictable, the entrepreneur operates in a context of uncertainty (and so "merits" the fresh return). In
fact, the entrepreneur may innovate not simply to earn money but
for the creative satisfaction or for its own sake. Schumpeter's later
pessimistic view of capitalism's future was based on his forecast that
entrepreneurial practices would wither as accumulation occurred,
motivation decreased, and the processes of production became routin-
ized. In Veblen's terms, the captains of finance would come to dominate the captains of industry. The creativeness of entrepreneurship is
overwhelmed by financial monopolies, spelling the end of development.

Accumulation

We may, in fact, distinguish two forms of profit: normal and supernormal. Normal profit is the return secured for innovations made in
conditions of uncertainty. It is different from wages, rents, and interest in that it cannot be contracted for and predicted in advance. Normal profit is not the result of calculated risks taken when probabilities
are known (Knight 1971 [1921]).

Normal profit is short term, because in perfect competition the new
profit is efficiently allocated among the factors and products of production. Due to competition and copying, the profit is temporary for
the initial holder. For example, if the price drops, part of the new
value is distributed among consumers. If wages rise or more workers
are employed, part of the increment flows to labor. A perfect market
efficiently reallocates input uses and products through the price system. When demand stabilizes, returns to the input factors become constant and represent a stable share in the now past innovation. In a
competitive system with profit ownership, the increment is distributed, and the standard of living rises.

A successful innovation, however, may be kept private in order to sustain the income flow and obtain a supernormal profit. The innovation becomes, I shall say, a "productivity niche" held as private property. It now yields a quasi-rent on analogy with a particularly fertile plot of corn land, a hillside conducive to high-quality viniculture, or a rich vein of ore. The holding of a productivity niche provides a monopoly over a scarce resource and yields a predictable income flow. The means of assuring monopoly control are various: financial, legal, social. For example, money capital may buy and sustain the productivity niche through patent rights, copyrights, and intellectual property rights. Oligopolies and cartels also are maintained by social networks based on gender, class, ethnicity, dialect, locality, and education: through cooperative ties that emerge from community, some potential competitors can be excluded. Such productivity niches – legal or illegal, monetary or community-based – convert profit from the realm of uncertainty to predictable risk.

But the difference between normal and supernormal profit may lie in the eyes of the beholder. For example, a monopoly profit may be increased by "efficiently" downsizing the labor force and raising the workload without changing production methods. Likewise, if a small monopoly is retained by a firm, part of this annual profit may be distributed as higher managerial wages. Some explain these earnings as a return for skills that add value, but others model them as a rent gained through control of resources. In Panama small landholders who grew sugar cane as a cash crop could secure a monopoly profit through their control of land, the productivity niche. The mills which purchased the raw product advanced their suppliers $1.50 for each work day needed in the crop. The planters employed other men to work their fields, but in addition to paying themselves a wage (though not working), they paid their workers $1.25 per day and withheld the remainder. They called both takings profit, but did compare it to a trader's gains. It was a mercantile profit made through exchange by having control of a resource and taking over part of existing value, not by adding it.

In my view, Marx's model of surplus value or value generation and exploitation provides one example of the way supernormal gains may be captured. According to Marx, normal profit arises through the exercise of labor; specifically, capitalist profit results from the difference between the value of labor-power purchased and the value produced when that labor-power is exercised. But Marx's distinction can arise only after an innovation has been established. Marx assumed that productivity niches already exist, so that through their financial possession capitalists can hold back on wages and sequester a profit. From the perspective of the innovation model, Marx offered a distribution not a generation model of profit, and he mystified value's origin as a "gift of nature" rather than seeing it as a result of human creativity.

Holders of capital can secure profit returns in other ways as well, especially through arbitrage, which has at least three forms. When the economy expands through use of existing technologies, more resources and labor are needed in response to the heightened demand. The holders of the needed raw materials or resources receive a gain as the value of their holdings increases (such holders have the resources in hand to sell, or firms themselves own the inputs). They are arbitrageurs between the present and future in that they purchase the property in anticipation that its value will rise. For this arbitrage they receive a part of the new, incremental return. Profit, accruing to the holders of needed inputs, is represented in rents.

An investment in stock markets represents an exchange of current money capital for rights to a possible future flow on the bet that the future flow will exceed the present value of the money stock. Purchasers of shares in a corporation gain rights to portions of the increasing profit. This form of arbitrage, like the preceding, does not create value but secures part of the profit from the firm's innovations and productivity niche. (I distinguish this investing from the innovation of new financial instruments, such as derivatives or junk bonds that yield their innovator a profit. In these cases, the innovation returns a normal profit – at least at first.) But the line between innovation and arbitrage is fuzzy. For example, FIRE (finance, insurance, real estate) interests – or financial property – in the USA during the period 1990–4 gathered 43 percent of the gross domestic product. Some of these returns were due to innovations (new financial instruments, new financial packages) but many FIRE investments produced streams of wealth in which new forms of value, rather than maintenance and expansion of existing forms (condos, insurance), were a small proportion (Henwood 1997: 76–84).

A subform of investment arbitrage revolves about holding "old objects," including houses, art, stamps, and other fashioned objects. Some objects from baseball cards to toys to Shaker furniture, may rise in value only after long delays and when periods of nostalgia pass through a community. In these cases, the original innovation is revalued by a community, but only the capital holder, not the innovator, receives the benefits, which is not unlike buying corporate stock and holding on in the expectation that it may rise. But in these cases, even the idea of a rise may not be anticipated – it is a windfall from innovation profit.

Finally, there may be arbitrage across separate or national labor markets – thus the explosion of off-shore manufacturing, light assembly plants and maquillas, and the use of immigrant labor, which are one facet of globalization today.

Arbitrage is part of the process of achieving efficiency; it occurs and disappears when prices adjust. Arbitrageurs are not innovators but calculators of risk and rewards; innovators create value, arbitrageurs use calculations to gather part of this value. But only holders of property have the opportunity to arbitrage between present and future value.

This ultimate sphere of appropriation, however, is never left unfettered by community. Taxes may limit it; force, consent, and ideologies sustain and encircle it. For example, in ethnographic contexts, chiefs may have the obligation to redistribute some of their takings. Among the Tiv, when wealthy men exchange goods for wives, material accumulations are dispersed. By contrast, among the Kachin high-ranking chiefs who receive marriage goods for lineage sisters must subsequently apportion the goods to followers (Leach 1954). In modern economies, corporate profits and individual shares of it may be taxed by governments and used to support community. In addition to this regulation on accumulation through fiscal means and transfer payments, central banks (e.g. the US Federal Reserve) may exert control over values through interest rates which can lead to adjustment of returns on corporate bonds, stock prices, corporate investments, and natural resources. This financial control, linked to the issuance of money, is often imbued with sacred powers, as exemplified by the motto "In God We Trust" imprinted on US coins, and the secret meetings of the Federal Reserve's Board of Governors – which raises the question: who controls these high priests of money?

Ultimate regulation is partial, and subject to leakage; the US discount rate does not control the entire economy because rentier returns are a function also of the pace of consumption, production expectations, and especially innovations.

NOTES

1 For recent anthropological analyses of markets as conceived and practiced, see the helpful introduction and case studies in Carrier (1997) and Dilley (1992). Also see Babb (1989), Beals (1975), Bohannan and Dalton (1965), Cook and Diskin (1976), Gell (1982), Malinowski and de la Fuente (1982), McBryde (1947), and Plattner (1985).

2 Hirschman (1992: 123) provides a summary critique: "The economists' claims of allocative efficiency and all-round welfare maximization are strictly valid only for this [ideal] market. Involving large numbers of price-taking anonymous buyers and sellers supplied with perfect information, such markets function without any prolonged human or social contact

among or between the parties. Under perfect competition there is no room for bargaining, negotiation, remonstration or mutual adjustment."

3   In *An Essay on Marxian Economics*, Robinson set out to compare Marx's theory of profits to orthodox or neoclassical theory; she soon ran into difficulties with the latter, which led her to observe that "academic economics fails to provide any theory (of profits) which is relevant to the real world" (1960 [1942]: 79). Her argument more completely was that "Even if we could form a clear conception of the equilibrium rate of profit, it would be irrelevant to the actual world. The equilibrium rate of profit is that rate which induces zero net investment. But over the course of history, since the Industrial Revolution began, net investment has always been going on. . . . The whole apparatus of equilibrium theory therefore seems to be without application to reality . . . [and] the orthodox notion of a definite supply price of capital thus disintegrates upon examination" (ibid.: 60–1). Thus, Robinson concluded, "the moral justification of profit as a necessary cost of production disappears, and the whole structure of the orthodox apology falls to the ground" (ibid.: 62). See also *Essays in the Theory of Economic Growth* (1962: 11, 13, 15).

     Thirty years after, Robinson reflected upon her discovery: "Many years ago I set out to write a little book on Marxian economics; when I had written a chapter on Marx's theory of profits, I thought I had to write a chapter on the orthodox theory for comparison, and blest if I could find one high or low. Ever since I have been inquiring and probing but I still cannot find out what it is" (1972: 8).

4   Obrinsky (1983) provides a recent discussion of the search for a theory of profit.

5   I also understand it to be one implication of Mirowski's studies of value theory in neoclassical economics (1989, 1991).

6   By some accounts, production should be understood as an entropic process, a view that rests very uneasily with the current emphasis on growth through use of non-renewable resources (Daly and Townsend 1993; Georgescu-Roegen 1971).

7   Useful sources on mercantilism include Heckscher (1935), Roll (1973), and Schumpeter (1954). For a contemporary application in the context of "underdevelopment," see Soto (1989).

8   This similarity of the mercantilist and Latin American models casts a different light on an argument put forward by George Foster. Foster suggested that peasant behavior, especially in Latin America, might be understood as if it were formulated in accord with an "Image of Limited Good" (1967). All good things, especially in the material realm, are available only in limited quantities, so that one's gains have to be at the expense of another. Using this model, Foster accounted for a variety of behaviors and beliefs, such as pervasive mistrust between people and the fear of envy. He interpreted various ritual actions as methods for warding off jealousy between villagers and calming suspicions. Treasure tales, too, were important, exculpatory accounts, for sudden increments in personal wealth holdings could be explained as due to the lucky finding of

buried wealth. Unlike Foster, who provides a perceptive ethnographic analysis, I see this model not so much as the product of an independent peasantry but as a mercantilist-like vision produced at the margin and perhaps inherited from Europe.

9   Ricardo showed that as the frontier or margin of agriculture expands, some of the profit on an existing plot becomes rent that flows to the plot's landowner; conversely, when the margin contracts, rent that flowed to landowners becomes profit. This pattern followed from Ricardo's marginalist view of rent. When the land area cultivated expands, new and poorer pieces of land are farmed. The extra income above costs that these last pieces secure makes up profit, but as the land is less and less fertile, this last or marginal profit continually falls. In contrast, each preceding plot – which had once been marginal – continues to produce as before; but now its revenues above costs are differently distributed. Profits on plots inside the margin fall – to match that of the poorest piece – whereas the rest of the extra above costs falls to the landowner. Thus, as profits fall, rents rise, for the overall productivity of each plot remains constant.

10 For simplicity, I omit the distinction between surplus value as measured in labor, and profit as measured in money. The difference, never fully reconciled by Marx, has given rise to the "transformation problem," or the problem of showing how value measured in labor is isomorphic with value measured in money. This unsolved problem or putative equation has exercised commentators and critics of the theory, leading many to reject it.

11 Thus he argues: "The essential difference between the various economic forms of society, between for instance, a society based on slave-labour, and one based on wage-labour, lies in the mode in which this surplus-value is in each case extracted from the actual producer, the labourer (1967 [1867]: 217). See also Marx 1967 [1894]: 785–6, 791.

12 The English version of *The Theory of Economic Development* was published in 1934, but Schumpeter traced the beginnings of the work to 1907; the first German edition was published in 1911.

13 For an early discussion of Schumpeter on innovation, see Ruttan (1959).

14 Schumpeter's first discussion (1934 [1926]) is the most suggestive, but he offered several later statements (1976 [1942]), (1989 [1947]), (1989 [1949]), and (1991 [1946]).

Chapter Seven

Profit on the Small

In industrial society, we have myths about the great inventor, such as Thomas Edison, and the innovator, such as Henry Ford; a museum in Nebraska is devoted to honoring American progress seen as the accomplishment of heroic entrepreneurs, including McCormick, Eastman, and others.[1] These folk narratives suggest that innovations are accomplished by flashes of intuition, experienced by isolated individuals. The same claim is found in some formal discourses. Schumpeter's entrepreneur exercises faculties that are independent of the impact of others.

But innovations – yielding new value – emerge within a heritage that they revise. Sometimes they are produced by a single person, sometimes by a group; sometimes they emerge in a leap, sometimes in small steps, as in learning-by-doing; often they are a mix. But innovations are always set within a community, because the learning and accomplishment are dependent on a social context (Merton 1957 [1942]).

Ethnography displays the creative processes that occur in market-dominated economies with the advantage that some features appear in sharpened form. I want to explore four cases of value creation to illustrate how innovation consists of learning-by-doing and is a new way of doing. It depends on community in complex ways, yet the returns may be appropriated by individuals, competitively allocated, or apportioned in community. My examples, which come from rural and urban Guatemala, also show some of the ways the four value domains of economy are linked in the creation of new value.[2]

A Potter's Profit

Consider the case of a successful woman potter outside Guatemala City, who was crafting new figurines for sale. She worked in a corner of her kitchen but had a separate store that was stocked with finished

pieces. Buyers came from the city to purchase in quantity, her husband spent much of his time overseeing the practical arrangements,
and the woman had accumulated enough money to make other small
investments in her village. The woman's items were selling well, but
she liked to invent new pieces and was experimenting with figures of
angels. Each figurine emerged from the potter's hands with a slightly
different form as the woman made adjustments to achieve greater balance or more stability. Looking at earlier angel figures, one could see
that the overall design of the angels had been evolving. The figures
had taken well to the firing, and the results were generally good. As
the potter explained, all her work was done by touch and testing
(*tantear*).

Feeling one's way also characterized the potter's pricing. For a batch
of figures, she knew what quantity of clay was used and the time she
spent. Each new figurine had a real cost basis derived from the cost of
the raw materials and labor return the potter had been receiving. (Unlike some household workers, the potter considered that her labor was
a monetary "cost" and not an unpriced "expense of the house" that
supported the market commodity through the use of "unaccounted"
housework). Still, the sum of her material costs and labor, a calculation the potter made with a high degree of precision, was not the price
she charged. For pricing, the ceramist would also feel her way; depending on what the market would bear, she raised or lowered her
price – and would or would not make a profit above costs.[3] Her expenditures were calculable and predictable for every angel figure, but
her profit was not; it was the "remainder" after costs, and it was always uncertain, depending on "the market."

The ceramist's profit also was temporary for a double reason. If her
product continued to sell well, eventually she would recalculate the
gain as an augmentation to the "value of her work"; she increased the
figured return to her own labor (or wage), which could have a long-
term effect on what she charged for her other pieces. But other potters
in the community would also see what she had done, how the figure
was made, and whether it drew buyers. They were adept artisans, too,
and would quickly copy her figurine if it became popular. Still, the
potter said that even with competition the eventual sale price of a new
figure usually did not fall to its original cost of production, for she
added that as she made more angel figures she would find ways to
produce them better and more quickly as she learned in the practices
of production. Although the price of new ceramic pieces might decline
through competition, the remuneration for her own labor almost always increased: even with competition, she was able to absorb some
of the initial profit as a return for her work. Over time, the value of all

her efforts had been rising; she had observed, for example, that although she had learned her craft directly from her mother at home, her standard of living was appreciably higher than that of her parent.

In miniature, the potter's case neatly displays the course and effects of innovation. The new product as well as the pricing were established by trial and error. The angel figure as a material creation in the household of the woman was initially an uncertain product. Then, its price was uncertain, as was its profit. Even so, profit on the innovation was temporary. But as it disappeared it was distributed as a higher imputed wage to the original maker, lower prices to consumers, and increased returns to other potters; what had been profit became higher wages and lower prices. The woman potter fits Schumpeter's model: the entrepreneur invents a new process, introduces it to the market, and holds a short-term monopoly; eventually, the improvement is distributed one way or another within the system and alters economic development, even as the originator continues to change her productivity niche through local learning.

The potter's example also shows how the market relies on a larger community and local reason. Fresh images for the figurines were often suggested by media and other outside sources; the potter's inspirations were then turned into products that varied with the batches of clay, the characteristics of the oven, and her own skills in relation to these conditions. The woman learned her skills by watching and working in her mother's kitchen, just as she continued to work in her own kitchen and her offspring learned from her. She added to this commons when her neighbors – who were also "competitors" – visited, watched, and copied her work just as she would benefit from their innovations. The series of innovations that emerged from and circulated among all the potters added to the local heritage. Apprenticeship and artisanship were performed and sustained by the house, village, and global communities, as were the practices of trial-and-error in conditions of uncertainty. The innovations emerged in a total situation that included practiced hands, glossy magazines, clay, international TV programs, and local artisans. The potter's case suggests how innovation – acts of creative destruction that engage uncertainty, alter the accepted heritage, draw a profit, and raise the standard of living – depends on and flourishes in community. Abstract, individualistic, instrumental reason does not illuminate or account for the potter's practices and success.

Innovation in Groups

The potter illustrates how the single innovator is embedded in a communal context, but groups themselves may be the source of innovation as illustrated by the case of a tinsmith who, with his two sons, operated a small business near the principal market in Guatemala City. Their equipment consisted of a few 10-year-old metal rollers that were operated and adjusted by hand, cutters, metal bars, tables, soldering irons, pliers, and hammers. The father, quick and dexterous, had learned the skills of sheetmetal-bending from his father – who kept a shop next door – and during his time as the foreman of a small tinsmith factory. His skills – the ability to adjust rollers by eye, to shape metal, to visualize and piece together new objects – were far superior to his father's, and his work was laid out very differently from a factory's. More important, the work arrangements of the three men were marked by continuous alterations that allowed them to produce better-quality work, take on a greater variety of projects, and produce more quickly. On each project the three worked together, whereas most tinsmiths labor independently. The work was undertaken as batch processing, as in the production of 12 or 24 drinking vessels, and the steps of production were planned as coherent sets of tasks. Each man took on several task sets, which occurred at different points of the batch flow. Assignment to a task set depended on personal interest and skill. These labor arrangements, as well as the details of production, such as the physical placement of a piece of sheeting, were calculated with the adeptness and care of an industrial engineer. Still, the plans were always adjusted in practice, which was the group's major innovation. As the men said, they "accommodated" themselves, and they had "to know the work well." For example, the sheeting, which varied in thickness and flexibility, might require more work at the stage of bending; or on a particular day one of the men might work more slowly; in addition, customers entered the shop and the person nearest or least occupied had to attend to them. Because the flow of work was constantly changing due to unpredictable influences, the men overlapped and interlinked their labor. If one completed a task set and was waiting on the output of another, he assisted that man in finishing his work or skipped ahead to unoccupied materials. When four or six hands were required on a task, one or two of the men would put down their work to assist the third. Then, to save time, as a man was finishing a task set he would often throw the first completed items to the next worker, who would look up just in time to make the catch and begin the subsequent stage. Unlike other sheetmetalmakers, the artisans never accumulated even a small inventory; they purchased materials as needed, their runs were short, and they practiced a form of "just-in-time" inventory control, all of which saved money. Their overriding aim was to turn out flawless items, requiring no corrections, an accomplishment in which they took much pride. To the observer, it looked as if the production team was putting on a dance, a performance – indeed, they listened to music throughout the day and clearly enjoyed working rhythmically. All the microadjustments were made without voiced communication; as the men repeated, each had to "know the work," which meant knowing how to adjust individual efforts to the materials given, knowing how to adjust for quality control, knowing how to do all the tasks in a production process, knowing what the others were doing at each stage, and knowing what was happening in the larger work context. The innovation consisted neither in what was produced nor in the materials and implements used. It lay in the knowledge of how to accommodate production practices to human variability, material variability, and the intrusions of others. The men did not see themselves as comprising a production line or a closed and integrated system. They drew on an artisan model and the Adam Smith image of functional specialization, but within the larger context of a fluid group that challenged their changing skills.

The men had constructed a production community through communal learning and learning-by-doing. Production was a play of trial-and-error practices, of adjusting and adapting to materials and one another. A production engineer might wish to script their performance, but a script would not capture its dynamic and changing form, and even if he could put on paper what the men did one day, their routines would shift by the next. The men practiced what Kash (1989), examining Japanese manufacturing, has called "continuous innovation." Their innovation lay not in what was produced or even in "the doing," but in "the doing of the doing" or what Bateson (1972) has termed "meta-learning." The men had learned how to learn as a group. The example shows how trial-and-error practices or extensions of a knowledge system are supported by community.

Competition among tinsmiths was fierce, entry costs were low, the market was limited to a less wealthy sector, and plastic and glass substitutes were appearing on the market. Did the innovations of the tinsmiths produce a profit, and was it figured by them? The father kept the daily return – the amount above running costs – in a "single pocket" from which he paid each son a daily sum larger than the prevailing wage in addition to providing their maintenance at home. The father also described how all three occasionally made another gain when, on a special order, materials were left over and could be fabricated into an object for sale. The father considered these extra payments and savings to be gains. But there was a further remainder that accrued to the father. He was so certain that this gain, which was the largest of the gains made by the enterprise and greater than that achieved by other tinsmiths, was due to their special practices that he never allowed a competitor or customer to stand in the shop for very long. The knowledge was kept secret to protect the innovation and preserve the monopoly profit.

The tinsmith operation is a shifting combination of three forms of production: premodern, modern, and postmodern. The tinsmith had learned the skills of shaping and making from his father. These traditional skills involved the use of tools developed 200 years ago, and many of the products were "traditional" as well. This artisanship or craftspersonship was the sort of Enlightenment activity extolled by Diderot in the eighteenth century.

As a former factory foreman, however, the tinsmith knew about assembly-line production, a regime that developed in the nineteenth century and culminated in Henry Ford's innovation of the mass production line in the early part of the twentieth. In this rationalized production system, products are moved to workers who perform specialized tasks in fixed places. This method of production requires careful managment and engineering control. Significantly, the tinsmith's own father, who had passed along the patrimony of artisanship to his son, did not practice Fordism. The father had a younger assistant, but both of them made objects alone, and both made one or two objects all the way through rather than by batches in stages. They practiced a premodern form of production, whereas the son and his offspring incorporated modernist methods.

Finally, the tinsmith placed special emphasis on "adjusting" and "accommodating" to the work, and on knowing all the work. He and his sons used batch processing; overlapped, replicated, and traded tasks (multispecialization); kept no inventory; made different products on demand in a short time; clustered themselves in space yet moved to the materials in their dance of production; did it right the first time so that quality control was not a separate overseeing function; labored ceaselessly while they worked; and learned what they needed to know on the job.

The tinmaking shop comprised a mix of premodern, modern, and postmodern practices; its method of incremental improvement encountered limits, however, as an innovation was explored and extended. The tinsmith accumulated profits but had no need to invest them in his business which could not incorporate more workers and did not need capital equipment. The money had to be hoarded or spent on consumer goods; in fact, the tinsmith had both a savings account and a television in every room of his house.

Extending the Base and Profit

Individual innovators depend on a community heritage, and groups innovate; but there is a third way in which community supports innovation – through extension of base across the boundaries of private operators and firms.[4] Innovations often build one on another, especially in passing from person to person.

I once observed how a Guatemalan innovator built a new type of furnace for baking clay bricks he was selling. This owner, who was in his late 50s, had already built several kilns and had expanded his operation over the years; but he spoke for several hours about his recent innovation. The man had designed a new type of furnace and brought into use a new resource or source of supply. The land underneath his kiln had previously been mined for clay and ordinarily would have been too unstable to support a furnace. The owner, however, had laid an extra thick, reinforced concrete floor, as he had seen done for the walls of buildings in towns, thus making possible a new use for an old excavation. His innovation was a metaphoric application whereby the floor of a brick kiln on unstable ground in a rural area was seen as being like the upright structure of a building in the city. He also hoped that this furnace would last longer than ordinary ones. Finally, the kiln was situated near a road, and the owner had constructured the furnace so that finished bricks could be unloaded directly from it onto trucks rather than be stacked first in the brickyard and then loaded for transport, saving worktime.

The owner described how he had worked with the "figure" of the kiln in his mind for several years – thinking about it in bed and talking about it during the day. He had been at once architect, planner, contractor, foreman, and financier. As the work progressed, everyone had told him that the project would fail, and he had known that he was breaking with established methods of making a kiln but was convinced that he could succeed. As his description of the innovation progressed, it became clear that he was motivated more by pride and the excitement of the project than by the possibility of gain, for he admitted that it would take many years before the effects of his innovation could be assessed, and the profit was uncertain. In all these respects – the pride, the obsession, the breaking with accepted wisdom, and the pleasure in the practice itself – the kilnmaker fit the model of the innovator who does something for its own sake.

His furnace was one of 20 in the community; each was slightly different, as each maker had adjusted his construction in relation to the terrain and was trying to achieve a slightly different purpose. The size of furnaces also had been growing as new materials became available and as makers learned from one another. The innovator with the reinforced concrete floor had many visitors, and he demonstrated freely what he had done, knowing that others would copy him. This sharing quickened the pace of local innovations. Clearly, if one has an innovation, such as a new way of producing tin buckets or baked bricks, it yields a profit as long as it is not copied by others who, by competing, will lower the market price. But within a community, sharing information may expand the base and benefit everyone, including the first innovator, because innovations often occur in series as one stimulates another.[5]

Profit, Base, and Capital

The kilnmaker was sharing his base within a face-to-face community in a situation where capital control did not markedly distinguish him from his competitors. In other cases, capital may control how a base is dispersed. For example, in Guatemala certain towns and regions are known for their weaving, and the textiles have a ready market. Until recently, most of the weaving methods and techniques, employing the footloom, had not changed dramatically, although weaving styles kept evolving. The weaving is done by women at home, and seemingly one and then another produces a new design. Each new design is an innovation and adds to the patrimony on which everyone can draw. But it would be difficult to specify exactly who added what to the stock of designs, and it would misrepresent the situation. These women are not purely competitive actors, as market models suggest, but co-holders of a base and participants in a community that includes responding to and learning from one another as well as teaching the next generation. Some are respected for their design skills and others for their weaving techniques, although these communal honors, which are the products of past sharing and which become shared in turn, may or may not be honored in the market through higher prices. Weaving designs are local, collective products.

One house in a weaving town, however, had considerably expanded its operations through sales to the United States. It had purchased additional footlooms and sewing machines, and was employing other villagers. But what seemed to be an expanded form of local production in fact had been absorbed by outside financial capital, for most of the output was sent to a California buyer who had secured exclusive rights to sell in the United States and made arrangements for local financing. Wages remained low and the organizing house was not holding onto a profit.

According to the traditional perspective on "underdevelopment," the weaving enterprise was an enclave industry, using external capital and low-cost domestic labor to produce a commodity for export. But a purely market analysis, focusing on differential labor and resource costs, leaves out the cultural transfer. The weaving techniques, designs, and labor skills of the women were the products of historical innovations, part of a shared base. The US entrepreneur, through his access to capital, was able to use this heritage for his private benefit

Sometimes, as in the case of building a new type of furnace or making tin products in a new way, we can clearly locate the beginning of an innovation. But innovation usually results from the application of shared know-how to new materials and contexts, often as it passes from person to person. Evolving products are community "properties" and help define the community's identity. In cases such as the textile-makers, drawing a line between common knowledge or a base and the private knowledge of an innovator is problematic (Brush 1996). Shared knowledge, however, can be easily appropriated for private use when protections, such as intellectual property rights, are lacking and financial control of productivity niches can be maintained.

Hidden support offered by a base and heritage is no less true of high technology sectors in the modern economy. Silicon Valley is not a collection of independent firms but a community of organizations that supports experimentation, learning, the passing of information, and extraordinary adaptation (Saxenian 1994). Silicon Valley is a network, a community of corporations with porous borders – information, people, and teams cross between the profit centers; and this creation of a larger, communal base enhances the market performance of each participant. In Italy small firms, connected to one another, innovate in the production of shoes and textiles; they have a community. In Germany, new machine tools and other equipment are produced by interlaced small firms. Part of the success of the Japanese automobile industry has been attributed to situated rationality exercised in work groups. In Silicon Valley, Hewlett-Packard's practice of managing by wandering around is a way of modeling that innovations emerge as connections are made.[6] In recent years, researchers too have turned to contextual reason in trying to understand practical business activity.[7]

Profit-making as a return to innovation and a function of community practices suspends belief in the exclusive role of instrumental rationality within the economy. Instrumental rationality is an excellent coping device given a measurement system and the possibility of assessing outcomes; it deals with calculated means and calculable ends, such as figuring the right road to take given a destination and traffic conditions. But when the consequences of an act are unknown and have no measure beforehand – can we predict the success of a hula hoop, an Edsel, 3-D movies, or a software program? – this mode of reason can hardly be used.

The idea that instrumental calculations, using a single measuring rod, anchor the market is threatened by the innovation view of profit because of the lack of predictable outcome it suggests in the central activity of the market. After the fact a successful practice can be assessed as having been rational, for it made a profit. But when the results are partly unknowable, the means can hardly be arranged to best fit the ends, because the entirety is a test, an experiment, or a matter of groping. Today, however, planned innovations within corporations, buttressed by advertising to persuade others of an innovation's worth, have almost hidden the unpredictable "making process" from view, so that instrumental calculation appears as the principal mode of practice.

Max Weber suggested that rational or efficient market behavior could not itself be justified as a rational act, for it is a value commitment. I offer a different paradox: profit-making, as a gain for innovations, is not a purely calculated act; but profit-making, as a monopolistic gain from control of a market, is a very rational one. Could the lack of an accepted theory of profit within neoclassical economics be a sign of the impossibility of developing a rational account for those contingent acts that result in gain?

NOTES

1 Pioneer Village, located in Minden, Nebraska.
2 This ethnography was developed with Alberto Rivera.
3 Walras's auctioneer calls out prices and works through a process that he termed *tâtonnements*, until equilibrium is created between supply and demand in a perfectly competitive market. English-speaking economists seldom translate this French cognate of *tantear*, or feeling one's way. Is equilibrium in the "rational" economy ultimately brought about by a non-rational activity?
4 "Individual initiative has no chance except on the ground afforded by the common stock, and the achievements of such initiative are of no effect except as accretions to the common stock. And the invention of discovery so achieved always embodies so much of what is already given

that the creative contribution of the inventor or discoverer is trivial by comparison" (Veblen 1942 [1908]: 28).

5 This point has been very effectively made by Allen (1983).
6 See Piore and Sabel (1984), Sabel (1982), and Womack et al. (1990).
7 See, for example, Sabel (1991, 1994) and Schön (1983).

Chapter Eight

Realms and Dialectics: Values in Production, Trade, and Use

Bankruptcy is a category mistake, or so ethnography suggests. Anthropology also explains why declaring bankrupcy is considered a disreputable act; why market arbitrage is usually disdained; why domestic budget discussions may become inflamed; and why the marketization of life is both alluring and loathsome. These moralities emerge when goods and services are transferred between economy's two realms.

Economies today are characterized by complex combinations of the impulses to build a base and capital. This economic dialectic links the comparable with the unique, or the tendency to commensurate values with valuing the incommensurate. One side of economy is connected to generalized exchange and the global; the other side is grounded in limited exchange and local practices. Yet the two intertwine, because outward-reaching practices and the commensurate are realized in local contexts and categories.

I have explored the community realm of economy and argued that profit-making depends on value creation and communal relationships. I want now to expand this thesis by considering value change, erasure, and conversion as economy's two realms are joined. Marx tried to show how monetary profit emerges when value is formed by human work or labor. In contrast, I have argued that value and profit are created by innovation and that Marx's theory of exploitation holds only when a new productivity is in place and can be used to gain a monopoly profit. But Marx (and Polanyi) also sensed that something substantive is lost when industrial production and markets grow and human efforts as well as the environment are commoditized. Drawing on ethnographic materials, we explore the contours of this value shift as it emerges in the connection between communities and trade, in the dynamics of turning base to capital and capital to base, in the practices by which communities contain circuits of trade and devise categories of commensurate goods, and in the way economic expansion is linked to innovations in community relationships as well as technology.

From Base to Base: Transforming Objects, Relationships, and Trade

To maintain their base, people trade with members of other communities through barter (Base ↔ Base') or via money (Base ↔ Money ↔ Base'). The community and trade realms are distinct, but objects and persons change value as they shift realms. In a first example, a community depends on trade for its sacra and prized possessions. Secured through exchange of ordinary items, these objects are transformed when they move from the trade realm to community, where in turn their use rearranges positions. Reapportioning the base and changing social standing depends on trade.

The Onabasulu, a group of some 400 people who reside on the Great Papuan Plateau of New Guinea, live in domestic groups that are part of larger longhouses, each based on a patriline.[1] Within a longhouse, the use of goods is shared on request; between these communities goods are traded. Onabasulu divide goods into two categories, *su* and *elebe*. *Su* are used in communal transactions and include mother-of-pearl shell crescents, steel axes, bush knives, and other items. The mother-of-pearl shell crescents – known as *kina* – are the core valuables or sacra. *Elebe* goods are used in trade and include cassowary bone implements, tobacco, black palm bows, arrows, plumes, and spears. But the contents of the two categories change over time. Before 1955 dog's teeth head-bands were sacra, and stone axes were important *su*. Both have been replaced by items secured in trade.

Elebe are traded either with non-Onabasulu or with Onabasulu who are not kin. If two longhouse members have *elebe* they want to exchange, they trade them through an intermediary with whom neither has familial ties. This circuitous trade is undertaken only when an Onabasulu wants to possess an item, because the use of *elebe* is shared in community.

Su and *elebe* also are traded one for another across community boundaries. Onabasulu produce some *elebe*, such as palm bows and tree oil, which they trade for the mother-of-pearl shell crescents and steel axes that become the most valued social objects. Through this conversion of trade items to *su*, the two types of value interact so that the amount of *su* needed in social transactions is influenced by the external rate of exchange at which they were secured.

Su are transferred between community members to mark changes in social position. For example, when a marriage is an exchange of sisters between men, it is accompanied by *su* collected from the groom's family and apportioned to the bride's – a double movement of base. When marriage is not a paired transaction, the groom offers mother-of-pearl shell crescents to the bride's brother who in turn may use the valuables to gain a wife for himself. To restore the social order, mother-of-pearl shell crescents are also paid:

- to the parents of a child by the parents of the child's namesake;
- by a man to his wife's brother when a child is born;
- in compensation for insult, injury, or homicide.

In these transactions base is reallocated in accord with shifting community positions.

Thus, the two types of good and of exchange are separate but formulated in relation to one another, for some trade items – secured by the manufacture of other trade objects – are converted to community goods. Never autarkic, community economy depends on trade.[2]

A complementary example to the Onabasulu is presented by the Hualu, a small group on the island of Seram. Hualu also distinguish sharply between communal and impersonal exchange, but in their case cross-border transactions may transform relationships from non-community to community by changing trade to reciprocity and sharing. As the meaning of payments is transformed, the local community is sustained.[3]

Hualu live in named, property-owning groups formed around patrilineal cores of males. They divide all people into the "other" or "different," and the "not-other." Members of a local group (not-other) share perishable goods and durable items out of compassion or to help. Accounts of this sharing are never kept, and the closer the kin relationship, the lower the expectation that there will be a return. At the inner core, sharing of the commons holds. But Hualu men also trade durable goods outside their communities, and these transactions take the form of barter, or buying and selling.

Marriage transactions shift people from other to not-other. Initially, a man "buys" a wife outside the group by paying antique plates (that were obtained by external trade). The marriage is an impersonal transaction. But this trade is soon negated or "crushed" when the bride's family offers gifts to the groom's. This new offering appears strange, for the bride's family has lost a woman while gaining plates, whereas the groom's side pays antique plates and receives a woman, and then obtains more valuables. But by offering gifts to the groom's family, the wife's side demonstrates that their daughter and sister was not sold for plates. Their presentation transforms the groom's offering of plates to a gift of base which is then reciprocated by the bride's side with gifts. Impersonal trade is transformed to an expansion of bases via reciprocity as a new community is created through marriage.

In these first two cases trade interacts with apportionment and reciprocity, as each may become the other. But they can also be kept separate yet connected when sociality is extended. For example, the Tiv used their traditional, local fetishes to consecrate marketplaces and ensure peaceful trading relations between antagonistic communities. Punishing breaches of the peace and promising calm trading relationships, the fetishes were sacra for a community encompassing trade. In this and other cases, trade is facilitated by innovations in community relationships.

This type of innovation by which communal relations are projected into the realm of trade is well illustrated by "ceremonial exchange." The expression refers to large exchange systems such as the Kula in the Trobriand Islands area or the potlatch of the Northwest coast, as well as smaller exchanges between two families (Stanner 1932–3, 1933–4; Thomson 1949). Through ceremonial exchange a created community surrounds trade that would otherwise be impersonal and difficult to sustain.[4] The community aspect of the exchange is maintained as an end itself, yet for the sake of ensuring trade; carrying out trade is also an end, yet for the sake of making community. A case from Australia shows how goods were shared between groups to build a larger community as valued items were traded between them. Both antagonism and mutuality were expressed in the ceremony as the base was extended to others.

The Gunwinggu of Western Arnhem Land (Northern Australia), who were hunters and collectors, and partly nomadic, practiced several ceremonial exchanges with their neighbors (Berndt 1951). *Dzamalag* was the name of a ceremony common to many. An actual trade might consist of cloth and blankets for spears but it was encased within dancing and singing, the exchange of sexual favors, and the circulation of tobacco between trading groups. A trading community was formed between the groups through the ceremony.

Dzamalag took place as follows. When visitors from a neighboring group arrived at a Gunwinggu camp laden with goods, everyone gathered at the dancing ground. Soon, two visiting men began to sing while a third played a pipe. Their music initiated *dzamalag*. Initially, two Gunwinggu women opposite in moiety (marriage half) to the singing men presented each with a piece of cloth; they hit and touched the men and uttered erotic jokes. (A male of opposite moiety was an appropriate marriage partner.) Shortly, another Gunwinggu woman – opposite in moiety to the pipe player – did the same with him. Then, other Gunwinggu women arose, and selecting a visiting man opposite in moiety, gave him cloth, struck him lightly, and invited him to have sexual relations. The pairs retired and copulated, after which the visiting men gave the Gunwinggu women tobacco and beads. Returning to the dancing ground, the Gunwinggu women gave the tobacco and beads to their Gunwinggu spouses.

Gunwinggu men then arose, and each gave a blanket to a visiting woman of opposite moiety. Striking her lightly and inviting her to copulate, the two retired to the bushes, after which the male offered his partner tobacco and beads, and she shared them with her spouse.

Finally, Gunwinggu women lined up in two rows. The visiting men, brandishing their spears, danced toward them saying, "We will not spear you, for we have already speared you with our penes" (Berndt 1951: 162). They gave the spears to the women, and a large food distribution was held which completed *dzamalag*.

Incorporating sex, food, music, dancing, and material things, *dzamalag* joined community and trade. Tobacco and beads circulated through the two groups – from the visiting men to Gunwinggu women of opposite moiety to them, to the latter's husbands (who were of opposite moiety to them), to the visiting women of opposite moiety to the Gunwinggu men, and back to the visiting men who started the transaction. Everyone was included in the exchange, as the tobacco and beads moved in a circle – to end where they started![5] As the items weaved between moieties, genders, and local groups, they built a larger – though temporary – community through apportionment and reapportionment of a base. The tobacco and beads, as well as the final food distribution, were shared for their own sake.

The cloth, blankets, and spears were handled differently. Gunwinggu women and men gave cloth and blankets to the visiting men and women in return for which the visiting men presented spears to Gunwinggu women (who passed them to their spouses). In this concluding act, the visitors expressed a transition between the groups from war to sex to peace.

Through this ceremonial exchange, communal elements reduced the uncertainties of trade by providing peace and a space for exchange, but through the material exchange a new community was forged between groups. Communities rupture their borders through trade that leads to new bonds.

Other ways of extending the base support trade. The Maring, located in the central New Guinea highlands, trade outside their local communities; but they do not practice anonymous exchange, for they trade only with kin, such as brothers (Healey 1978, 1984). The kin ties are constructed, however, after trading begins. Maring explain that kin are related because they share substance from their parents and from products of the land made fertile by the ancestors.[6] Traders eat together as they transact, and so become brothers. Kinship through trade is created by extending the base of food, land, and, ultimately, ancestors, and this mutuality – modeled after at-hand experience – stabilizes a dangerous, uncertain, and impersonal transaction.[7]

From Base to Capital: Appropriation, Production, Trade

Base can be transformed to capital through modes of appropriation, through trade and through production forms that combine economy's two realms. For example, in some cases base is appropriated as tribute or leaves via trade (Base → ∆Base → Market); in more complex instances it is combined with capital to yield a product for sale in markets (Base + Capital → Commodity → Capital). This last process, joining the unpriced and the priced or community resources, labor, and relationships with capital, can can lead to *debasement*.

Collection of tribute represents the exercise of coercion in the economy, backed by state or military force. Tribute and slavery systems can be exercised on both community and market institutions, and can be in the service of community leaders (czars) or market agents (plantation owners). But such appropriation often turns base to capital. For example, after the Spanish conquest of the New World, the granting of *encomiendas* and lands to soldiers quickly destroyed native groups. The *encomienda* (or entrustment) was a grant from the Crown to a Spaniard of (limited) rights to use native labor for agricultural, pastoral, or mining enterprises; in "return," the *encomendero* was expected to offer religious training in Christianity, and limited protection. The powers were much abused. Separately, land grants to Crown supporters were illegally extended in the far-flung conditions of the New World, and the two appropriations soon pushed native groups to marginal land areas. Then, by the laws of the *repartimiento*, tribute from native groups could be demanded as well, and this triple process of sequestering land, appropriating tribute labor (under conditions approximating slavery), and extracting tribute in kind, all backed by military power, had devastating effects on the indigenous economies and their bases.[8] As market actors gained command of the more fertile areas, community economies were left with the least productive, setting forth a skewed pattern of land control that persists in many areas of Latin America today.[9]

The results of this appropriation process were far-reaching, because when a community economy loses control of its base, members must enter the market, offering their goods or labor for cash. By the eighteenth century in Latin America, *hacendados*, or owners of large land tracts, frequently owned more land than they could use in order to limit competition and force local inhabitants to work on haciendas or become low-paid laborers at mines or plantations.[10] Today, on the frontiers of Guatemala, Colombia, and Brazil, dispossessed workers often become squatters who cut the native forest, farm for a year, and then are replaced by more powerful agricultural or pastoral interests, forcing them to retreat farther and cut more forest.

In the general case, however, appropriation is not so direct: base and capital are joined through political, social, or economic pressures, so that uncounted parts of the base are used in production, and what would be the full monetary cost of a product need not be recompensed in the market. This combination of base and capital occurs in agriculture, pastoralism, and manfacturing, and is found in a diversity of institutions where it sometimes persists but usually leads to debasement.[11] For example, Polish estates from the sixteenth through the eighteenth century relied on the dialectical connection of base and capital (Kula 1976 [1962]). These agricultural entities produced crops for the market, but to reduce costs they generated many of the required inputs – such as tools and subsistence food – on the estate itself. This use of uncosted base allowed noblemen to reap money gains, while working peasants lost an unmeasured volume of effort and estate land deteriorated:

> In a dual sector economy (monetary and natural) it is the natural sector which generally is of prime importance to the peasant, whereas for the nobleman it is the monetary one. The nobleman eagerly takes up anything that serves to increase his revenues in money. Whether or not such an increase is obtained at the expense of the sum total of properties is a question to which one cannot give an unequivocal answer within this socio-economic system. This accounts for the contradiction between the desire to increase money revenues and the frequent accusations of *dezolacja*. (Kula 1976 [1962]: 37)

The Polish word *dezolacja* means devastation, which is close to my term "debasement." The Polish devastation process remained hidden from view, because it occurred within estates, and because the "natural" economy had no value scale for measuring its "diminution in productive potential" (Kula 1976 [1962]: 36). A like process occurred in other European manorial forms (Petrusewicz 1996) and Latin American haciendas.

In the Colombian uplands today, rural householders combine the two economic realms. They distinguish between "counting" by different measures and "accounting" by money. When referring to cash crops, the people talk about "making money" and give a verbal *account* of money costs and returns. When referring to home crops (such as maize, beans, and potatoes), they say "we don't account that," even when part of the crop is sold. Rural folk do *count* the harvests and material expenditures of their domestic crops, but they are speaking about the incommmensurability of maize, eggs, and hogs, each of which has a distinct use and is kept "apart." In rural Panama, I observed much the same. A neighbor there once gave me exquisite details for his domestic crops. He recounted the labor, land size, seed volume, and harvest quantities for each of his household crops – principally rice, maize, and beans. The land was measured by hectares, the seed and harvest by container size, and labor by tasks and time. The measures used to count the seed and harvest volumes as well as the labor were not comparable across the crops, and land size was deduced from the amount of seed or labor that had been used. Each crop input and output was counted by a different measuring rod, and no common scale was used to unite a production process. But my neighbor also grew sugar cane for sale, and he gave me an accounting of this crop in money so that all the expenditures and returns were brought together. This distinction between *counting* in one sphere and *accounting* in the other, between "expending" materials (*gastos*) and "spending" money (*costos*), reflects the difference between the community and market realms of economy.

But the two realms are connected by cross-flows of labor or goods. For example, a house may raise two crops, one for domestic consumption and one for sale. In theory, the market crop requires the expenditure of money and yields a cash revenue, with the difference constituting profit. But if market crops are grown by purchasing all the needed materials and labor, financial losses result due to the extra-marginal or non-competitive land the house must use and the competitive sales price – established by capitalized producers – it must meet. In place of purchasing productive materials, a house draws on its self-supported labor and domestic products. For example, men who are fed by home foods and clothed by the sale of domestic crops may work in their cash crop for no pay; the household may sell some of a domestic crop to purchase pesticides for the cash crop; or outside laborers may be fed from a domestic harvest to lower the cash wage paid to them. In these cases, the house expends base to sell a market crop and receive money. The pattern has many variations. During the 1980s, the older generation in Hungary would sell "excess" pigs, onions, or lettuce for cash, so using their base to secure a market return. (In contrast, the younger generation calculated costs and sales prices, and raised musk or planted tobacco, depending on the return – see Lampland 1991.) Similarly, men in a community economy may devote some of their time to earning cash. Because their subsistence is supplied at home, the market wage may be low, boosting profits for employers and low- ering product prices. As more such local efforts are devoted to the market sphere, the intensity of female work may rise in compensation.

When the two value realms of economy are thus joined, products reach the market from conditions that would be unprofitable if cash values were applied to land and labor. A house can use extra-marginal land to sustain itself and produce for the market because its expendi- tures are not accounted in the trading calculation: the home crop, raised with few monetary costs, is sold at a competitive price, because it re- ceives a subsidy from the base. Thus, dispossessed agriculturalists some- times "open" frontier land that lies beyond the margin of profitable use. Their domestic economies buffer the market at its frontier and hide the market's effects on land and labor, making it appear as if the drawing down of resources is a consequence of other than market practices.

In the Latin American countryside, the debasement process is modeled in terms of exchange. Many rural folk claim that financial profits are made only by market traders. In their view, the same prac- tice of thrift that yields leftovers in a household secures money gains in the market. Rural folk argue that market traders gather house re- mainders through unfavorable terms of exchange. The people say that when they go to the market, they have to sell a household product to buy something else; but buyers who have large reserves of goods and money do not have to purchase from them. This inequality in control of money and the power to withhold allows a trader to buy a good at one price and then sell a smaller amount of it at the same price. The merchant keeps the material remainder for subsequent sale, which pro- vides the profit. In support of their argument, rural folk observe that if they sell a volume of goods, with the money received they can buy back a smaller quantity only; the leftover stays in the hands of the trader and awaits sale.

This folk model of merchant's profit is a projection of their house experience. The house practices thrift – cutting expenditures and costs – to have a physical remainder; the trader economizes – cutting costs – to make a monetary gain. The two practices are alike and they are connected, for the merchant, by using his financial power, captures and withholds exactly what was a physical remainder in the house- hold. A double process of modeling is involved. First, the model of house practices is projected onto merchant behavior; then the two are connected by the argument that the tangible remainder in one is appropriated by and becomes the monetary leftover in the other. In its construction of market processes, the household applies its model of internal operations to make sense of the larger market experience and interactions.

For the people, the implication of this local model of profit is precisely that market exchange results in debasement for the house and gain for the trader. Business profit is the money form of tangible household remainders that were secured by working in the fields (gathering nature's force) and economizing at home; business gains (or the conversion of substantive to monetary wealth) are taken at the expense of a household's base. And this transformation happens each time householders, who lack withholding power, transact with traders who command wealth. The household construction provides a scathing critique of market traders, and underlies the folk accusation that market prices are "unjust" or "unfair" in relation to rural dwellers. In this reproach, the folk voices add to a long, community conversation about the immorality of external trade that starts with Aristotle.

In fact, the "accounting" bifurcation has long been recognized in Western householding manuals. It can be found as early as Roman times (Cato 1933) and is implicit in the important medieval texts, such as Walter of Henley (Oschinsky 1971).[12] But the process is general and encountered outside agriculture, for it involves the provision of a no-cost subsidy from community to market. It may characterize the production process of home-based artisans, such as tailors, weavers, leather-makers, or potters: the artisan sells his product on the market, while being provisioned by his family. The production form holds for small market sellers, too, when the members of a domestic group provide no-cost labor in a market stall; and it characterizes much of the informal sector and what has been called "petty commodity production," in which goods reach the market from conditions in which not all the factors of production are purchased.

Today's economist might count resources of the base as "externalities." Externalities are the unpriced effects that one market actor has on another. Usually, they are considered to be negative: one manufacturer pollutes the stream that another uses for commercial fishing. By pricing this externality – the expense of cleaning up the water or of losing the fish – a cost can be attributed to one or the other actor and then internalized; the polluter or affected cleans the water or covers the fish loss, and through a rise in the manufacturer's or fisherman's prices the market reflects the damage. The externality is brought within the realm of prices and the market.

For economists, the use of base in market contexts is similar, except that the community realm offers positive externalities: unpriced land is used, below market labor is employed, or low-cost goods reach the market through community subsidies so lowering prices. One could argue that this subsidy should be repaid at its market value. But applied in this way, the externality model converts base to capital value, for it assumes that all actors are market participants. I argue that to consider community values – a sacra, basket of corn, and sack of potatoes – as comparable and reducible to market prices is a category mistake and an example of projecting one realm on the other to "interpret," reconstruct, and subsume it. Demsetz (1967), for example, claims that the Naskapi of Northern Canada switched from holding communal land to private plots in order to have bounded hunting grounds, accumulate furs, and earn cash. On his account, they internalized an externality (the "free" land) which led to an efficient allocation of resources, thus explaining a transformation in property rights that was actually powered by external conquest and colonialism on the grounds of choice and the desire to maximize. But before the arrival of British and French traders, Cree hunted to survive, to communicate with the other world, and to maintain several levels of community. Demsetz reduces actions carried out for their own sake to instrumental behaviors, and presumes that values are commensurate across all spheres.

I do not hold that shifts across value realms always represent benefits to one side and losses to the other, because these transformations cannot be measured against one scale. Consider the Blue Nile Scheme, by which participants in a Sudanese village raise cotton as a cash crop and sorghum for subsistence (Bernal 1994). Villagers hold usufruct to state land if they raise cotton; the state purchases the cotton for export. Each tenant devotes one-third of the allotted land to cotton and one-third to fallow; the remainder can be used for subsistence crops. The government advances cash for raising the cotton, to be repaid at the harvest, but tenants use the money to cultivate sorghum which they eat, and they build up debts for the cotton. In effect, the state, through the project, provides a space for building a base.

The story has further complexities. Young men leave the village for years to earn cash in urban areas and in Saudi Arabia, but the employment is insecure and the pay is low, so the men cannot afford to bring their families with them. The Blue Nile market project, by its support of a subsistence crop, subsidizes the low wages of the men in the national and international labor markets, yet some of these wages are sent home.

In this project the two realms of economy are joined. Sorghum is raised on "market" land, and planters must also grow cotton; but the cash advances they receive for the cotton pay for the subsistence crop that supports the emigrant labor force and subsidizes part of the global market. The Sudanese government – making use of international loans – acts as a communal force supporting both a village economy and a larger market (the political advantage of keeping people in rural areas may be a motivating factor). Should this set of flows that starts with loans from industrialized nations be called development? Can its multiple transformations between market and community values be measured? Who gains – local communities or corporations in Saudi Arabia that employ low-cost labor and accumulate capital?[13]

From Capital to Base: Resilience and Resistance

Even in market-dominated economies, communities may use trade to sustain themselves, by limiting consumer demand or transforming goods as they enter community. The Jukumani – whose system of land allotment we previously considered – mine tin for cash when subsistence needs have been met, but they use the return only to purchase goods for home use, avoid making a capital commitment in mining, and often stop work before fully exploiting a deposit, leaving it for others (Godoy 1990).[14]

Recent events in two highland towns to the west of Guatemala City show how markets can be used to maintain a local heritage by transforming the market practices so that capital sustains the base.[15] The two communities contain *cofradías* or religious brotherhoods, each of which possesses a saint's idol in whose honor it mounts a procession. The festivities, featuring bands, dancers, and a float, are expensive to produce. They draw tourists, which benefits local businesses, but their costs have risen and the *cofradías* have been facing financial collapse.

In one community, municipal authorities – at the urging of local businesses – offered financial support, but they asked the *cofradías* to perform on non-religious days for tourists, who would be charged for the entertainment. In response, the *cofradías* said they would collect for religious processions something less than their expenses, because the performances were a "commitment," but they would charge a higher rate for the tourist performances. They separated market payment from community service. Distinguishing performance by context, the *cofradías* used local businesses to perpetuate their base.

In the second town, hotels, restaurants, and shops agreed to pay for the *cofradía* processions, but the brotherhoods responded that they were not charging for their religious services and suggested that businesses offer donations or alms (*limosna*), "in accord with their hearts." Imposing a community lexicon on the interaction, the *cofradías* drew the commercial establishments into their realm, while securing market wealth.

In each case, *cofradías* refused to sell their base. In one, they separated community from market; in the other, they compelled market actors to change the meaning of their recompense as it crossed realms.

A different but remarkable example of converting capital to base comes from Malaysia. Drawing on fieldwork in the 1930s, Raymond Firth (1966) showed how cash returns from the sale of fish were divided among the members of a boat and the owners of fishing equipment. The returns were converted to small coins, and, at the end of each week, the boat leader piled up the coins and sorted them into different sized piles with divisions and subdivisions for the different participants from boat owners, to fishing guides, to crew. Each participant received a ratio return or several fractions, just as visitors to a monastery once received rations. The separate rewards to the boat owners and workers were not based on marginal inputs, size of capital invested, amount of labor performed, or work productivity. The market allocation was converted to a community apportionment. Some years after, Janet Carsten (1989, 1995a, 1995b, 1995c) reaffirmed Firth's findings and showed that the money the men received was transferred to women, who placed it in the household where it became a commons. When household need arose, any member could use the collected cash for group purposes. Thus, starting in the market sphere, where the size of a fishing team's return was determined by luck and market conditions, the money was transferred to the communal sphere by apportioning it to males, shifting control from males to females, pooling a household's returns, and spending the result on household needs. By this complex transformation, fishing communities converted money's value from capital to base as they set boundaries on the market realm.[16]

Trade Within the Base: Circuits and Budgets

Communities contain value spheres – that is, categories of substitutible or commensurate items. Sometimes a category contains only one good that has a determined distribution, such as manioc soup among the Nambicura. But often a value sphere includes several, commensurate items. When these goods are traded one for another, the spheres are "circuits of exchange." Exchange circuits reveal the dynamic between limited and generalized exchange. For example, in Panama men traded work in the same crop and occasionally across similar efforts; but labor was never traded across all work. In contrast, general exchange mixes categories by transforming one thing to another through money, and by this alchemy it can dissolve an existing cultural world. The Tiv, whom we have considered for their allotment practices, present the paradigm case of spheres or limited exchange as linked to generalized exchange; markets, morality, arbitrage, and value circuits are involved.[17]

Tiv traditionally separated market from community: they traded with other subsistence producers both to sustain the base and to gain money; and they exchanged with itinerant traders, and capitalized agents who arrived via the colonial powers. In addition, Tiv traded inside their community through circuits of exchange, and senior males practiced a kind of arbitrage between these internal circuits that was both morally approved and disdained.

When engaging in external exchange, Tiv distinguished between trading to replace the base and trading to make a gain. When Tiv said they knew what they needed to maintain the house and would look around to find something to sell, they were replacing the base; women engaged in such trade (B → M → B′). In contrast, Tiv sometimes went to a market with money in order to buy, sell, and return with a profit; Tiv men traded for gain (M → B → M′). Tiv also said that Ibo men would enter markets for this purpose only: leaving a compound carrying an empty tray, they bought in one market and transported goods for sale in another. In contrast, Tiv men who traded for profit practiced agriculture, because a Tiv who did not farm cut himself off from his ancestors and ceased being Tiv. Tiv deprecated living by trading alone and were contemptuous of wealth in money. But Tiv observed that their agricultural base was being lost in markets to wealthy external traders who accumulated profits.[18]

Tiv males also tried to augment their holdings in community, for a compound head gained influence and power by increasing the size of his family and number of dependents. A larger family provided more farm workers and produce, and the foods in turn supported more dependents, which yielded higher standing in community. (Each wife in a polygynous family also tried to "accumulate" (*kem*) or enlarge her yam field, but this goal was difficult to achieve given her work obligations and relative inability to control labor.[19])

Accumulation within community was connected to crossing between the three spheres of exchange. Transactions within each sphere were market-like or forms of trade, but exchanges between them were morally freighted, and involved shifts in social standing. The lowest exchange circuit was made up of foods, craft products, tools, and raw materials that were also exchanged in markets. Tiv traded these items among themselves at bargained rates. Prestige items made up the second sphere, and included slaves, cattle, horses, ritual offices, large white textiles known as *tugudu* cloths, medicines, magic, and brass rods. Brass rods and *tugudu* cloths provided the standards of measure for all the items, although actual payment was usually made in cash or other goods. The rates of exchange varied, depending on kinship position of the transactors and their command of wealth; there also might be adjustments when payment was made in items from the market sphere, because subsistence goods could be traded for prestige items. The third circuit consisted of transactions in rights over women and children. At marriage, a groom incurred a debt to his wife's family that could be met in several ways. He could return a sister or see that his eldest daughter married into the mother's group. Alternatively, a group of males might form a ward-sharing group, with each man becoming the guardian of one or more females. Ward-sharing groups exchanged females at marriage. The preferred way to contract a union, however, was by *kem* or "accumulating" marriage, according to which a man, by paying brass rods from the second sphere, gained economic, domestic, and sexual rights to a woman in the third. (Tiv distinguished marital rights between man and woman from rights to a woman's children. The payment in brass rods established only the first type of right. A man's lineal relation to the children who issued from his *kem* wife had to be established by further payments of brass rods.) *Kem* marriage required a "strong heart," because, as he accumulated wealth, a male had to ward off the envy of others and meet legitimate requests from close kin.

Tiv men tried to move up the circuits by converting subsistence to prestige values and then acquiring a woman via *kem* marriage. Such arbitrage once was "fairly common" and seen as a measure of a man's worth (Bohannan and Bohannan 1968: 235). In converting subsistence to prestige to more valued forms of wealth, a male both expressed and denied community. He demonstrated command over his compound group and its accumulated wealth as communal obligations outside it were denied. By displaying social freedom and autarky of his immediate community, a man's *kem* marriage realized the Tiv aspiration that compounds be self-sufficient.

Tiv thus participated in a complex system of value conversions. Markets, that surrounded communities, were used both to maintain the base and to make gains (and these markets relied on a communal element through their use of fetishes ensuring peace). Within Tiv economy, exchange was divided into commensurate circuits but exchanges across these domains allowed compound groups to deny larger communal obligations, assert their self-sufficiency and identity, and assure their own reproduction as a community. In these transactions, new social ties (marriage) were created as others were lost (siblings, offspring, wards). Relationships became instrumentalities for securing wealth, and goods were converted to relationships kept for their own sake. Mutuality was marketed, accumulated wealth was converted to sacra – women.[20]

Tiv economy, and like systems, appear strange when viewed through the spectacles of standard market theory. But we can also see Tiv circuits as a cultural budget that specifies how wealth is to be spent and invested. In fact, budgets are community distributions in which categories are made up of substitutible items and sometimes exchange circuits. In the community realm, people trade in circuits or within budget categories, and sometimes across them. For example, the Lawondanese who live on the island of Sumba in Eastern Indonesia have ranked circuits of exchange, and they have long been exposed to cash economies (Vel 1994). The Lawondanese transform money earned to community use, but they also stream and ration it according to their circuits of exchange. The Lawondanese initially used money, the old Dutch-Indian ringgit, to replace the golden ornament or treasured sacra of lineages, and these colonial coins are still worn on special occasions. Today, the use of currency is more widespread. The Lawondanese divide goods into three ranked circuits of exchange (with subdivisions within them), and money is similarly apportioned or budgeted, and morally ranked. The highest use of money is for university education, medical treatment, transport vehicles, and luxurious consumer goods. All fall within the same category or circuit, and should be funded by cash earnings or revenues from lower-ranked activities. The second category and circuit consists of payments for secondary schools, houses, some medical treatments, and small feasts. The third and lowest circuit consists of contributions, taxes, and some foods and house utensils. Finally, money is never spent on maize, tubers, roots and staples that can be raised at home. The more money a person has, the more she or he can participate in the higher circuits, but close relatives will also make claims on it for expenditures in those spheres as well. For the Lawondanese, the ranked circuits of exchange are a budget scheme.

We use budgetary schemes in government, homes, corporations, and other institutions, such as universities. On the consumption side, a budget rations funds, but the scheme is a product of political debate over different values: what budget categories are to be used, what shall be their relative size, and who benefits by an expenditure? A university community, for example, is continually rent by struggles over the size of expenditures for administrative salaries, faculty salaries, fringe benefits, new buildings, technology upgrades, and graduate students. Household budgets often contain categories such as food, clothing, mortgage payments, utilities, transportation, school, entertainment and savings. But their management may give rise to stress and disagreements between partners. Bankruptcy results from two issues concerning the transformation of money to spheres of value. First, some households seem unable to set up the categories of a budget or to convert general exchange to limited categories of exchangeable items. What falls into entertainment, and how important should it be? Other households are unable to keep the incommensurate circuits separate (savings are diverted to entertainment). As wages and wealth rise, so apparently do the declared number of bankruptcies. This correlation may be due to the expansion of the legal profession or to consumer desires that grow faster than the means of satisfying them, but it may also owe itself to the fact that as participation in the market increases and encompasses greater parts of our lives, so the faculties of making a community economy – budgeting, rationing, economizing, and making-do – receive less emphasis, and the skills dwindle. In fact, we now buy these skills by hiring financial planners, reading books, and taking courses on the internet.

The Base in Trade

I have distinguished growth and development as different ways of achieving economic expansion. Growth refers to extending existing production methods. Hayami (1998) broadly terms this form of expansion the Marx model. By contrast, development designates expansion powered by changes in the production function and rises in efficiency. (Hayami calls this pattern the Kuznets model.) I have argued that the second mode of expansion is dependent on innovation which relies on a base. I now want to extend this argument to innovations in the form of community to suggest that these innovations also are important in economic expansion.

Community relationships provide security and certainty in new market contexts, through the extension of existent ties and the modeling of new ones. The example of ceremonial exchange and cases from New Guinea display some of the imaginative, local, and cultural ways that communities fashion new connections between themselves as they trade. Much the same happens when community members engage in market exchanges and trading for gain. For example, in many parts of Latin America small-scale market exchanges are given stability and longevity by being sealed to *compadrazgo* (shared godparenthood) bonds that are formed before or after the market relationship. In early modern Europe, trading networks of merchants spread across large geographic areas. Based on ethnicity, language, religion, or kinship, these communities of traders or diasporas underwrote trust in long-range relationships, especially when information was sparse and imperfect (Curtin 1984: 46). Lacking laws of contract and a shared political order, the community commitment protected traders from chicanery among themselves and by others.[21]

Dispersed communities can be very flexible and innovative in the way they fit themselves to the market. In the nineteenth century the Zuwaya of southern Libya controlled a string of desert oases and formed a network of traders. Today, Zuwaya own trucks and transport goods; in fact, they have a near monopoly on the transport business. A Zuwaya man gains access to this trade and a truck by working for a kinsman, perhaps on a share arrangement. Eventually, he purchases a truck with the help of others; and he has significant trade advantages because he can borrow money and parts, and receive help and information from other Zuwaya in route. The Zuwaya community, keeping a tight grip on its trade sector, reduces the uncertainty and costs of operating in an anonymous market. Zuwaya, as they say of themselves, do not speculate, which is an accurate assessment, for they combat uncertainty (not risk) through the maintenance of community (Davis 1992).

The ethnography from Australia, New Guinea, Africa, and elsewhere displays the integral connection of trade and community, and suggests its generality. But these general practices also resemble ones in the center of industrial markets, such as the Japanese keiretsu (corporate group with a lead bank) and the Korean chaebol (large conglomerate) which played important roles in the market expansion of those economies and were modeled after existent communal forms (Platteau and Hayami 1998). Use of community ties in a market, however, can sustain monopolistic practices. In the United States, a very high executive in the country's leading retail firm once called the company's tire supplier (in Akron, Ohio) to ask if the retailer's tire prices could be lowered in this oligopolistic market. The answer reflected a community presence in this market: "Wait until Saturday when I play golf with my friends," was the reply. This same merchant was denied the firm's presidency, because – the board of directors agreed – he could not be a member of the city's social clubs due to his religion, a fact that might harm the firm's connections.

Social connections are used not only to create scarcity, as in market monopolies, they may be used to mitigate scarcity in centrally planned economies. In the former East Germany, personal relationships – expressed through acts of barter, reciprocity, and gift-giving – helped assure access to goods and resources (Berdahl 1999). Similar patterns were encountered in other socialist economies (Ledeneva 1998). But much depends on the viewer and perspective: we decry mutuality in the context of crony capitalism, as in Indonesia and Russia, but esteem the effects of infrastructural trust when looking at Italy's market development (Putnam 1993).

Should we support community development as a precursor to economic growth? Should we foster community development for the purpose of market success? For example, the Grameen (village) Bank in Bangladesh uses community modeling to achieve its putative successes.[22] (A similar project has been operated by *Fundación Social* in Colombia.) The Grameen bank contravenes standard economic theory and banking practices by loaning small sums of money to impoverished individuals, especially women, who lack financial collateral but have a viable business project, such as selling milk or raising poultry. To receive loans, the women must first form a small group (about five) and receive training in business and cooperation; they also agree to practice certain community values, such as limiting family size and starting vegetable gardens. When the community skills have been mastered, loans are given. Each member then becomes responsible for the payments and actions of the others, so if one defaults, the rest – at risk of losing their credit – are obliged to assist in repayment. As the group evolves, it becomes a community presence in the market: one member may share market information or refer a customer to another. According to some reports nearly 60 percent of the participants have been able to work themselves out of extreme poverty. The new communities are instituted through a market initiative which then relies on mutuality for its success, and the community base of people, values, and heritage provides a new influence in the market.

The Grameen strategy, which has been used in the United States, initially was shunned by development agencies and governments, including the World Bank. Our economic discourses, built on the image of isolated but resource-endowed, market actors, played a role in limiting the World Bank's capacity to comprehend the Grameen project. But can communities be built in this fashion? The Grameen method seems almost like the old turn-key mode of development by which an outside firm would build a new manufacturing facility in a "less developed country" and then turn it over to local owners and managers; it has analogues as well with the structural adjustment programs that have been imposed by the World Bank and IMF on many countries. None of these strategies, whether focused on fiscal and monetary policies, production methods and products, or the building of communities and trust, begins with innovation. Can communities be imposed or must they develop through use of past images and extensions?

There is a larger issue. If social relationships are created simply to increase wealth, people become a means, which was Collingwood's observation about the effects of economic practices and Polanyi's concern that the substance of society would be commoditized in capitalism. Mutuality valued for itself becomes valued for the sake of something else. Veblen provided a gloomier picture. He divided the market sector into finance and industry: the former revolved about property holding and money, the latter was concerned with good workmanship and production. In Veblen's view, the "captains of finance" held and traded property to make money. However, they drew on the work of the "captains of industry," who took care of production. As capitalism developed, driven by competitive emulation, the captains of finance themselves were credited with the honorable qualities of industry and workmanship. For Veblen, this final projection – by which an activity carried out for the sake of something else (accumulation) was attributed with the value of being done for its own sake (workmanship) – was a derangement, peculiar to market economy.

Material exchanges have a necessary component – that is community. When we reduce this mutuality to an instrumental calculation – as something done for the sake of establishing trade – the residual itself becomes a contract, and another social agreement to encompass this contract must be formed. But if we admit the presence, importance, and necessity of the commitment – for its own sake yet used for the sake of the market – the market exchange is not autonomous. The value of mutuality cannot be given a price, for even when viewed as an instrumentality, we cannot know to what extent or how it may be used in the future. The Zuwaya in the late nineteenth century could not have predicted that their ethnicity would benefit their progeny who operate trucks in the late twentieth century. Such is the nature of community: it often provides a free gift to the market realm. It is an innovation and has a place in development, but can it be planned?

NOTES

1   For this section, I have drawn on the study by Ernst (1978).
2   A very similar picture, in which salt may have both base and trade uses, was reported by Godelier (1977b) for the Baruya of New Guinea. The basic resource, salt land, is socially allotted and shared; salt itself is in-

dividually produced, used, apportioned, and exchanged for other ceremonial objects among Baruya themselves. Externally, however, salt is traded in accord with changing and competitive rates of exchange, but old salt bars are kept as reminders of these past relationships.

3   This material is based on Valeri's study (1994).

4   The term "ceremony" understood as ritual can be misleading; it refers to the social aspect of the exchange or communal commitment.

5   Terming the intermarrying moieties A and B, using capitals for females and lowercase for males, and employing 1 for the visitors and 2 for Gunwinggu, one circuit of tobacco and beads runs from a1 to B2 to a2 to B1 to a1, and the other cycles from b1 to A2 to b2 to A1 to b1.

6   See, for example, Strathern (1973). I found something rather similar in rural Panama (Gudeman 1976).

7   See also Mintz's (1961) description of *pratik*, an enduring bond formed between buyer and seller in Haitian markets.

8   For an overall view of the brutality and reasons for the high mortality in the Americas after the conquest, see Stannard (1992).

9   The studies of land distribution in Colombia provide one example; see Fals Borda (1979), Gaitán (1984), LeGrand (1986), and Villamarín (1975).

10   The Dutch Culture System in Indonesia had much the same effect (Geertz 1963). See Wilk (1991) for nineteenth-century illustrations from Belize.

11   There are many ways of modeling this appropriation or transfer of resources. See, for example, Bartra (1982), Gudeman (1978), Gudeman and Rivera (1990), and Meillassoux (1981 [1975]).

12   Kula (1976 [1962]: 39) also remarks: "In this respect it is interesting to analyse the bookkeeping system used on the nobility's demesnes. . . . Gostomski (1588) gives advice [that] . . . they ought to have a separate account for each item in money or in kind that enters into the production and consumption of the estate . . . in all, one hundred and fifty-six distinct accounting items without, we might add, any common denominator! . . . 'The clerk must carefully see to it that nothing decreases; nay, he must see to it that *everything* increases.' But how can one assess the operation of the estate if the amount of wheat in the barn increases while the stock of apples decreases?"

13   A recent and detailed study in Peru of raising potatoes for house and market displays the impossibility of measuring these dialectical shifts of value (Mayer and Glave 1990, 1992, 1999).

14   Today, on the island of Ponam in Papua New Guinea, remittances from workers living abroad are used to sustain local ceremonies and ties of kinship, not to buy private goods; the market injection has led to a flowering of communal rituals (Carrier and Carrier 1989). In the fourteenth century, the monks of Peterborough Abbey raised grain for consumption and kept herds to pull ploughs as well as to provide milk and meat. But the abbey also bought and sold cattle – to rid itself of mature animals, secure young ones, and help reproduce itself (Biddick 1989).

15   This material is drawn from Gudeman and Rivera (2001).

16   Zelizer (1994) has explored changing gender control of cash in American households during the past century and a half. In the early nineteenth century, wives received a "dole" from their husbands. Toward the end of the 1800s, the dole became an "allowance" which was a set entitlement. Later, families began to keep "joint control" of funds, by establishing a single bank account, although husbands often held sums aside for their own use. Finally, when women began to earn large sums of money, many kept these returns to spend as they wished. These shifts in household disbursement of cash reflect changing gender roles and consumption patterns. But the forms – dole, allowance, joint control, separation of a stream – are modes of communal apportionment exercised on market returns.

17   For other examples of exchange spheres, see Armstrong (1924, 1928), Firth (1965 [1939]), and Malinowski (1961 [1922]). Kopytoff (1986) presents a recent reanalysis. Generally, exchange spheres designate cases in which goods are exchanged one for another within a circuit but do not circulate outside it. Exchanges within a sphere usually take the form of barter, but a single currency may serve as the measuring rod for the exchange rates. Exchanges between circuits also occur, but these are less frequent and are morally weighted, for the spheres are socially ranked. To trade "upward" represents a gain in prestige, exchanging "downward" loses status.

A Western interpretation of spheres was provided by Armstrong (1924, 1928) who tried to show how disparate transaction circuits on Rossel Island were tied together through shell "money." Different sized shells had to be paid for goods in different spheres; their linking measure was time elapsed and interest. The ethnography did not support his model (Barić 1964), however, because the amounts borrowed and repaid had to do with status claims and social maneuvering, not interest rates.

18   When the activities of trading and marketing intersected, Tiv could end up selling their base. In marketing, money is the measure and means of exchange; in trading, money serves as means, measure, and end of exchange. Tiv observed that trucks arrived at their markets empty and left with foodstuffs, complaining that their livelihood seemed to disappear in trade. The Bohannans noted that "When Tiv men engage in subsistence marketing, they seldom make computations; but when engaged in trade, they almost universally count their profits and losses." (Bohannan and Bohannan 1968: 209–10)

19   Men seed yams; women weed and harvest.

20   In his discussion of entrepreneurs and exchange spheres in Darfur, Barth (1967) provides a related picture. Local entrepreneurs, interested in securing a money profit, could mobilize costless labor for their projects. They offered (in the traditional fashion) beer, made from the subsistence millet crop, to those who labored in their fields; but the entrepreneurs purchased the inexpensive millet, and they used the low-cost labor to plant their profitable cash crops rather than more millet. One sphere thus grew by debasing the other, and profit was made by strategic exchanges or arbitrage between different economic spheres.

21   For an example of family firms and their use in the geographic spread of business ties, see Benedict (1968). In the eleventh, twelfth, and thirteenth centuries, Maghribi traders who spread into North Africa from Europe made use of their community. They relied on one another, at great distance, to oversee shipments of goods, provide information, and handle funds. By drawing on a religious and communal patrimony, they could provide a collective front to others who might embezzle them (Grief 1993, 1994).

22   For one version of the Grameen story, see Counts (1996). Rotating credit associations are found in many parts of the world. Associates contribute regularly to a fund, which by turns goes to a member to purchase a bicycle, pay for a funeral, or meet another need. According to the theory of rational choice, it would pay an associate to drop out after receiving the fund and renege on making future contributions from which only others will benefit. But members usually keep their promises, because successful associations are built on kinship, residential, godparenthood, or other enduring bonds that would be lost if the monetary obligation were denied. See Ardener (1964), Dewey (1964), Geertz (1962), and Vélez-Ibañez (1983).

Chapter Nine

Political Economy Today

Spreading rapidly and on a global scale, markets are subsuming greater portions of everyday life. Increasingly, we commoditize things, leisure, body parts, reproductive capacities, DNA, and social relationships. As people flock to cities, sell their hardwood trees, change clothing styles, and watch television, community economy shrinks. Even the role of the modern nation may be diminishing in the face of economic globalization: states are coordinating regulatory policies and environmental controls, adopting common currencies, and standardizing welfare benefits to "stabilize" international labor markets. As a result of capital's spread, new global currents include rapidly changing technologies, increased communications, heightened flows of information, the blurring of state boundaries, and the increased effects of others' actions on ourselves from the devastation of Chernobyl to Asian economic crises. Yet globalization refers not simply to the growing reach of capital but to the double fragmentation of communities and corporations. As both forms of organization splinter and become interwoven, their once sharp and lasting outlines now seem ephemeral.

Has the era of community economy passed, and is the knowledge gained from ethnography an anachronism? How are we to conceptualize the recent changes? Since Adam Smith, we have modeled economies as made up of discrete, bounded units. Durkheim's two forms of solidarity – organic and mechanical – exemplify this modern view. With Adam Smith, he pictured industrial society as held together through a division of labor: the model of organic solidarity applies to the production line, which is made up of complementary tasks, and to the relation between corporations who trade for what they lack in markets. The separate tasks in the production line and the independent trading units in the market reach completion through exchange. Durkheim's second organizational form, mechanical solidarity, refers to self-sufficient units, such as lineages, households, or local clusters, which are economic atoms. The two models are ideal types, because self-sufficient units do trade, and corporations are infused with social connections.

These models do not capture today's fluidity. The borders of market participants are porous, shift, and disappear; units overlap and fragment; and different organizational modes conjoin and oppose one another. Consider the contemporary corporation. Temporary workers increasingly are used: initially hired by a "temp" firm, they invade and work for another where eventually they may receive a permanent offer. In the early part of this century, textile, shoe, and other manufacturers had on-site machine shops to produce and maintain their capital equipment: today these workshops are museums, because specialist maintenance workers are hired by contract and brought by helicopter when needed. Accountants, tax advisors, lawyers, public relations experts, long-range planners, management consultants, and financial advisors are hired to complete specific tasks, but later they may may work for competitors. Food and custodial services are "outsourced." Head-hunting firms, replacing personnel divisions (that have "morphed" into human relations groups), are hired to scan the labor market for high executives and managers, whose own tenure may be short. Within a firm, project teams are brought together to solve immediate problems, then they disperse; corporate floors have movable partitions to accommodate frequent reorganization; and office workers may not be allotted permanent desks so that space and equipment can be jointly and efficiently utilized. Employees in a department may not even compose a face-to-face unit, because they work from home, work flexible hours, or work part-time in retirement. Corporations once integrated backwards to provide their own parts and raw materials. Today, they contract with parts suppliers (who may provide the same parts to competitors); the separate suppliers have no interconnections, and they may have subcontractors who in turn subcontract. These relationships among producer, suppliers, and subsuppliers shift quickly in response to product turnover, changes in the price of labor, and exchange-rate movements in the global economy. The fixed production line has been changing, too. It is shorter and less permanent, firms are more artisan-like, and labor skills are less fixed as producers adapt to purchasers (Harvey 1989; Piore and Sabel 1984).

If today's corporation cannot be interpreted as a fixed, bounded unit, the same conclusion holds for traditional images of community. People today belong to many communities that fragment and reform. The solidarity of many nation-states is contested and undermined by new coalitions, such as ethnic identities, which challenge established state boundaries. Alliances across national borders are forged: Native

American confederations now unite people from North to South America; human rights and environmental groups draw on global membership to assert local claims; neighborhood groups demand better supplies, from cleaner water to street lighting to schools. These communities do not resemble Robert Owen's unified towns, enclave utopian ventures, or guilds, but they do form around interests that give them identities, and these assertions of ethnicity, commonness, and nationalism are not simply expressions of nostalgia for old identities but the making of new ones in the context of the information explosion, migrations, and diasporas.

In this shifting situation, what can we say about economic structure? Do the successes of capitalism and the demise of socialism point to the future? Or, does the anthropological model of economy offer a different picture? Let us turn first to innovation and the way this dynamic not only unites the sometimes opposed parts of economy but introduces history, change, and a Maussian view into the anthropological model of economy. Then, I shall consider the dialectic of market choice and central planning to suggest how each might be viewed anthropologically, before taking up some of today's questions concerning the environment, community, development, identity, and our shared life.

Innovating Relations

The anthropology of economy starts with the act of creating or innovating, for without this efficacy there is no economy or world transformation. The innovator makes tools in the broad sense; his act changes the instruments surrounding people, the way they interact with the environment, their relationships as they produce, and sequent relations and identities. The innovator, who is individual or group, acts in a field of traces, fashioning something and distributing it to others. His field of effects makes up new base.

Let us consider how this perspective departs from Schumpeter's notion of the innovator as an isolated, gifted individual. In my pragmatic and Maussian view, the innovator creates relations by influencing others. An innovation connects innovator to others who mimic or "consume" his process or thing and so are affected by his presence. The innovation mediates the innovator's action.

The innovator's act becomes a cultural trace. Like a memory distributed among members of a community, or like the bits and pieces of equipment and the shards that I found in the Guatemalan tilemaker's shop, the innovation is good to keep. The innovator has a distributed presence which alters the world and adds to base, the reservoir of traces bequeathed at different times.

The innovator has never been a Schumpeterian isolate, but part of a thick historical stream. The innovator draws together traces and leavings from others (the potter learned from her mother and villagers) and from himself (the tilemaker accumulated his tangible successes, failures, and techniques; the tinmakers kept learning new ways of fashioning objects). This latter reflexive use of an innovation – or innovation on one's own innovation – makes up an historical trajectory or personal "style," such as an artisan's way of making furniture, a shopkeeper's manner of selecting, arranging, and selling merchandise, or an investment manager's style of selecting stocks. Through the use of traces from himself, the innovator creates a way of doing, indexed in an object or service, that becomes a model for others.

In Schumpeter's model, the innovator is the prototypical agent who causes development in an economy. In my view, the innovator is an agent because he is a node, a moment of transformation, in a stream of innovations that are instruments linking people. Through tools the innovator absorbs predecessors, and by tools he creates connections to the future.

But what the innovator leaves may have unintended consequences, because the tool is responded to, interpreted, and used in a context of relations; and the use of a new instrument may stimulate innovations: the furnace man saw reinforced concrete being used in the walls of buildings, and he adopted this tool when devising the floor of his new furnace.

I have argued that making and maintaining a base are fundamental economic processes, and that distribution is "prior" to reciprocity. But my account rejoins a Maussian perspective in that I see innovation as creating relations between people through things. The relationship between people as mediated by things – whether in the market or in community, whether via capital or the base – is the stuff of economy.

The distribution of innovation, however, does take different forms. In community, an innovation is distributed through copying and by allotment and apportionment. The Nambicuara hunter who brings his catch to the village for equal sharing draws on a legacy and distributes and leaves his traces in community. In community, the steps in a physical distribution are usually well known, because they occur through personal relations (as in the Gunwinggu distribution or the Wogeo reapportionment of chestnuts).

In the market, distribution occurs through copying and contract, but the immediate link between efficacious act and its visible trace may not be brought to consciousness, for the chain of linkages that bring the object or service to a locale is often forgotten or suppressed. We do not know where the meat comes from in a MacDonald's hamburger or who made the inexpensive running shoes we buy – often to our physical detriment or embarrassment. Based on time-bound contracts between people, and independence from others, markets allow us to forget our ties to others. Unlike a Kula valuable, a Kenmore washer does not convey to us how it developed, who made it, the significance of its name, or how it moved through a physical distribution chain (in which design, purchase, pricing, trucking, inventory, display, and advertising were all involved).

Interesting, then, that the innovation relationship is made prominent and hidden in opposite ways in community and market. In community, the innovative act is often effaced or "distributed" among people ("the old ones" did it), or attributed to God, ancestors or another agent who "sanctifies" the distribution for the participants and invokes obligations. The Spanish community that distributes timber relied on its forest which, on the people's account, was given to them by the Crown in return for armed help; it is sustained and protected by a saint who helped them in the battle and is annually revered. In community, goods are indices, though the relations they indicate are various: divine force and sanctification by God, paternity and blessings of the ancestors, authority and power of a kingship, power of a social group, efficacy of a hunter. The innovation is recounted, and lies in the distribution and in the everyday lives of people who are obliged by it.

In the market, goods may be indices of their makers – the Ford car, Hewlett-Packard printer, Microsoft program, Kenmore dishwasher, or Homart appliance indexes the innovative act and production. But the purchaser's relation to the innovator is seemingly inconsequential and short term, it is denied by the myth of free choice and contracts; yet the impact, influence, and effect of innovator on recipient is profound; with reason, markets have copy protections.

But the two realms are united by the same act that underlies them: creating, making, and doing. And both eclipsing the relation and exonerating the innovator (as in the market), and recognizing the relation and effacing or hypostatizing the innovator (as in community) are mystifications of economy's basis. In fact, I shall suggest that it was exactly the eclipsing of both innovation and mediated relations that may have hampered socialism.

The Rationality of Capitalism and Socialism

Both market capitalism and centrally planned socialism use rationality as their warrant – in the individual or in the larger system – but some mischief has been perpetuated by measuring one against the other, that is, seeing socialism as economically "inefficient" and the market economy as immoral and alienating. In contrast, I model economy as built on the tension between making rational calculations and maintaining connections with others, and between the desire for certainty and want of serendipity in material life. For example, consider the place of corporate profit-making in the market. Given that the expansion of capital depends on base, does this reliance have implications for the way profit could be distributed in the future?[1]

In the standard model, the corporation is a capital-endowed entity surrounded by markets where it purchases raw materials, tools, and labor, and sells products to make a profit. In the anthropological model, the corporation also has a base consisting of people with skills, social knowledge, experience, memory, and connections. Guided by a charter or mission statement – often promulgated by a founding entrepreneur – the corporation has a sacra, although this anchor changes through reflexive planning. Corporate identity is made up of emblems – a saying, a logo – and a way of doing. The "Hewlett-Packard way," or management by walking around, originating with the firm's founders, constitutes that corporation's identity as well as its products (Zell 1997). In contrast, when Wall Street bond traders say. "Whatever money you make is what you're worth," they are abstracting from the real practices that bring the gains (Abolafia 1996:30). The core activity of a market actor is not accumulating money but creating value for which a resilient base is needed.

The corporate base extends beyond the boundaries of private property or corporate capital, for the corporation is nestled in other communities, its base intersects others. A generation ago, corporations listed goodwill as a financial asset on their balance sheets to denote the value of their social connections; the base was given a monetary value. Corporations today forge connections with buyers, sellers, and competitors, for loyalty, trust, and long-term cooperation between firms can be crucial to success. Cooperation between buyers and sellers, or producers and suppliers may grow as products are created and adjusted to taste; competitors share knowledge that expands the total market; supplementors (such as movies and fast foods) work to enhance each other's products by sharing place of sale, serving size, taste, and advertising.[2] The Great Harvest Bread Co. is a franchise operation with individually owned stores that are separate profit centers. But it is a "richly cross-linked community" in which innovations are passed among the separate franchises, and this shifting set of interconnections and ideas keeps the company ahead of its competitors, which copy its innovations.[3] Viewed through the standard model, Great Harvest is a collection of private, profit-making units. In the anthropological model, it is a collection of units with capital and bases, linked within a larger base.

The corporate base is extended through allotment and apportionment, and by reciprocity and gifts. At its legal, property margins, the corporation engages in contractual relationships, buying and selling. But it may share product, plan, and market information, or solve problems with suppliers or purchasers. Sometimes, corporations share machines or extend financial help to one another. Such sharing represents an allocation from the base, but it may sustain contractual relationships. Ceremonial exchanges on the golf course, in social clubs, and in trade associations also support the contractual arena through familiarity and personal attraction. Finally, corporate innovations have spillover effects or deposit traces, stimulating new products and services, as in the case of Ford and the tire, petroleum, steel, and concrete industries.

Given this interweaving of the two realms, who merits a share in corporate earnings, and in what proportion? The measurement of profit is subject to accounting methods, such as rates of depreciation, the form of write-offs, and variant ways of valuing inventory. Profits are absorbed as dividends, stock options, warrants, bonuses, and more; in fact, so hidden are profits in the language of corporate accounting that many Wall Street analysts use price-to-sales in place of price-to-earnings as a fundamental ratio when evaluating a stock. But given that profit is partly constructed by the language of accounting, how is the dependence of profit on base to be manifested? What are the obligations of the corporation as private owner and controller of accumulated capital to its communal rooting?

Some economists argue that if the return from profit does not flow to innovators, they will have no motivation to create. This justification presumes that people only create to accumulate. But people have long devised forms of production, consumption, and exchange outside markets. Innovation and the creation of surplus are multiply impelled and nestled in communal bonds. The rationale for profit's distribution cannot be traced to a single psychological propensity. Consider the Guatemalan potter, who made figurines, took pleasure in her work, and was accumulating wealth. Did she owe something to her mother from whom she learned skills and styles? Was her base a "free" gift from others? The father and sons who made tin items for profit, and took pleasure in working together, drew on knowledge from their family and from market institutions. Who should receive a share in their profits – their deceased predecessors, the father's father, the market entities in which the father had participated, each man separately, their group, or charity? In today's corporation, group work often is rewarding as it increases capital, but managerial power plays a major role in profit's allocation, as shown by the widening gap in the distribution of corporate returns. Will this appropriation debase corporations and hinder their ability to function? What does a corporation owe to its past members, its local setting, the knowledge generators (schools and universities) on which it draws, the state that provides an infrastructure enabling it to operate, the families and schools that provide it with workers, other corporations with which it maintains unmeasured exchanges that enhance products, or the community economies that provide unpriced subsidies? The global spread of business, with outsourcing and property boundaries lying outside national control, further obscures communal obligations. What happens to the local donations of a corporation when it is taken over by foreign capital? In my two-sided model, profit is the accounted return on both capital and base, but the communal contribution needs to be made transparent. Rethinking the distribution of corporate returns lies at the heart of a new political economy.

But let us now turn our gaze from triumphant capitalism to "failed" socialism. Because socialism might be seen as an exemplar of community economy, should we conclude that, because socialism failed, so the community realm of economy must be extinguished?

In Eastern Europe and elsewhere, variant forms of socialism emerged in response to capitalism and local conditions. I distinguish two types: market socialism, exemplified by Hungary and other economies, and centrally planned socialism that characterized the Soviet Union, Cuba, and Bulgaria. I shall attend only to the central planning model, because most forms of market socialism were a combination of central planning and open pricing, and often represented a moment of transition from the more centralized form.[4]

Centrally planned socialism displayed features of community economy, including self-sufficiency of a local, national, or larger trading bloc, and transfer of resources by allotment and apportionment. With rationing, money had a lesser role than in market systems, and prices were partially disconnected from scarcity and demand. In fact, because money was not a general measuring rod or medium of exchange, circuits of exchange developed. Within and between nations, barter sometimes took place (Cuban sugar was exchanged for Soviet oil); and reciprocity preceded by gifting arose as a way of securing goods and services outside the formal allocation system.

Public ownership of the means of production was general throughout the Soviet Union, although some farms remained collective (or cooperative) after the revolution (Humphrey 1983). Through central planning a relatively high savings rate was achieved, and as the state controlled the allocation of investment funds, resource commitments could be deepened in targeted sectors where expansion was desired, such as industry. Given investment allocation, central planners specified production targets for industry and agriculture, and directed where the outputs would flow. In this fashion, central planning emphasized vertical control and flows of information as opposed to horizontal connections through markets.

Socialism also has similarities to contemporary capitalism. Both presume that rational control of the economy may be achieved. Central planners rationally arrange a total economy according to "economic laws" (Humphrey 1983). Input–output tables or matrices (at least in theory) define exchanges among enterprises. In contrast, market participants themselves are presumed to be rational choosers. Both economic systems assume that information is sufficient to make rational decisions at the national or individual level. But central planning probably places more reliance on acquiring information, because planning boards must specify what products will be produced, how they will be produced, which factories produce them, from where the resources for production come, and who shall receive the output. Central planners must also presume that orders will be enacted, and they must erect quality control and reward systems.

In light of central planning's totalizing focus and dependence on adequate information, I draw a distinction between socialism and the community economies known to anthropology. The latter systems are far smaller than the Soviet and even Cuban economies. Often the ethnographic economies are face-to-face groups or have subcomponents, such as chiefdoms, compound groups, and households in which group planning is more easily exercised. I do not wish to imply that socialism was simply community economy wrongly applied to large populations, from the top down, because the difference is more complex. Few, if any, economies studied by anthropologists represent attempts to organize a totality. In the ethnographic cases, units at different levels exercise degrees of control, and different goods and services are managed differently. For example, all members of a Nambicuara village share manioc soup and fresh game (as might members of a centrally planned economy), but other important foods are gathered and apportioned in households, and sometimes between them. This pattern of multiple distribution systems is found from Papua New Guinea, to Southeast Asia, to Latin America, to Africa. Land possession is allotted one way, its use is apportioned differently, with temporary access gained in yet a different manner; control over other natural resources may be gained by other connections, and the division of cooked foods may be managed still separately. No one set of distribution rules characterizes or penetrates an entire economy. This non-systemic feature makes the ethnographic economies more diversified than a centrally planned economy, and the multiplication of allocation systems, vested at different levels of organization and involving different goods and services, seems to lower risk and offer insurance against failure in distributional or entitlement mechanisms (Sen 1981). One reason for the "failure" or perhaps fragility of centrally planned socialism – in addition to the problems of managerial and information control – may have to do with its totalizing character, the insistence that an economy be organized by a single method.

Strong political authority linked to central planning socialism also distinguishes it from community economies that draw on kinship relationships as backbone. Certainly, tribute-taking and top-down decision-making may characterize an ethnographic economy (tribute may be owed to a brother-in-law, a maternal uncle, or a chief), but these systems are partial. Socialism itself need not take an authoritarian direction, and can be operated through democratic control, as in the case of the Spanish villagers who share their timber resources on the basis of luck. But most centrally planned socialist economies tied force and power to economic management.

In both centrally planned and market socialism, economic management starts at the national level with the formation of a national budget defining sectors for investment. But, to simplify, at this stage the two forms of socialism diverge. In market socialism, given state investment in specific areas, bidding and price-making among enterprises allocates their resources and outputs, and profit-making operates. In a centrally planned system, however, transfers of goods between industries are a function of central command, not purchasing power; resources are allocated by rationing (as in the European monastery), and enterprises cannot legally obtain inputs without state licenses. Production units, in turn, are directed to meet defined output levels. Money is issued but is largely disconnected from the flow of goods and services; currency transfers mark exchanges already executed. Within a sector or enterprise, however, money is used to pay salaries, and wages fluctuate depending on productive efficiency, because an enterprise may exceed or fail to meet its target levels. Wage money is used to purchase goods, but these items may be rationed at set prices, so shortages occur.

Several features of the socialist enterprise do invite comparison with the ethnographic cases, however. Given output specification, enterprises probably placed more emphasis on economizing and thrift – as in community economies – than on profit-making, because conserving resources allowed for more output that in turn could be used "outside" the planned transfers in what became known as the "second economy." (Humphrey (1983: 85) reports a slight variation for collective farms where aggregate production, measured in rubles, was the principal indicator of success. This assessment method led farms to produce more expensive products than necessary by selecting costly resources. Still, the collective farms also would try to raise labor and investment productivity by economizing.)

Under a rationing system, one way to gain access to resources is by queuing, as exemplified by lines that formed outside consumer shops. A different method of gaining access was through the second economy, using bribes, gifts, and reciprocity (Berdahl 1999, Humphrey 1983, Ledeneva 1998, Pérez-López 1995). Reciprocity in goods and services forged horizontal connections and represented an exchange across incommensurate sectors. In these respects, an industrial sector made up a circuit of exchange. Within the sector, transactions in labor, goods, and money took place, but no stable unit of value was used.

A crucial difference between socialism and community economies revolves about innovation. Central planning can successfully foster large projects, as illustrated by space and armaments programs, or water-control and hydroelectric schemes. But central planning did not foster innovation by serendipity. I suggest that socialist economies seem to have been productivity-takers. They could induce high rates of saving and investment leading to growth using known technologies (Marxist growth), but they do not induce the production of new values (Schumpeterian development) and unexpected change. Socialism is not constructed to provide positive externalities or the interdigitation of bases across enterprises that nourish innovation. I qualify these comments, however, by pointing to the contradictory nature of many socialist economies. There is a difference between the project of capitalism which is profit-making and capital accumulation, and the project of a community economy which is maintenance and augmentation of the base. Twentieth-century socialism may have found itself caught between the two aims. It did provide goods and necessities to a large number of citizens, and large-scale innovations were not required for the achievement of this end. Assessing socialism by market measures, such as productivity growth, may be a category mistake, because the system cannot meet these standards. Socialism's rationality lies in carrying out community values of distribution as opposed to creating productivities. Was growth in socialist economies due to internal technological change or to savings and investment in known technology using available resources and labor? I surmise it was the latter.

Much attention has been given to the problems socialist economies face in shifting to market systems.[5] Explanations invoke Polanyi on the disruption caused by disembedding market relationships from social connections, or point to the problem of establishing a national currency and budget, the importance of raising entrepreneurial motivations, and the difficulty of constituting systems of private property. But given the circuits of exchange, the reliance on allotting and apportioning, the material versus currency transfers, and the emphasis on internal economizing, I would emphasize that the transition also revolves about adopting the notion of commensuration. What had been unlike becomes similar and exchangeable. The categories of the world dissolve when suddenly one item can be transformed to another through the magic of the market. Who is equipped to manage this cultural transformation that affects both productive practices and consumer behavior? It may be that the final or consumer goods sector of an economy more quickly adapts to generalized exchange than does the industrial side, which suddenly faces choice and competition that deeply affect interdigitated productive practices. The difficulty of achieving this cultural transformation was hardly anticipated by most economists.

The Questions Today

How should we comport ourselves in a mixed economy, where we are caught between self-interests and shared concerns? Does the anthroplogy of economy provide a language for discussing our conditions? I think three questions frame today's debates on political economy.

- What do we want to produce and distribute through the market, and what not?
- What do we want to produce and apportion in community, and what kinds of community do we want involved in economic life?
- How shall the two realms of value value be mixed together?

Let us consider these contemporary questions in relation to the environment, the transglobal economy, development, identity, and our shared life.

The environment

The "environmental problem" refers to using up resources, generating excessive waste, and degrading the planet. Certainly, population growth increases environmental pressures, and human life is entropic, but consider environmental issues through the model of market and community.

Some innovations have a negligible effect on the use of materials. A smaller computer chip is thrifty; the potter who made angel figurines sold new ones in place of others; automobiles may be made with lighter materials or designed to use less gasoline. Studies suggest that US output, measured in tons, hardly increased in the twentieth century, although gross domestic output is now more than 20 times larger in monetary terms (Neef 1998: 4).

Profit-making also may diminish the base. Nobles who overused their estates in Poland to secure a cash profit, and farmers who raise market crops in place of subsistence ones while depleting the land debase community resources. Copper-mining by transnational corporations on the island of Bougainville has brought little wealth to the people and has profoundly changed their environment (Wesley-Smith and Ogan 1992). The James Bay hydroelectric project, cultivated by the Quebec government, wrought enormous changes in the economy of the Cree, with loss of their traditional hunting areas. Attempts to log rare woods in the forests of Papua New Guinea are resisted by those who use the forests, though welcomed by others.[6] I do not argue against all instances of capital accumulation and market expansion, but for modeling the environment as a heritage. Transforming it changes current and possible identities.

Some economists analyze environmental change through cost/benefit calculations. We decide how to manage a forest or another resource by considering its alternative uses, figuring the monetary value of its benefits, arranging the returns as a stream of wealth realized at different periods, and discounting these flows to their present value in order to weigh one use against another. This commensuration technique is an elegant and rational market exercise designed to save the environment – from market forces.

But we cannot know how a base will be used in fifty or one thousand years. To place a price on a forest, a river, the air, or a lake implies its future value is determinant and not subject to repositioning.[7] By assigning the environment a price, we transform base to capital and limit our legacy. I do not assume that a community will manage the environment well. But potential uses of the foundation must be addressed in light of economy's many values, for we cannot predict the meanings and uses that may be supported by a current base.

Community in the transglobal economy

Globalization increases as trade crosses communities (it is "balanced" by foreign claims to property that also undermine singular communities).[8] Economic globalization does not simply mean an increased flow of goods and services across borders, for it involves profit-making through trade and by expanding control of resources, while ownership of capital remains relatively local.

Global corporations outsource across national boundaries, and profits grow by arbitrage across resource and labor markets: bauxite is mined in Australia and shipped to Iceland for processing into aluminum, because the latter has low electric power rates; light assembly plants (an innovation) allow corporations to shift production among competing national labor markets. By accounting techniques, global corporations can register their profits in different nations, depending on exchange rates and taxes. These tactics of globalization disconnect profit centers from production and the nation that hosts a processing plant. Morality, obligation, and commitment are loosened as shared language and culture disappear. Yet light assembly plants – that characterize the Asian Pacific rim and parts of Latin America, deposit wage returns in an area, and vest managerial control in non-national forces – affect gender experience, authority, and spending power in local communities (Mills 1997, Ong 1987).

In contrast to the global spread of production, recent evidence suggests that innovation remains locally rooted (Doremus, Keller, Pauly, and Riech 1998). Will innovation be the last to go global? What are the possibilities for innovating in a global context? Some innovations, as in the case of the Guatemalan weavers, are appropriated across national borders by the power of financial capital, a fact that raises new legal issues about intellectual property rights (Brush and Stabinsky 1996). But the global flow of information and ease of travel also raise possibilities for innovation. Shaman Corporation in California sent small teams to different parts of the world looking for local medicines and remedies in forests and elsewhere. Bringing these remedies to its labs in San Francisco, it refined them in search of the active agents. For Shaman, a people's heritage, honed through use and refinements, constituted preclinical trials which shortened the usual innovation process that for most drug-makers begins with countless experiments in laboratories. Shaman built a cross-national base through its financial power to bring together practical and published information. Yet, this constitution of a base from global fragments is not new, as the study of Appfel-Marglin (1990) suggests for smallpox vaccination. In India, a similar preventative against smallpox was used for centuries, and knowledge of it probably spread to England where Jenner subsequently "discovered" it. When the British in colonial India compelled use of their vaccination technique and banned the traditional practice, the incidence of smallpox grew before the new method became established.

Anthropology and development

Most development practices are powered by market forces and models. I have seen development programs that emphasize building infrastructure, such as roads and market-distribution centers; establishing property rights and legal systems; creating rotating loan funds; distributing land plots and extending agricultural technology; fostering irrigation schemes, livestock improvement, pasture projects, and backyard fish tanks; and constructing schools and medical centers. These franchising operations extend to others what we know and have created. In this form development involves a one-way flow of techniques, goods, and services. But should we not focus on nurturing innovation? Base-building will require new ways of thinking about development, because the problem transcends technical and engineering solutions, or even making savings for investment. How do we strengthen a local base to foster innovations?

Ultimately, development has to do not with capital accumulation but innovation in the relationships of society. Community offers a reservoir of possibilities. For example, Platteau and Hayami (1998) compare growth in Asia and Africa to suggest that the development of African markets was hampered by existant redistribution systems, whereas a key to the success of Asian markets was the prevalence of reciprocity. Convincing or not, the argument raises the question: which community processes are useful in market contexts? Do cronyism and nepotism enhance or damage growth? What allocation rules are helpful? Is some equity in assuring access to necessities a nurturant influence? Does equality in access to productive resources or sharing technical knowledge enhance economic performance (Humphrey 1998)? From the perspective of the dual model, the conversation on "development" must become more complex. We know something about the dynamics of the market realm, but how are they connected to the community sphere? How do we support innovation – by techni-

cal training, by offering opportunities and encouraging experimentation, by building support groups?

Identity and community

Innovation, predation, and development present problematic issues in
the global market. Others revolve about identity in relation to production and consumption. With globalization, the base and social
aggregations fragment – and communities multiply from imagined
associations to communities of demanders. Consider the place of "base
products" in the market. Automobiles, milk, tissues, shaving cream,
hamburgers, and breakfast cereals are basic goods in many areas, and
they can be produced anywhere. But "place" of origin for a group of
products, such as wine and cheese, determines their identity and value.
In France, these products are termed *produits de terroir*, which I gloss
as base products because they convey the message of community production.[9] In Europe, beans, ham, chicken, cider, asparagus, sausages,
olive oil, peppers, and more fall into this class: there are generic beans
and Tarbais beans; there is Breese chicken, Varzi salami, and Gascon
pork. In France and Italy, these products represent over 10 percent of
foods purchased, and regulations or property rights protect use of the
labels, for their production supposedly brings together a physical
microregion and a group of people. The labels convey the linking of
patrimony, inherited skills, know-how, and local resources. Similarly,
one seller of Florida orange juice, advertising that its juice is produced
by cooperatives, implies that the product receives more care and has
greater sweetness as a result of its community legacy. These foods,
and others such as a "traditional" wine or syrup, are tokens of community sold in the market. The communal base is extended to include
others through purchase not reciprocity. The buyer, by consuming,
makes the community and its identity part of himself. The products
are imagined sacra and satisfactions that the consumer participates in
a community by sharing its substance. But defining who has "authen-
tic" rights to a protected label is often a political negotiation, for the
assemblages of product, name, people, and technique are usually fab-
rications. These communities are usually innovations or illusions, that
is, mystifications of the "real" relations of production.

Keeping the base and forming identity are key issues, as the
transglobal market extends its reach through the processes of commensuration and commodification. We create identities through communities, as in the instance of base products, and resist losing them,
as in the case of the Japanese and rice. We also maintain residual

communities in the market context. For example, migrants from the Caribbean island of St. John living in North America and elsewhere keep their rights to family land on the island.[10] The plots are small, no one has rights to specific pieces, and the land cannot support its holders. But the land signifies family, home, a community. Cared for and used by some, it is a burial place for all. Manipulating local laws to gain private rights to use agricultural plots or sell them is considered to be immoral, for the acts deny the community by alienating its core.

In a very different way, a real community may enter the market today as a successful producer of goods, but find itself transformed by the experience. In Spencer, Massachusetts, the monks of St. John's Abbey produce – through their company Trappist Preserves – 31 flavors of jellies, jams, and preserves (Weil 1995). Their annual revenues, exceeding one million dollars, provide two-fifths of the Abbey's income, and only 11 of the 75 monks are engaged in the endeavor. To remain successful, however, the monks must participate in a world where the strawberry pickers are underpaid migrants, kickbacks for shelf space are customary, and jams are hawked at raucous trade shows. With market success, the monastery strengthens its base, and debases itself, for the monks are part of a community whose principles are antithetical to the practices of competitive accumulation; but the jams and preserves project remains a livable contradiction.

Consider yet a different combination of community in market: barter clubs. These associations have grown in the United States as market competition has increased.[11] Some argue that barter clubs are formed to avoid taxes. But barter takes place for broader reasons; for example, when communal trust in money breaks down barter may emerge (Humphrey 1985). Barter communities or clubs, which exchange within a larger market, often grow in response to slack times. They promote business for members who, lacking fluid capital, are motivated to transact with other associates; members are able to produce and consume more than they would if all trades had to be cash mediated. Some clubs keep a central account of debits and credits so that participants do not even need to exchange one with another but can build up and draw credits through offers and purchases. As a community market within a larger market that determines its exchange rates, a barter club is an agreement to use a private medium of exchange, even if it is imaginary and never issued.

In contrast, more than 30 US communities – including Madison, Austin, Detroit, and Ithaca – have issued their own currencies (Graham 1996). Legal tender, the monies pay for goods, wages, rents, and services among the merchants who accept them. Payments in these currencies also may be combined with federal money. Use of the currencies promotes local businesses – that are resisting the undercutting effects of global competition – and some of the local monies may be "taxed" and donated to local charities or used as seed money for start-up businesses in the area. Finally, these two forms of community-in-market – barter clubs and local communities – may be combined. In Massachusetts, the Valley Trade Connection is a barter group that also issues dollars for use by members (Graham 1996); barter, market, local money, and community are combined.

Today, with a heightened flow of information connected to the internet, new methods of sending messages, and the expansion of media systems, knowledge about people, events, ideas, and goods is transmitted at a speed that would have astounded anthropological theorists of cultural diffusion a century ago. This new geography makes possible the formation of a base that is wider and more complex than anything experienced. Things of value are turning from steel, rubber, and glass to skills and conceptual products, just as affiliations with communities multiply and become more contingent. But people still seek shared spaces, as on the internet, that has "home" sites, "rooms" for conversing with others, and even consumer clubs where buyers create trustworthy identities so that others will transact with them. These identities replace older social markers, and exchange sites keep the records of legitimacy for others to see, even if the identity is a fabrication and the histories are only 30 days old.

If the internet makes possible one way of forming communities and constructing identities, new reproductive technologies also make the notion of a foundation problematic. A person now may have several mothers – the ovum donor, surrogate, care-taker and legal – as well as several fathers. But still we seek such foundations in juxtaposition to the flux of contracts that enable the new communal forms.

Shared life

What should be the commonness in our economy today? Should every citizen in the USA have the right to a basic food? Should every school-child be given a serving of milk as a member of community? Should we provide national tax advantages to heterosexual nuclear families? What portion of corporate profit should flow to communities to support basic relationships on which profit-making rests? In recent years, many public services have been partially or completely shifted to the market sphere, including hospitals, public schools, prisons, roads, fire departments, and garbage collection. Some argue that welfare agencies themselves should be privatized, so that helping the impoverished becomes a profitable activity. Can we identify the interests and identities of our many communities? How should these be intertwined with the market?

Because we live in different types and sizes of community, one question concerns the base most appropriate for type of association: at what level of community should decisions about street-lighting, police, roads, public transport, or education be made? The same question holds for a university and its budget. Which academic unit – a department, a college, a division, the university itself – comprises a community and what does it share? The library may be a shared resource of the university and should be supported by the entirety, but in what proportions from the units? How should other resources be supported, such as buildings (especially ones dedicated to expensive equipment that brings external funding), admission and advising offices that benefit students, fundraising staff, telephone systems, and technology centers? Are these units and services the responsibility of the university or should their support be differentially attributed to the component colleges and departments that use them? Should these services, goods, and buildings be freely available, or rationed, or are they "market centers" to be supported by rents charged for their use? Finally, what mix of public subsidy, earned income, private gifts, and tuition money should fund different units, from the humanities to the hard sciences and professional schools?

Today's debates about these issues are dominated by the notion of efficiency and phrased as trade-offs between efficiency and equity. But equity has multiple meanings, and the debates actually concern incommensurate value realms. With a broader lexicon, we can revisit these issues that concern the balance of community and market, and the identities we establish. Consider US national parks and monuments. The national budget for parks has declined in the last dozen years, while maintenance expenses are rising, as is the number of visitors, from 207 million in 1983 to 270 million in 1996. The entry fee at Yellowstone National Park has remained at $10 per automobile since 1916. Should this fee be raised? Should more tax money be devoted to park support? Should some park land be sold, so shrinking the area to be supported and raising an endowment, or should parks be privatized? Perhaps we should rent space for corporate advertising inside parks. (Target stores of Minneapolis donated money for renovating the Washington Monument and advertises its contribution, presumably in hopes of attracting customers who admire its communal commitment.[12])

How should we pay for the sacred objects in Washington, D.C.? Many would argue that our national holdings should be subjected to market forces. Arches National Park would be open to those willing to pay an entry fee; and its upkeep would be determined by the dollar votes. More popular parks will expand and be in better condition. But consider: if a small entrance fee to see the US Constitution or the White House were collected, many people might not object; however, if an admission fee to the Vietnam Memorial were charged, an outcry would result. Should we rank our national sacra to charge differential fees?

Parks and monuments are our national commons, our base, our mutual commitment and identity. If we market the commons – whether a national park or a community drinking-fountain, whether the Lincoln Memorial or a child's swing in a pocket park, whether our once-vaunted school system or a boulevard tree in the city – we lose our commonality, our community. Part of our national commitment is that minorities and the poor, as well as majorities and the rich, should share our sacra and commons. This value of living in community has no market price. So, the question is not which goods should be private and which kept public, as determined by individual wants and what the market will bear, but which should be public and which private in terms of what a community needs to be just that community. We should not simply assign to community what cannot be sustained in the market; rather, the market can be allowed to exchange what a community does not need.

Sharing community emblems and beliefs conflicts with our idealization of the choosing, maximizing individual, but these sacra provide identities, such as cultural character and kinship, locality, religion, and gender as well as the rational person himself, even if these identities are in greater flux than ever before. Because these disparate identities place on us incommensurate demands, the conversation concerning how to divide our economic life between community and market must take place outside the market discourse. We ought not let ourselves be persuaded that the coin has only one side.

The model of economy with multiple and interwoven sources makes us less certain of our own system and induces a greater understanding of others. I cannot picture an economic finality or utopia, given the cultural legacies that make variant arrangements fitting, and the shifting balances that deny the possibility of stasis. This book represents a plea for openness to the values of equity, merit, and identity as well as efficiency in economy, and for openness with ourselves and others in trying new combinations of community and market that compose economy. With its historical and cross-cultural perspective, the anthropology of economy offers tools for undertaking these conversations and imagining such other outcomes.

NOTES

1   The work of Gibson-Graham (1996; Gibson-Graham and O'Neill 2001), and conversations with them have been very helpful in developing my own views of profit.
2   For related discussions, see Brandenburger and Nalebuff (1996) and Reichheld (1996).
3   Wall Street Journal, Nov 21, 1997 (Section B, p. 1).
4   For one analysis of market socialism and its reliance on neoclassical theory and the presumption of perfect information, see Stiglitz (1994). For useful descriptions of variant forms of socialism see Centeno and Font (1997), Humphrey (1983), Ledeneva (1998), Ritter (1998), and Woodruff (1999).
5   See, for example, Burawoy and Verdery (1999), Kideckel (1995), Lampland (1991, 1995), and Verdery (1996).
6   San Francisco Chronicle, May 29, 1996, p. A8.
7   I wish to acknowledge the influence of conversations with and the work of Stephen A. Marglin on my understanding of uncertainty (1996).
8   For a contemporary instance in which the two realms are mixed together in fishing quotas, see Pálsson and Helgason (1995).
9   "Local land products" would be a more direct translation. I draw on the work of Bérard and Marchenay (1996).
10 This material is drawn from Olwig (1994, 1999).
11 Recent studies suggest that, in general, barter arises for different reasons in different areas (Helgason and Pálsson 1996; Humphrey 1985).
12 Minneapolis Star Tribune, July 7, 1996.

References

Abolafia, Mitchel Y. 1996. *Making Markets*. Cambridge: Harvard University Press.

Allen, Robert C. 1983. Collective Invention. *Journal of Economic Behavior and Organization* 4: 1–24.

Anderson, Benedict. 1991. *Imagined Communities: reflections on the origin and spread of nationalism*, 2nd edn. London: Verso.

Anderson, David G. 1998. Property as a Way of Knowing on Evenki Lands in Arctic Siberia. In *Property Relations: renewing the anthropological tradition*, ed. C. M. Hann, pp. 64–84. Cambridge: Cambridge University Press.

Appadurai, Arjun. 1986. Introduction: commodities and the politics of value. In *The Social Life of Things*, ed. Arjun Appadurai, pp. 3–63. Cambridge: Cambridge University Press.

Appfel-Marglin, Frédérique. 1990. Smallpox in Two Systems of Knowledge. In *Dominating Knowledge: development, culture, and resistance*, ed. Frédérique Appfel-Marglin and Stephen A. Marglin, pp. 102–43. Oxford: Clarendon Press.

Ardener, Shirley. 1964. The Comparative Study of Rotating Credit Associations. *Journal of the Royal Anthropological Institute of Great Britain and Ireland* 94: 201–29.

Aristotle. 1926. *The Nicomachean Ethics*, trans. H. Rackham. London: William Heinemann.

Aristotle. 1946. *The Politics of Aristotle*, trans. Ernest Barker. London: Oxford University Press.

Aristotle. 1953. *The Ethics of Aristotle*, trans. J. A. K. Thomson. London: Penguin Books.

Aristotle. 1984. *The Complete Works of Aristotle*, ed. Jonathan Barnes. Princeton: Princeton University Press.

Armstrong, W. E. 1924. Rossel Island Money: a unique monetary system. *Economic Journal* 34: 423–9.

Armstrong, W. E. 1928. *Rossel Island*. Cambridge: Cambridge University Press.

Aspelin, Paul L. 1979. Food Distribution and Social Bonding Among the Mamaindê of Mato Grosso, Brazil. *Journal of Anthropological Research* 35: 309–27.

Babb, Florence E. 1989. *Between Field and Cooking Pot*. Austin: University of Texas Press.

Barić, Lorraine. 1964. Some Aspects of Credit, Saving and Investment in a "Non-Monetary" Economy (Rossel Island). In *Capital, Saving and Credit in Peasant Societies*, ed. Raymond Firth and B. S. Yamey, pp. 35–52. London: George Allen and Unwin.

Barth, Fredrik. 1967. Economic Spheres in Darfur. In *Themes in Economic Anthropology*, ed. Raymond Firth, pp. 149–74. London: Tavistock Publications.

Bartra, Armando. 1982. *El Comportamiento Económico de la Prodúccion Campesina*. Mexico: Universidad Autónoma Chapingo.

Bateson, Gregory. 1972. *Steps to an Ecology of Mind*. New York: Ballantine Books.

Beals, Ralph L. 1975. *The Peasant Marketing System of Oaxaca, Mexico*. Berkeley: University of California Press.

Becker, Gary S. 1976. *The Economic Approach to Human Behavior*. Chicago: University of Chicago Press.

Becker, Gary S. 1981. *A Treatise on the Family*. Cambridge: Harvard University Press.

Benedict, Burton. 1968. Family Firms and Economic Development. *Southwestern Journal of Anthropology* 24(1): 1–19.

Bérard, Laurence, and Philippe Marchenay. 1996. Tradition, Regulation, and Intellectual Property: local agricultural products and foodstuffs in France. In *Valuing Local Knowledge*, ed. Stephen B. Brush and Doreen Stabinsky, pp. 230–43. Washington, DC: Island Press.

Berdahl, Daphne. 1999. *Where the World Ended*. Berkeley: University of California Press.

Bernal, Victoria. 1994. Peasants, Capitalism, and (Ir)rationality. *American Ethnologist* 21: 792–810.

Berndt, Ronald. 1951. Ceremonial Exchange in Western Arnhem Land. *Southwestern Journal of Anthropology* 7: 156–76.

Biddick, Kathleen. 1989. *The Other Economy: pastoral husbandry on a medieval estate*. Berkeley: University of California Press.

Bird-David, Nurit. 1990. The Giving Environment. *Current Anthropology* 31: 189–96.

Bird-David, Nurit. 1992a. Beyond "The Original Affluent Society." *Current Anthropology* 33: 25–47.

Bird-David, Nurit. 1992b. Beyond "The Hunting and Gathering Modes of Subsistence." *Man* (N.S.) 27: 19–44.

Bird-David, Nurit. 1993. Tribal Metaphorization of Human–Nature Relatedness. In *Environmentalism: the view from anthropology*, ed. K. Milton (ASA Monogr. 32), pp. 112–25. London: Routledge.

Bloch, Marc. 1961. *Feudal Society*. Chicago: University of Chicago Press.

Bloch, Maurice, and Jonathan Parry. 1989. Introduction: money and the morality of exchange. In *Money and the Morality of Exchange*, ed. Jonathan Parry and Maurice Bloch, pp. 1–32. Cambridge: Cambridge University Press.

Boeke, J. H. 1942. *The Structure of Netherlands Indian Economy*. New York:

Institute of Pacific Relations.

Bohannan, Paul. 1955. Some Principles of Exchange and Investment Among the Tiv. *American Anthropologist* 57: 60–70.

Bohannan, Paul, 1959. The Impact of Money on an African Subsistence Economy. *The Journal of Economic History* XIX: 491–503.

Bohannan, Paul and Laura Bohannan, 1968. *Tiv Economy*. London: Longmans.

Bohannan, Paul, and George Dalton, eds. 1965. *Markets in Africa*. Garden City: Doubleday & Co.

Bourdieu, Pierre. 1977. *Outline of a Theory of Practice*. Cambridge: Cambridge University Press.

Bourque, Susan, and Kay Warren. 1981. *Women of the Andes*. Ann Arbor: University of Michigan Press.

Brandenburger, Adam M., and Barry J. Nalebuff. 1996. *Co-opetition*. New York: Doubleday.

Braudel, Fernand. 1982. *The Wheels of Commerce*, trans. Siân Reynolds. New York: Harper and Row.

Bruner, Jerome. 1985. Vygotsky: a historical and conceptual perspective. In *Culture, Communication, and Cognition: Vygotskian perspectives*, ed. James V. Wertsch, pp. 21–34. Cambridge: Cambridge University Press.

Brush, Stephen B. 1996. Is Common Heritage Outmoded? In *Valuing Local Knowledge*, ed. Stephen B. Brush and Doreen Stabinsky, pp. 143–64. Washington, DC: Island Press.

Brush, Stephen B., and Doreen Stabinsky, eds. 1996. *Valuing Local Knowledge*. Washington, DC: Island Press.

Buck, P. H. 1930. *Samoan Material Culture*, Bulletin 75. Honolulu: Bernice P. Bishop Museum.

Burawoy, Michael, and Katherine Verdery, eds. 1999. *Uncertain Transition: ethnographies of change in the postsocialist world*. Lanham: Rowman and Littlefield Publishers.

Cardoso, Fernando Enrique, and Enzo Faletto, 1979. *Dependency and Development in Latin America*. Berkeley: University of California Press.

Carrier, James G. 1992. The Gift in Theory and Practice in Melanesia: a note on the centrality of gift exchange. *Ethnology* 31: 185–93.

Carrier, James G. 1995. *Gifts and Commodities*. London: Routledge.

Carrier, James. G. ed. 1997. *Meanings of the Market*. Oxford: Berg.

Carrier, James. G. 1998. Property and Social Relations in Melanesian Anthropology. In *Property Relations: renewing the anthropological tradition*, ed. C. M. Hann, pp. 85–103. Cambridge: Cambridge University Press.

Carrier, James G., and Achsah H. Carrier. 1989. *Wage, Trade and Exchange in Melanesia*. Berkeley: University of California Press.

Carsten, Janet. 1989. Cooking Money: gender and the symbolic transformation of means of exchange in a Malay fishing community, In *Money and the Morality of Exchange*, ed. J. Parry and M. Bloch, pp. 117–41. Cambridge: Cambridge University Press.

Carsten, Janet. 1995a. Houses in Langkawi: stable structure or mobile homes? In *About the House: Lévi-Strauss and beyond*, ed. Janet Carsten and Stephen

Hugh-Jones, pp. 105–28. Cambridge: Cambridge University Press.

Carsten, Janet. 1995b. The Politics of Forgetting: migration, kinship and memory on the periphery of the southeast Asian State. *Journal of the Royal Anthropological Institute* (N.S.) 1: 317–35.

Carsten, Janet. 1995c. The Substance of Kinship and the Heat of the Hearth: feeding, personhood, and relatedness among Malays in Pulau Langkawi. *American Ethnologist* 22(2): 223–41.

Cato. 1933. *On Farming*, trans. Ernest Brehaut. New York: Columbia University Press.

Centeno, Miguel Angel, and Mauricio Font. 1997. *Toward a New Cuba? legacies of a revolution*. Boulder: Lynne Rienner Publishers.

Chamberlin, Edward. H. 1933. *The Theory of Monopolistic Competition*. Cambridge: Harvard University Press.

Coase, R. H. 1988. *The Firm, the Market, and the Law*. Chicago: University of Chicago Press.

Cole, Michael. 1991. Conclusion. In *Perspectives on Socially Shared Cognition*, ed. Lauren B. Resnick, John M. Levine, and Stephanie D. Teasley, pp. 398–417. Washington: American Psychological Association.

Cole, Michael. 1996. *Cultural Psychology*. Cambridge: Harvard University Press.

Collingwood, R. G. 1989. *Essays in Political Philosophy*. Oxford: Clarendon Press.

Cook, Scott, and Martin Diskin, eds. 1976. *Markets in Oaxaca*. Austin: University of Texas Press.

Counts, Alex. 1996. *Give Us Credit*. New York: Random House.

Curtin, Phillip. 1984. *Cross-cultural Trade in World History*. Cambridge: Cambridge University Press.

Cushner, Nicholas P. 1980. *Lords of the Land*. Albany: State University of New York Press.

Dalton, George. 1960. A Note of Clarification on Economic Surplus. *American Anthropologist* 62: 483–90.

Daly, Herman E., and John B. Cobb, Jr. 1994. *For the Common Good*, 2nd edn. Boston: Beacon Press.

Daly, Herman E., and Kenneth N. Townsend, eds. 1993. *Valuing the Earth*. Cambridge: MIT Press.

Davenport, William H. 1986. Two Kinds of Value in the Eastern Solomon Islands. In *The Social Life of Things*, ed. Arjun Appadurai, pp. 95–109. Cambridge: Cambridge University Press.

Davis, John. 1992. Trade in Kufra (Libya). *In Contesting Markets*, ed. Roy Dilley, pp. 115–27. Edinburgh: Edinburgh University Press.

Demsetz, Harold. 1967. Toward a Theory of Property Rights. *The American Economic Review* LVII :347–59.

Denholm-Young, N. 1937. *Seignorial Administration in England*. New York: Barnes and Noble.

Derrida, Jacques. 1992 [1991]. *Given Time*, trans. Peggy Kamuf. Chicago: University of Chicago Press.

Dewey, Alice. 1964. Capital, Credit and Saving in Javanese Marketing. In

Capital, Saving and Credit in Peasant Societies, ed. Raymond Firth and B. S. Yamey, pp. 230–55. London: George Allen and Unwin Ltd.

Diderot, D. 1751. Art. In *Encyclopédie, ou Dictionnaire Raisonné des Sciences, des Artes et des Métiers*, ed. Diderot and D'Alembert, I: 713–17. Paris: Briasson, David, Le Breton, Durand.

Diderot, D. 1965. Art. In *Encyclopedia: selections*, trans. Nelly S. Hoyt and Thomas Cassirer. Indianapolis: Bobbs-Merrill.

Dilley, Roy. 1992. *Contesting Markets*. Edinburgh: Edinburgh University Press.

Dore, Ronald. 1992 [1983]. Goodwill and the Spirit of Market Capitalism. In *The Sociology of Economic Life*, ed. Mark Granovetter and Richard Swedberg, pp. 159–79. Boulder: Westview.

Doremus, Paul N., William W. Keller, Louis W. Pauly, and Simon Reich. 1998. *The Myth of the Global Corporation*. Princeton: Princeton University Press.

Du Boulay, Juliet. 1974. *Portrait of a Greek Mountain Village*. Oxford: Clarendon Press.

Duby, Georges. 1968 [1962]. *Rural Economy and Country Life in the Medieval West*, trans. Cynthia Postan. Columbia: University of South Carolina Press.

Duby, Georges. 1974. *The Early Growth of the European Economy*, trans. Howard B. Clarke. Ithaca: Cornell University Press.

Dumont, Louis. 1977. *From Mandeville to Marx: the genesis and triumph of economic ideology*. Chicago: University of Chicago Press.

Durkheim, Emile. 1933. *The Division of Labor in Society*, trans. George Simpson. Glencoe: Free Press.

Durkheim, Emile. 1995 [1912]. *The Elemental Forms of Religious Life*, trans. Karen E. Fields. New York: The Free Press.

Engels, Frederick. 1972 [1884]. *The Origin of the Family, Private Property and the State*. New York: International Publishers.

Epstein, Richard A. 1995. *Simple Rules for a Complex World*. Cambridge: Harvard University Press.

Ernst, T. M. 1978. Aspects of Meaning of Exchanges and Exchange Items Among the Onabasulu of the Great Papuan Plateau. *Mankind* 11: 187–97.

Evers, Hans-Dieter. 1994, The Trader's Dilemma. In *The Moral Economy of Trade*, ed. Hans-Dieter Evers and Heiko Schrader, pp. 7–14. London: Routledge.

Fals Borda, Orlando. 1979. *El Hombre y la Tierra en Boyacá*, 3rd edn. Bogotá: Tercer Mundo.

Filifer, Marija. 1995. Legacy: time and kinship in urban Serbia. University of Minnesota: PhD dissertation.

Finley, M. I. 1970. Aristotle and Economic Analysis. *Past and Present* 47: 3–25.

Firth, Raymond. 1965 [1939]. *Primitive Polynesian Economy*, rev. edn. London: Routledge & Kegan Paul.

Firth, Raymond. 1966. Malay Fishermen: their peasant economy. New York: W. W. Norton & Co.

Fortune, R. F. 1963 [1932]. *Sorcerers of Dobu*. New York: E. P. Dutton & Co.

Foster, George. 1967. *Tzintzuntzan*. Boston: Little, Brown.

Frank, Andre Gunder. 1967. *Capitalism and Underdevelopment in Latin America*. New York: Monthly Review Press.

Frank, Andre Gunder. 1969. *Latin America: Underdevelopment or Revolution*. New York: Monthly Review Press.

Freeman, J. D. 1958. The Family System of the Iban of Borneo. In *The Developmental Cycle in Domestic Groups*, ed. J. Goody, pp. 15–52. Cambridge: Cambridge University Press.

Freeman, J. D. 1970 [1955]. *Report on the Iban*. London: Athlone Press.

Friedman, Milton. 1953. *Essays in Positive Economics*. Chicago: University of Chicago Press.

Fukuyama, Francis. 1995. *Trust: the social virtues and the creation of prosperity*. New York: The Free Press.

Furtado, Celso. 1976. *Economic Development of Latin America*, 2nd edn. Cambridge: Cambridge University Press.

Gaitán, Gloria. 1984. *La Lucha por la Tierra en la Década del Treinta*, 2nd edn. Bogotá: El Ancora.

Gambetta, Diego, ed. 1988. *Trust: making and breaking cooperative relations*. Oxford: Basil Blackwell.

Gates, Hill. 1996. *China's Motor: a thousand years of petty capitalism*. Ithaca: Cornell University Press.

Geary, Patrick. 1986. Sacred Commodities: the circulation of medieval relics. In *The Social Life of Things*, ed. Arjun Appadurai, pp. 169–91. Cambridge: Cambridge University Press.

Geertz, Clifford. 1962. The Rotating Credit Association: A "middle rung" in development. *Economic Development and Cultural Change* 10: 241–63.

Geertz, Clifford. 1963. *Agricultural Involution*. Berkeley: University of California Press.

Geertz, Clifford. 1973. *The Interpretation of Cultures*. New York: Basic Books.

Geertz, Clifford. 1973 [1962]. The Growth of Culture and the Evolution of Mind. In *The Interpretation of Cultures*, pp. 54–83. New York: Basic Books.

Geertz, Clifford. 1973 [1966]. The Impact of the Concept of Culture on the Concept of Man. In *The Interpretations of Cultures*, pp. 33–54. New York: Basic Books.

Gell, Alfred. 1975. *Metamorphosis of the Cassowaries*. London: Athlone Press.

Gell, Alfred. 1982. The Market Wheel: symbolic aspects of an Indian tribal market. *Man* 17: 470–91.

Gell, Alfred. 1992. Inter-tribal Commodity Barter and Reproductive Gift-exchange in Old Melanesia. In *Barter, Exchange and Value*, ed. Caroline Humphrey and Stephen Hugh-Jones, pp. 142–68. Cambridge: Cambridge University Press.

George, Kenneth M. 1996. *Showing Signs of Violence: the cultural politics of a twentieth-century headhunting ritual*. Berkeley: University of California Press.

Georgescu-Roegen, Nicholas. 1971. *The Entropy Law and the Economic Process*. Cambridge: Harvard University Press.

Gibson-Graham, J. K. 1996. *The End of Capitalism (as we knew it)*. Oxford:

Blackwell Publishers.

Gibson-Graham, J. K., and Phillip O'Neill. 2001. Toward a New Class Politics of the Enterprise. In *Re-presenting Class: essays in postmodern political economy*, eds. J. K. Gibson-Grahm, S. Resnick, and R. Wolff. Chapel Hlll: Duke University Press.

Gies, Frances, and Joseph Gies. 1990. *Life in a Medieval Village*. New York: Harper & Row.

Godelier, Maurice. 1977a. The Concept of "Social and Economic Formation": the Inca example. In *Perspectives in Marxist Anthropology*, trans. Robert Brain, pp. 63–9. Cambridge: Cambridge University Press.

Godelier, Maurice. 1977b. "Salt money" and the Circulation of Commodities Among the Baruya of New Guinea. In *Perspectives in Marxist Anthropology*, trans. Robert Brain, pp. 127–51. Cambridge: Cambridge University Press.

Godelier, Maurice. 1995a. L'Énigme du don, I. Le legs de Mauss. Social Anthropology 3:15–47.

Godelier, Maurice. 1995b. L'Énigme du don, II. De l'existence d'objets substituts des hommes et des dieux. *Social Anthropology* 3: 95–114.

Godoy, Ricardo A. 1990. *Mining and Agriculture in Highland Bolivia*. Tucson: University of Arizona Press.

Godoy, Ricardo. 1991. The Evolution of Common-Field Agriculture in the Andes: a hypothesis. *Comparative Studies in Society and History* 31: 395–414.

Goody, Esther N, ed. 1995. *Social Intelligence and Interaction*. Cambridge: Cambridge University Press.

Graham, Ellen. 1996. Community Groups Print Local (and Legal) Currencies. In *Wall Street Journal*, June 27: section B, pp. 1, 6.

Granovetter, Mark. 1992 [1985]. Economic Action and Social Structure: the problem of embeddedness. In *The Sociology of Economic Life*, ed. Mark Granovetter and Richard Swedberg, pp. 53–81. Boulder: Westview.

Granovetter, Mark. 1992b. The Nature of Economic Relations. In *Understanding Economic Process*, ed. Sutti Ortiz and Susan Lees, pp. 21–37. Lanham: University Press of America.

Gregory, C. A. 1982. *Gifts and Commodities*. London: Academic Press.

Gregory, C. A. 1997. *Savage Money: the anthropology and politics of commodity exchange*. Amsterdam: Harwood Academic Publishers.

Greif, Avner. 1993. Contract Enforceability and Economic Institutions in Early Trade: the Maghribi traders' coalition. *American Economic Review* 83: 525–48.

Greif, Avner. 1994. Cultural Beliefs and the Organization of Society: a historical and theoretical reflection on collectivist and individualist societies. *Journal of Political Economy* 102: 912–50.

Gudeman, Stephen. 1976. *Relationships, Residence and the Individual: a rural Panamanian community*. London: Routledge.

Gudeman, Stephen. 1978. *The Demise of a Rural Economy*. London: Routledge & Kegan Paul.

Gudeman, Stephen. 1986. *Economics as Culture*. London: Routledge & Kegan

Paul.

Gudeman, Stephen. 1992. Remodeling the House of Economics: Culture and Innovation. *American Ethnologist* 19(1): 141–54. 1991 American Ethnological Society Distinguished Lecture.

Gudeman, Stephen, and Alberto Rivera. 1990. *Conversations in Colombia.* Cambridge: Cambridge University Press.

Gudeman, Stephen, and Alberto Rivera. 2001. Sustaining the Community, Resisting the Market: Guatemalan perspectives. In *Land, Property and the Environment*, ed. John F. Richards, pp. 355–81. Oakland: ICS Press.

Hardin, G. 1968. The Tragedy of the Commons. *Science* 162: 1243–8.

Harris, Marvin. 1959. The Economy Has No Surplus? *American Anthropologist* 61: 185–99.

Harrison, Simon. 1992. Ritual as Intellectual Property. *Man* (N.S.) 27: 225–44.

Hart, Keith. 1986. Heads or Tails? Two Sides of the Coin. *Man* (N.S.) 21: 637–56.

Hart, Keith. 1992. Market and State after the Cold War: the informal economy reconsidered. In, *Contesting Markets: analyses of ideology, discourse, and practice*, ed. Roy Dilley, pp. 214–30. Edinburgh: Edinburgh University Press.

Harvey, David. 1989. *The Condition of Postmodernity.* Oxford: Basil Blackwell.

Harvey, David. 1996. *Justice, Nature and the Geography of Difference.* Oxford: Blackwell Publishers.

Hayami, Yujiro. 1998. Toward an East Asian Model of Economic Development. In *The Institutional Foundations of East Asian Economic Development*, ed. Yujiro Hayami and Masahiko Aoki, pp. 3–35. New York: St. Martin's Press.

Healey, Christopher J. 1978. The Adaptive Significance of Systems of Ceremonial Exchange and Trade in the New Guinea Highlands. *Mankind* 11: 198–207.

Healey, Christopher J. 1984. Trade and Sociability: Balanced Reciprocity as Generosity in the New Guinea Highlands. *American Ethnologist*, 11: 42–60.

Heckscher, Eli. 1935. *Mercantilism.* London: George Allen and Unwin.

Helgason, Agnar, and Pálsson, Gísli. 1996. Contested Commodities: mapping the moral landscape of exchange. Paper presented at the European Association of Social Anthropologists, Barcelona, July 12–15.

Helliwell, Christine. 1995. Autonomy as Natural Equality: inequality in "Egalitarian" societies. *J. Roy. anthrop. Inst* (N.S.) 1: 359–75.

Henry, Jules. 1951. The Economics of Pilagá Food Distribution. *American Anthropologist* 53: 187–219.

Henwood, Doug. 1997. *Wall Street: how it works and for whom.* Verso: London.

Herzfeld, Michael. 1984. The Significance of the Insignificant: blasphemy as ideology. *Man* (N.S.) 19: 653–64.

Herzfeld, Michael. 1987. *Anthropology Through the Looking Glass.* Cambridge: Cambridge University Press.

Hirschman, Albert O. 1977. *The Passions and the Interests: political arguments for capitalism before its triumph*. Princeton: Princeton University Press.

Hirschman, Albert O. 1992 [1986]. *Rival Views of Market Society*. Cambridge: Harvard University Press.

Hogbin, H. Ian. 1938–9. Tillage and Collection: a New Guinea economy. *Oceania* IX–X: 127–51, 286–325.

Hornborg, Alf. 1994. Environmentalism, Ethnicity and Sacred Places: reflections on modernity, discourse and power. *Canadian Review of Sociology and Anthropology* 31(3): 245–67.

Humphrey, Caroline. 1983. *Karl Marx Collective: economy, society and religion in a Siberian collective farm*. Cambridge: Cambridge University Press.

Humphrey, Caroline. 1985. Barter and Economic Disintegration. *Man* (N.S.) 20: 48–72.

Humphrey, Caroline. 1998. The Domestic Mode of Production in Post-Soviet Siberia? *Anthropology Today* 14 (3): 2–7.

Hutchins, Edwin. 1995. *Cognition in the Wild*. Cambridge: MIT Press.

Hyden, Goran. 1980. *Beyond Ujamaa in Tanzania*. Berkeley: University of California Press.

Ingold, Tim. 1996a. Growing Plants and Raising Animals: an anthropological perspective on domestication. In *The Origins and Spread of Agriculture and Pastoralism in Eurasia*, ed. David R. Harris, pp. 12–24. London: UCL Press.

Ingold, Tim. 1996b. Hunting and Gathering as Ways of Perceiving the Environment. In *Redefining Nature: ecology, culture and domestication*, ed. Roy Ellen and Katsuyoshi Fukui, pp. 117–55. Oxford: Berg.

Ingold, Tim. 1996c. The Optimal Forager and Economic Man. In *Nature and Society: anthropological perspectives*, ed. P. Descola and G. Pálsson, pp. 25–44. London: Routledge.

Janowski, Monica. 1995. The Hearth-Group, the Conjugal Couple and the Symbolism of the Rice Meal among the Kelabit of Sarawak. In *About the House*, ed. Janet Carsten and Stephen Hugh-Jones, pp. 84–104. Cambridge: Cambridge University Press.

Johnson, Allen W. 1971. *Sharecroppers of the Sertão*. Stanford: Stanford University Press.

Kash, Don E. 1989. *Perpetual Innovation*. New York: Basic Books.

Keith, Robert G. 1976. *Conquest and Agrarian Change: the emergence of the hacienda system on the Peruvian coast*. Cambridge: Harvard University Press.

Kenny, Michael. 1961. *A Spanish Tapestry*. New York: Harper & Row.

Kideckel, David, ed. 1995. *The Struggle for Balance in Turbulent Times: Eastern European communities*. Boulder: Westview Press.

Klamer, Arjo. 1983. *Conversations with Economists*. Savage (Maryland): Rowman & Littlefield.

Klamer, Arjo, and David Colander. 1990. *The Making of an Economist*. Boulder: Westview Press.

Klein, Herbert S. 1993. *Haciendas and Ayllus*. Stanford: Stanford University Press.

Knight, Frank H. 1971 [1921]. *Risk, Uncertainty and Profit*. Chicago: University of Chicago Press.

Kopytoff, Igor. 1986. The Cultural Biography of Things. In *The Social Life of Things*, ed. Arjun Appadurai, pp. 64–91. Cambridge Cambridge University Press.

Kula, Witold. 1976 [1962]. *An Economic Theory of the Feudal System*, trans. Lawrence Garner. London: Verso.

Lampland, Martha. 1991. Pigs, Party Secretaries, and Private Lives in Hungary. *American Ethnologist* 18: 459–79.

Lampland, Martha. 1995. *The Object of Labor*. Chicago: University of Chicago Press.

Lave, Jean, and Etienne Wenger. 1991. *Situated Learning*. Cambridge: Cambridge University Press.

Leach, Edmund. 1954. *Political Systems of Highland Burma*. London: G. Bell and Sons.

LeClair, Edward E., and Harold K. Schneider. 1968. *Economic Anthropology*. New York: Holt, Rinehard and Winston.

Ledeneva, Alena V. 1998. *Russia's Economy of Favours: blat, networking and informal exchange*. Cambridge: Cambridge University Press.

LeGoff, Jacques. 1988. *Your Money or Your Life*. New York: Zone Books.

LeGrand, Catherine. 1986. *Frontier Expansion and Peasant Protest in Colombia, 1850–1936*, Albuquerque, New Mexico: University of New Mexico Press.

Leibenstein, Harvey. 1966. Allocative efficiency and X-efficiency. *American Economic Review* 56: 392–415.

Leibenstein, Harvey. 1976. *Beyond Economic Man*. Cambridge: Harvard University Press.

Lévi-Strauss, Claude. 1969 [1949]. *The Elementary Structures of Kinship*. London: Eyre and Spottiswoode.

Lewis, Oscar. 1951. *Life in a Mexican Village*. Urbana: University of Illinois Press.

Locke, John. 1960 [1690]. *Two Treatises of Government*, ed. Peter Laslett. Cambridge: Cambridge University Press.

Lowry, S. Todd. 1969. Aristotle's Mathematical Analysis of Exchange. *History of Political Economy* I: 44–66.

MacIntyre, Alasdair. 1988. *Whose Justice? Which Rationality?* Notre Dame: University of Notre Dame Press.

Malinowski, Bronislaw. 1920. Kula: The Circulating Exchange of Valuables in the Archipelagoes of Eastern New Guinea. *Man* 51: 97–105.

Malinowski, Bronislaw. 1961 [1922]. *Argonauts of the Western Pacific*. New York: Dutton.

Malinowski, Bronislaw and Julio de la Fuente. 1982. *Malinowski in Mexico*. London: Routledge & Kegan Paul.

Marglin, Stephen A. 1990. Losing Touch: the cultural conditions of worker accommodation and resistance. In *Dominating Knowledge*, ed. Frédérique Apffel-Marglin and Stephen A. Marglin, pp. 217–82. Oxford: Clarendon Press.

Marglin, Stephen A. 1996. Farmers, Seedsmen, and Scientists: systems of agriculture and systems of knowledge. In *Decolonizing Knowledge: from development to dialogue*, ed. Frédérique Apffel-Marglin and Stephen A. Marglin, pp. 185–248. Oxford: Clarendon Press.

Marks, S. A. 1976. *Large Mammals and a Brave People*. Seattle: University of Washington Press.

Marx, Karl. 1967 [1867]. *Capital*, I, trans. Samuel Moore and Edward Aveling. New York: International Publishers.

Marx, Karl. 1967 [1894]. *Capital*, III. New York: International Publishers.

Marx, Karl. 1970 [1859]. *A Contribution to the Critique of Political Economy*, trans. S. W. Ryazanskaya, ed. Maurice Dobb. New York: International Publishers.

Matos Mar, José. 1976. *Yanaconaje y reforma Agraria en el Perú*. Lima: Instituto de Estudios Peruanos.

Mauss, Marcel. 1990 [1925]. *The Gift*, trans. W. D. Halls. London: Routledge.

Mayer, Enrique, and Manuel Glave. 1990. Papa Regaladas y Papas Regalo: rentabilidad, costos e inversión. In *Peru: el problema agrario en debate*, ed. Alberto Chirif, Nelson Manrique, and Benjamin Quijandría, pp. 87–120. Lima: SEPIA.

Mayer, Enrique, and Manuel Glave. 1992. Rentabilidad en la Produccion Campesina de Papas. In *La Chacra de Papa*, ed. Enrique Mayer, pp. 29–179. Lima: Centro Peruano de Estudios Sociales.

Mayer, Enrique, and Manuel Glave. 1999. *Alguito Para Ganar* (A Little Something to Earn): profits and losses in peasant economies. *American Ethnologist* 26 : 344–69.

McBryde, Felix W. 1947. *Cultural and Historical Geography of Southwest Guatemala*. Washington: Smithsonian Institution.

McCracken, Grant. 1988. *Culture and Consumption*. Bloomington: Indiana.

McCreery, David. 1994. *Rural Guatemala: 1760–1940*. Stanford: Stanford University Press.

McNeill, Desmond. 1990. Alternative Interpretations of Aristotle on Exchange and Reciprocity, *Public Affairs Quarterly* 4: 55–68.

Meikle, Scott. 1995. *Aristotle's Economic Thought*. Oxford: Clarendon Press.

Meillassoux, Claude. 1981 [1975]. *Maidens, Meal and Money: capitalism and the domestic economy*. Cambridge: Cambridge University Press.

Mertes, Kate. 1988. *The English Noble Household 1250–1600*. Oxford: Basil Blackwell.

Merton, Robert K. 1957 [1942]. Science and Democratic Social Structure. In *Social Theory and Social Structure*, pp. 550–61. Glencoe: The Free Press.

Mills, Mary Beth. 1997. Contesting the Margins of Modernity: women, migration, and consumption in Thailand. *American Ethnologist* 24: 37–61.

Mintz, Sidney W. 1961. *Pratik*: Haitian Personal Economic Relationships. Symposium: *Patterns of Land Utilization and Other Papers*, pp. 54–63. Seattle: American Ethnological Society.

Mirabeau, Marquis de. 1973 [1760]. The *Tableau Économique* and Its Explanation. In *Precursors of Adam Smith*, ed. Ronald Meek, pp. 115–46. London: Dent.

Mirowski, Philip. 1989. *More Heat Than Light*. New York: Cambridge University Press.

Mirowski, Philip. 1991. Postmodernism and the Social Theory of Value. *Journal of Post-Keynesian Economics* 13: 565–82.

Morgan, Lewis Henry. 1963 [1877]. *Ancient Society*, ed. Eleanor Burke Leacock. Cleveland: World Publishing Co.

Mosko, Mark. 1985. *Quadripartite Structures: categories relations and homologies in Bush Mekeo culture*. Cambridge: Cambridge University Press.

Mosko, Mark. 1989. The Developmental Cycle Among Public Groups. *Man* (N.S.) 24: 470–84.

Neef, Dale. 1998. The Effect of Knowledge on National Economies. In *The Economic Impact of Knowledge*, ed. Dale Neef, G. Anthony Siesfeld, and Jacquelyn Cefola, pp. 1–16. Boston: Butterworth-Heinemann.

Neusner, Jacob. 1990. *The Economics of the Mishnah*. Chicago: University of Chicago Press.

Nussbaum, Martha C. 1986. *The Fragility of Goodness*. Cambridge: Cambridge University Press.

Obrinsky, Mark. 1983. *Profit Theory and Capitalism*. Philadelphia: University of Pennsylvania Press.

Ohnuki-Tierney, Emiko. 1993. *Rice as Self: Japanese identities through time*. Princeton: Princeton University Press.

Ohnuki-Tierney, Emiko. 1995. Structure, Event and Historical Metaphor: rice and identities in Japanese history. *J. Roy. Anthrop. Inst.* (N.S.) 1: 227–53.

Olwig, Karen Fog. 1994. *"The Land is the Heritage": land and community on St. John*. Denmark: St. John Oral History Association.

Olwig, Karen Fog. 1999. Caribbean Place Identity: from family land to region and beyond. *Identities* 5(4): 435–67.

Ong, Aihwa. 1987. *Spirits of Resistance and Capitalist Discipline*. Albany: State University of New York Press.

Orlove, Benjamin. 1986. An Examination of Barter and Cash Sale in Lake Titicaca: a test of competing approaches in economic anthropology. *Current Anthropology* 27: 85–106.

Orlove, Benjamin. 1995. Beyond Consumption: meat, sociality, vitality and hierarchy in nineteenth-century Chile. In *Consumption and Identity*, ed. Jonathan Friedman, pp. 119–45. Reading: Harwood Academic Publishers.

Orlove, Benjamin. 1997. Meat and Strength: the moral economy of a Chilean food riot. *Cultural Anthropology* 12: 234–68.

Oschinsky, Dorothea. 1971. *Walter of Henley and Other Treatises on Estate Management and Accounting*. Oxford: Clarendon Press.

Ostrom, Elinor. 1990. *Governing the Commons*. Cambridge: Cambridge University Press.

Pálsson, Gísli. 1993. Introduction: beyond boundaries. In *Beyond Boundaries*, ed. G. Pálsson, pp. 1–40. Oxford: Berg.

Pálsson, Gísli. 1994. Enskilment at Sea. *Man* (N.S.) 29: 901–27.

Pálsson, Gísli, and Agnar Helgason. 1996. The Politics of Production: enclosure, equity, and efficiency. In *Images of Contemporary Iceland: everyday lives and global contexts*. ed. Gísli Pálsson and E. Paul Durrenberger, pp. 60–84. Iowa City: University of Iowa Press.

Parry, Jonathan. 1986. *The Gift*, the Indian Gift and the "Indian Gift." *Man* (N.S.) 21: 453–73.

Parry, Jonathan. 1989. On the Moral Perils of Exchange. In *Money and the Morality of Exchange*, ed. J. Parry and M. Bloch, pp. 64–93. Cambridge: Cambridge University Press.

Parry, Jonathon, and Maurice Bloch. 1989. *Money and the Morality of Exchange*. Cambridge: Cambridge University Press.

Pérez-López, Jorge F. 1995. *Cuba's Second Economy*. New Brunswick: Transaction Publishers.

Petrusewicz, Marta. 1996. *Latinfundium: moral economy and material life in a European periphery*, trans. Judith C. Green. Ann Arbor: The University of Michigan Press.

Piore, Michael J., and Charles F. Sabel. 1984. *The Second Industrial Divide*. New York: Basic Books.

Platt, Tristan. 1982. The Role of the Andean *Ayllu* in the Reproduction of the Petty Commodity Regime in Northern Potosi (Bolivia). In *Ecology and Exchange in the Andes*, ed. David Lehmann, pp. 27–69. Cambridge: Cambridge University Press.

Platteau, Jean-Philippe, and Yujiro Hayami. 1998. Resource Endowments and Agricultural Development: Africa versus Asia. In *The Institutional Foundations of East Asian Economic Development*, ed. Yujiro Hayami and Masahiko Aoki, pp. 357–410. New York: St. Martin's Press.

Plattner, Stuart, ed. 1985. *Markets and Marketing*. Lanham: University Press of America.

Plattner, Stuart, ed. 1989. *Economic Anthropology*. Stanford: Stanford University Press.

Polanyi, Karl. 1944. *The Great Transformation*. New York: Rinehart.

Polanyi, Karl. 1968. *Primitive, Archaic, and Modern Economies*, ed. George Dalton. Garden City: Anchor Books.

Polanyi, Karl. 1968a. The Self-regulating Market and the Fictions Commodities: labor, land, and money. In *Primitive, Archaic and Modern Economies*, ed. George Dalton, pp. 26–37. Garden City: Anchor Books.

Polanyi, Karl. 1968b. Aristotle Discovers the Economy. In *Primitive, Archaic and Modern Economies*, ed. George Dalton, pp. 78–115. Garden City: Anchor Books.

Polanyi, Karl. 1977. *The Livelihood of Man*, ed. Harry W. Pearson. New York: Academic Books.

Polanyi, Karl, Conrad Arensberg, and Harry Pearson, eds. 1957. *Trade and Market in the Early Empires*. Glencoe: Free Press.

Postan, M. M. 1975. *The Medieval Economy and Society*. Harmondsworth: Penguin.

Price, John A. 1975. Sharing: The integration of intimate economies. *Anthropologica* XVII(1): 3–27.

Putnam, Robert D. 1993. *Making Democracy Work*. Princeton: Princeton University Press.

Quesnay, François. 1963 [1766]. General Maxims for the Economic Government of an Agricultural Kingdom. In *The Economics of Physiocracy*, ed. Ronald L. Meek, pp. 231–62. Cambridge: Harvard University Press.

Radcliffe-Brown, A. R. 1958 [1952]. The Comparative Method in Social Anthropology. In *Method in Social Anthropology*, ed. M. N. Srinivas pp. 108–29. Chicago: University of Chicago Press.

Raheja, Gloria. 1988. *The Poison in the Gift*. Chicago: University of Chicago Press.

Reichheld, Frederick F. 1996. *The Loyalty Effect*. Boston: Harvard Business School Press.

Resnick, Lauren B., John M. Levine, and Stephanie D. Teasley, eds. 1991. *Perspectives on Socially Shared Cognition*. Washington: American Psychological Association.

Ricardo, David. 1951 [1815]. *The Works and Correspondence of David Ricardo*, IV, ed. P. Sraffa. Cambridge: Cambridge University Press.

Ricardo, David. 1951 [1817]. *On the Principles of Political Economy and Taxation*, I, ed. P. Sraffa. Cambridge: Cambridge University Press.

Richards, A. I. 1939. *Land, Labour and Diet in Northern Rhodesia*. London: Oxford University Press.

Ritter, Archibald R. M. 1998. Entrepreneurship, Microenterprise, and Public Policy in Cuba: promotion, containment, or asphyxiation? *Journal of Interamerican Studies and World Affairs* 4: 63–94.

Rivera Gutiérrez, Alberto. 1986. Material Life and Social Metaphor. PhD Thesis. University of Minnesota.

Robbins, Lionel. 1969 [1932]. *An Essay on the Nature and Significance of Economic Science*. London: Macmillan.

Robinson, Joan. 1933. *The Economics of Imperfect Competition*. London: Macmillan.

Robinson, Joan. 1960 [1942]. *An Essay on Marxian Economics*. London: Macmillan.

Robinson, Joan. 1962. Essays in the Theory of Economic Growth. New York: St. Martin's Press.

Robinson, Joan. 1972. The Second Crisis of Economic Theory. In *The Second Crisis of Economic Theory*, ed. Rendigs Fels, pp. 1–11. Morristown: General Learning Corporation.

Robinson, Joan, and John Eatwell. 1973. *An Introduction to Modern Economics*. Maidenhead: McGraw-Hill.

Rogoff, Barbara. 1990. *Apprenticeship in Thinking*. New York: Oxford University Press.

Rogoff, Barbara and Jean Lave, eds. 1984. *Everyday Cognition: its development in social context*. Cambridge: Harvard University Press.

Rogoff, Barbara, Jayanthi Mistry, Artin Göncü, and Christine Mosier. 1993. Guided Participation in Cultural Activity By Toddlers and Caregivers. *Monographs of the Society for Research in Child Development* (serial no. 236), vol. 58: 8.

Roll, Eric. 1973. *A History of Economic Thought*. London: Faber & Faber.

Rösener, Werner. 1992 (1985). *Peasants in the Middle Ages*, trans. Alexander Stützer. Urbana: University of Illinois Press.

Rothenberg, Winifred Barr. 1992. *From Market-Places to a Market Economy.* Chicago: University of Chicago Press.

Ruttan, Vernon W. 1959. Usher and Schumpeter on Invention, Innovation, and Technological Change. *Quarterly Journal of Economics* LXXIII: 596–606.

Sabel, Charles F. 1982. *Work and Politics.* Cambridge: Cambridge University Press.

Sabel, Charles. 1991. Moebius-Strip Organizations and Open Labor Markets: some consequences of the reintegration of conception and execution in a volative economy. In *Social Theory for a Changing Society*, ed. Pierre Bourdieu and James S. Coleman, pp. 23–61. Boulder: Westview Press.

Sabel, Charles F. 1994. Learning by Monitoring: the institutions of economic development. In *The Handbook of Economic Sociology*, ed. Neil J. Smelser and Richard Swedberg, pp. 137–65. Princeton: Princeton University Press.

Sahlins, Marshall. 1972. *Stone Age Economics.* Chicago: Aldine.

Sahlins, Marshall. 1976. *Culture and Practical Reason.* Chicago: University of Chicago Press.

Saxenian, Annalee. 1994. *Regional Advantage: culture and competition in Silicon Valley and Route 128.* Cambridge: Harvard University Press.

Scheper-Hughes, Nancy. 1984. Infant Mortality and Infant Care: cultural and economic constraints on nurturing in Northeast Brasil. *Social Science and Medicine* 19: 535–46.

Scheper-Hughes, Nancy. 1992. *Death Without Weeping.* Berkeley: University of California Press.

Schneider, Harold K. 1974. *Economic Man.* New York: Free Press.

Schön, Donald A. 1983. *The Reflective Practitioner: how professionals think in action.* New York: Basic Books.

Schumpeter, Joseph A. 1934 [1926]. *The Theory of Economic Development.* Cambridge: Harvard University Press.

Schumpeter, Joseph A. 1954. *History of Economic Analysis.* New York: Oxford University Press.

Schumpeter, J. 1976 [1942]. *Capitalism, Socialism and Democracy.* New York: Harper and Row.

Schumpeter, Joseph A. 1989 [1947]. The Creative Response in Economic History. In *Essays*, ed. R. V. Clemence, pp. 221–31. New Brunswick: Transaction Publishers.

Schumpeter, Joseph A. 1989 [1949]. Economic Theory and Entrepreneurial History. In *Essays*, ed. R. V. Clemence, pp. 253–71. New Brunswick: Transaction Publishers.

Schumpeter, Joseph A. 1991 [1946]. Comments on a Plan for the Study of Entrepreneurship. In *Joseph A. Schumpeter: the economics and sociology of capitalism*, ed. R. Swedberg, pp. 406–28. Princeton: Princeton University Press.

Scott, James. 1976. *The Moral Economy of the Peasant.* New Haven: Yale University Press.

Scott, James. 1998. *Seeing Like a State.* New Haven: Yale University Press.

Scott, Julie. 1998. Property Values: ownership, legitimacy and land markets in Northern Cyprus. In *Property Relations: renewing the anthropological tradition*, ed. C. M. Hann, pp. 142–59. Cambridge: Cambridge University Press.

Seguino, Stephanie, Thomas Stevens, and Mark Lutz. 1996. Gender and Co-operative Behavior: economic *man* rides alone. *Feminist Economics* 2: 1–21.

Semo, Enrique. 1993. *The History of Capitalism in Mexico: its origins, 1521–1763*, trans. Lidia Lozano. Austin: University of Texas Press.

Sen, Amartya K. 1978. Rational Fools: a critique of the behavioral foundations of economic theory. In *Scientific Models and Men*, ed. H. Harris, pp. 317–44. London: Oxford University Press.

Sen, Amartya K. 1981. *Poverty and Famines: an essay on entitlement and deprivation*. Oxford: Clarendon Press.

Sikkink, Lynn. 1994. House, Community, and Marketplace: women as managers of exchange relations and resources on the southern *altiplano* of Bolivia. Dissertation, University of Minnesota.

Sikkink, Lynn. 1997. Water and Exchange: the ritual of *yaku cambio* as communal and competitive encounter. *American Ethnologist* 24: 170–89.

Simon, Herbert A. 1957. *Models of Man*. New York: Wiley.

Simon, Herbert A. 1959. Theories of Decision-Making in Economics and Behavioral Science. *American Economic Review* XLIX: 253–83.

Siskind, Janet. 1973. *To Hunt in the Morning*. New York: Oxford University Press.

Smedal, Olaf H. 1989. *Order and Difference: an ethnographic study of Orang Lom of Bangka, West Indonesia*. Oslo: Department of Social Anthropology (University of Oslo).

Smelser, Neil J. 1976. On the Relevance of Economic Sociology for Economics. In *Economics and Sociology*, ed. T. Huppes, pp. 1–26. Leiden: Martinus Nijhoff.

Smith, Adam. 1976 [1776]. *The Wealth of Nations*, ed. Edward Cannan. Chicago: University of Chicago Press.

Solow, Robert M. 1997. *Learning From "Learning by Doing."* Stanford: Stanford University Press.

Soto, Hernando de. 1989. *The Other Path*. New York: Harper and Row.

Southern, R. W. 1967. *The Making of the Middle Ages* London: Century Hutchinson Ltd.

Spinosa, Charles, Fernando Flores, and Hubert L. Dreyfus. 1997. *Disclosing New Worlds: entrepreneurship, democratic action, and the cultivation of solidarity*. Cambridge: MIT Press.

Stannard, David E. 1992. *American Holocaust: the conquest of the New World*. Oxford: Oxford University Press.

Stanner, W. E. H. 1932–3, 1933–4. The Daly River Tribes: a report of field work in North Australia. *Oceania* III: 377–405; IV: 10–29.

Stevenson, H. N. C. 1937. Feasting and Meat Distribution Among the Zahau Chins of Burma. *Journal of the Royal Anthropological Institute* LXVIII: 15–32.

Stevenson, H. N. C. 1943. *The Economics of the Central Chin Tribes*. Bombay: The Times of India Press.

Stewart, Michael. 1992. Gypsies at the Horse-Fair. In *Contesting Markets*, ed. Roy Dilley, pp. 97–114. Edinburgh: Edinburgh University Press.

Stiglitz, Joseph E. 1994. *Whither Socialism?* Cambridge: The MIT Press.

Strathern, Andrew. 1973. Kinship, Descent and Locality: some New Guinea examples. In *The Character of Kinship*, ed. Jack Goody, pp. 21–33. Cambridge: Cambridge University Press.

Strathern, Marilyn. 1988. *The Gender of the Gift*. Berkeley: University of California Press.

Sunkel, Osvaldo, ed. 1993. *Development From Within*. Boulder: Lynne Rienner.

Taussig, Michael T. 1980. *The Devil and Commodity Fetishism in Latin America*. Chapel Hill: University of North Carolina Press.

Theodossopoulos, Dimitrios. 1999. The Pace of the Work and the Logic of the Harvest: women, labour and the olive harvest in a Greek island community. *Journal of the Royal Anthropological Institute* (N.S.) 5: 611–26.

Thomson, Donald F. 1949. *Economic Structure and the Ceremonial Exchange Cycle in Arnhem Land*. Melbourne: Macmillan.

Töennies, Ferdinand. 1988 [1887]. *Community and Society*, trans. Charles P. Loomis. New Brunswick: Transaction Publishers.

Tord, Javier, and Carlos Lazo. 1981. *Hacienda, Comercio, Fiscalidad y Luchas Sociales (Peru Colonial)*. Lima: Biblioteca Peruana de Historia, Economia y Sociedad.

de la Torre Arauz. 1989. *Patrones y Conciertos*. Quitos: Corporacion Editora Nacional.

Toulmin, Stephen. 1990. *Cosmopolis*. New York: The Free Press.

Turgot, Anne Robert Jacques. 1898 [1770]. *Reflections on the Formation and the Distribution of Riches*. New York: Macmillan.

Turner, Victor. 1967. *The Forest of Symbols*. Ithaca: Cornell University Press.

Valeri, Valerio. 1994. Buying Women But Not Selling Them: gift and commodity exchange in Hualu alliance. *Man* (N.S.) 29: 1–26.

Veblen, Thorstein. 1884. Kant's Critique of Judgment. *The Journal of Speculative Philosophy* XVIII: 260–74.

Veblen, Thorstein. 1914. *The Instinct of Workmanship, and the State of the Industrial Arts*. New York: Macmillan.

Veblen, Thorstein. 1942 [1908]. On the Nature of Capital. In *The Place of Science in Modern Civilisation*, pp. 324–51. New York: Viking Press.

Veblen, Thorstein. 1942 [1919]. *The Place of Science in Modern Civilisation*. New York: Viking Press.

Veblen, Thorstein. 1953 [1899]. *The Theory of the Leisure Class*. New York: Mentor Books.

Veblen, Thorstein. 1978 [1904]. *The Theory of Business Enterprise*. New Brunswick: Transaction Books.

Veblen, Thorstein. 1983 [1921]. *The Engineers and the Price System*. New Brunswick: Transaction Books.

Vel, Jacqueline. 1994. *The Uma-Economy*. Wageningen: Thesis.

Vélez-Ibañez, Carlos G. 1983. *Bonds Of Mutual Trust*. New Brunswick: Rutgers University Press.

Verdery, Katherine. 1996. *What Was Socialism, and What Comes Next?* Princeton: Princeton University Press.

Villamarín, Juan A. 1975. *Factores que afectaron la Producción Agropecuaria en la Sabana de Bogotá en la Época Colonial*. Bogotá: Pato Marino.

Vygotsky, L. S. 1978. *Mind in Society*. Cambridge: Harvard University Press.

Wagner, Günter. 1956. *The Bantu of North Kavirondo*, II, ed. L. P. Mair. London: Oxford University Press.

Weber, Max. 1958 (1920). *The Protestant Ethic and the Spirit of Capitalism*, trans. Talcott Parsons. New York: Scribner.

Weber, Max. 1961 [1923]. *General Economic History*, trans. Frank H. Knight. New York: Collier Books.

Weber, Max. 1978. *Economy and Society*, I, ed. by Guenther Roth and Claus Wittich. Berkeley: University of California Press.

Weil, Elizabeth. 1995. It's Just Jam, My Brother, Just Jam. *Boston Magazine*, (November): pp. 45–58.

Weiner, Annette. 1978. The Reproductive Model in Trobriand Society. *Mankind* 11: 175–86.

Weiner, Annette. 1980. Reproduction: a replacement for reciprocity. *American Anthropologist* 7: 71–85.

Weiner, Annette. 1992. *Inalienable Possessions*. Berkeley: University of California Press.

Wesley-Smith, Terence, and Eugene Ogan. 1992. Copper, Class, and Crisis: changing relations of production in Bougainville. *Contemporary Pacific* 4: 245–67.

Wilk, Richard R. 1991. *Household Ecology: economic change and domestic life among the Kekchi Maya in Belize*. Tucson: University of Arizona Press.

Wilk, Richard R. 1996. *Economics and Cultures: foundations of economic anthropology*. Boulder: Westview Press.

Williamson, Oliver. 1975. *Markets and Hierarchies*. New York: The Free Press.

Womack, James P., Daniel T. Jones, and Daniel Roos. 1990. *The Machine That Changed the World*. New York: HarperCollins.

Woodburn, James. 1998. "Sharing is not a Form of Exchange": an analysis of property-sharing in immediate-return hunter-gatherer societies. In *Property Relations*, ed. C. M. Hann, pp. 48–63. Cambridge: Cambridge University Press.

Woodruff, David. 1999. *Money Unmade: barter and the fate of Russian capitalism*. Ithaca: Cornell University Press.

Yack, Bernard. 1993. *The Problems of a Political Animal*. Berkeley: University of California Press.

Zelizer, Viviana A. 1994. *The Social Meaning of Money*. New York: Basic Books.

Zell, Deone. 1997. *Changing By Design*. Ithaca: Cornell University Press.

Index